THE MAJORS

GOLF

TRIVIA

Q+A

ALSO BY MIKE McGUIRE

1001 U.S. Geography Trivia Q & A
500 Ohio State Football Trivia Q & A
800 Ohio State Football Trivia Q & A
500 Heisman Football Trivia Q & A
1220 Ohio State Football Trivia Q & A

The Majors
Golf Trivia Q+A
by Mike McGuire

978-0-9772661-5-9

FIRST EDITION

Published by Mike McGuire

Order copies from
Mike McGuire
27081 N. 96th Way
Scottsdale, AZ 85262-8441
(480) 563-1424

Printed in the United States of America

DEDICATION

My dedication is short, simple and serious. I dedicate this golf trivia book to all golf enthusiasts around the world from touring golf professionals to beginners and everyone in between. My hope is that after you have read and played golf trivia you will have a newfound respect and understanding of the great history and traditions of the game we all love to play.

AUTHOR MIKE McGUIRE'S GOLFING BIO

Like thousands of other young boys, I was very fortunate to be introduced to the wonderful game of golf by my father. My early years were spent playing "cowboys and Indians," riding my bike (without a helmet), drinking water from a garden hose, playing all the sports, building tree forts and sand castles, and climbing up (and falling out of) trees. My buddies and I shot our Red Ryder BB guns at bottles (and squirrels), played cards and other board games, and we collected baseball cards. On the black and white TV, we watched cartoons, sports and movies. My first girlfriend was Brigitte Bardot. I played hide-and-seek at night, and my mother just blew a whistle when it was time to come home and eat dinner. It was a great childhood, but what I really wanted was to play golf with my dad on the weekends. That day happened when I was about 10 years old.

At first, I was just "going along" on The Ohio State University golf courses (Scarlet & Gray) — tending the pin, raking the traps, watching the ball, hitting an occasional chip shot or putt — and just learning how the game was played. On my 11th birthday, I got my first set of golf clubs: Sam Snead Model by Wilson Sports. I wish I still had that first putter; I made a lot of putts and money over the years with that baby. With my first set of golf clubs, my dad also thought it was time to go to work and learn how to be a caddy.

Well, I got a job at Scioto Country Club (home of Jack Nicklaus) in Columbus, Ohio. Boy, did I learn a lot about life as a young caddy: four-letter words and then some, buying low and selling high, what a real "gimme" is and was, all the parts of the female anatomy, the rules of golf and golf etiquette, the differences between a republican and a liberal, and how to shoot seven, say six, and write down five. The list could go on, but the best thing was the talk about a young local player named Jack Nicklaus.

At first, after I had completed a loop, I would call my mom to come and pick me up. But I quickly learned that if Jack was practicing, it was well worth my time to sit by the practice range and watch his swing. It was something else to watch! I was a quick learner, and now I wanted to play golf more and caddy less.

I followed Jack's career through Upper Arlington High School (the Golden Bears) and on to The Ohio State University (Buckeyes), a National Championship, and a U.S. Amateur Championship before he went on to the pro tour and won his 18 major championships. I learned about other golfing greats—Ben Hogan, Sam Snead, Arnold Palmer, Lee Trevino and Tom Watson, to name just a few. My enjoyment of the game continued to grow.

Fast forward. I now have been playing golf for more than 50 years. I have played in numerous scrambles, as members' guests, in charity events, in weekend pick-up games, in Daytona and Nassau games, and during road trips around the United States with my golfing buddies (aka the RATS). I have traveled to my fatherland, Scotland, and played all the British Open Championship courses. My enjoyment of the game continues to grow annually. I finally became a member of Scioto Country Club, where it all started, but now I live in Scottsdale, Arizona, and I play at The Estancia Club.

Now living in the third quarter of my life, and after crushed ankles, back surgery, knee replacement, lap-band surgery and just plain getting older, I still love to drop the ball on the ground, hit it and keep moving. An emergency nine holes is always welcome and fun, as the enjoyment of the game is still very much with me. I have all the shots, but I just don't know which one is coming out of my bag next.

I hope you enjoy my book, and I hope the pleasure of playing the great game of golf continues to grow with you. Keep your head down, with a slow backswing.

INTRODUCTION

The Majors Golf Trivia Q+A is my sixth in a series of trivia books, and it's one of my most enjoyable projects. I wanted to capture the great history and traditions of the four major golfing championships in a way that would be more of a teaching tool, so that readers of *Golf Trivia Q+A* will have a newfound understanding and respect for the great game of golf. Almost all of the questions relate to the major championships, players, courses, scores and records, architects, and sayings or players' comments. Just a few relate to unique historical golfing facts and terms. As I have always stated, trivia questions are meant to be fun, tricky, thought-provoking, or confusing. They should be able to bring back old memories and test your knowledge of a particular subject. Laugh, cry, argue...or all of the above. I hope this book is a learning experience for you, and I hope you will have fun with the trivia.

Many of the questions and answers were taken right off the top of my head because I have spent many years as a golf fan, following the tour and major championships. I used the Internet to verify and double check several of the questions and answers, and I read extensively from my golf book collection of more than 500 books, which has been donated to the Fownes Foundation Golf Library at Oakmont Country Club.

The one thing that sticks with me about all the great players in the history of the four major championships is this one thought: All you can be is the best player of your era; you can't compare players from different eras. After you have played and read *The Majors Golf Trivia Q+A,* and contemplated and discussed my statement with other golf enthusiasts, I believe you will agree.

When I was nearly finished with the 1,500 trivia questions about the four major championships, I decided to add 100 questions about the Ryder Cup and 20 questions concerning the President's Cup. Both these events are greatly affected by the four major championships, and I thought they fit in nicely. Finally, I completed the book with a variety of tables and lists that cover all the dates, courses and winners of the four major championships and two cup championships.

Author's note: With all due respect and for the sake of clarity, I refer to "The Open Championship" as "The British Open Championship" in this book. Most Americans recognize the championship by that name.

Enjoy!

Mike McGuire

HOW TO USE
THE MAJORS GOLF TRIVIA Q+A

Trivia questions are always meant to be fun, tricky, thought-provoking, and confusing, and to bring back good ole' memories, while testing your knowledge of a particular subject. *The Majors Golf Trivia Q+A* is no different.

We do offer the following suggestions on "How to Use" *The Majors Golf Trivia Q+A* book for greater enjoyment. It's great to use as a "party starter" for any golf fan gathering before tee-off, and an excellent way to meet new people while also learning about the wonderful traditions and history of the major golf championships. The book is laid out in a format of 20 questions and 20 answers so golf fans can go along at their own pace. Or you could make each correct answer worth 5 points for an individual or a team, and award some prizes for their knowledge of major golf trivia.

OTHER SUGGESTIONS

Corporate Tents... A fun way to meet new people, sponsors, guests, customers and others as you wait for players or play between holes.

On-the-Road... Driving to or from a tournament, trivia can help make the miles pass faster. Play to see who drives, who asks the questions, and who buys the next tank of gas, food or drinks.

On-an-Airplane, Bus or Train... A good way to study and improve your knowledge of golf's great championships, the traditions and history of the tournaments, the players, records, famous quotes, and the courses. Impress your friends with your expanded golf trivia knowledge.

19th Hole... A pizza or sandwich and beer always taste better with great sports trivia conversations, discussions and arguments, and it doesn't get any better than major golf trivia.

In-your-Golf-Bag... You should carry a good copy of this book in your bag in case of a long rain delay while on the course or any occurrences of delay while in the clubhouse.

In-the-Bathroom... OK! But please keep the book on your night stand or a bookshelf.

Note: Handy reference material, facts and figures about the major golf championships, players, and their records are located in the back of this book.

Send me the unique ways you have used *The Majors Golf Trivia Q+A* book to enjoy and enhance your respect and love for the game of golf.

TABLE OF CONTENTS

Dedication iv

Mike McGuire's Golf Bio iv

Introduction vi

How to Use this Book vii

Golf Trivia Q+A 9

Ryder Cup Q+A 159

The Presidents Cup Q+A 169

The Masters Tournament Winner's Data 171

U.S. Open Championship Winner's Data 174

The British Open Championship Winner's Data 179

PGA Championship (Stroke-Play Era) Winner's Data 186

PGA Championship (Match-Play Era) Winner's Data 189

The Ryder Cup Winner's Data 191

The Presidents Cup Winner's Data 193

Major Championship Winner's Data 194

Top Major Championship Winner's Data 199

The 13 Original Rules of Golf 200

GROUP **1** QUESTIONS

1-1 What was the first public municipal facility to host a major championship?

1-2 Name each of the four major championships and the month the tournament is held.

1-3 Who was the first native-born American to win the U.S. Open Championship?

1-4 How many yards is the longest Par 3 in U.S. Open Championship history?

1-5 Which one of the four major championships is always played on the same golf course?

1-6 How many U.S. Amateur and British Amateur titles did Bobby Jones win when they were considered major golf championships?

1-7 The Golf Champion Trophy is better known by what name?

1-8 Who was the first player to win both the U.S. Open and the British Open in the same year?

1-9 Who is the oldest winner of the PGA Championship?

1-10 How many of his 18 major championship wins did Jack Nicklaus win in a play-off?

1-11 What was "the fifteenth club in my bag," as stated by Ben Crenshaw when he won the 1995 Masters?

1-12 Who was the only player to win the British Open three straight years in the 20th century?

1-13 Who won the 1964 U.S. Open Championship at Congressional Country Club in a 36-hole final day played in the "scorching heat?"

1-14 Who was a runner-up four times in the 1969, 1972, 1974 and 1975 Masters Tournament?

1-15 Who was the first golfer to win four U.S. Open Championships?

1-16 Who was the first amateur to win the U.S. Open and the U.S. Amateur in the same year, 1916?

1-17 Orville Moody won which major by one stroke over Deane Beman, Al Geiberger and Bob Rosburg?

1-18 In what year was the only time the British Open was held outside of Scotland or England?

1-19 What year and where was the first PGA Championship held?

1-20 Walter Hagen was the first club professional at what famous Michigan championship course?

ANSWERS

GROUP
1

1-1   Bethpage State Park (Black Course), New York, 102nd U.S. Open Championship 2002

1-2   The Masters Tournament (April), The U.S. Open Championship (June), The Open Championship (British Open) (July), and The PGA Championship (August)

1-3   John McDermott, 1911 and he also won in 1912

1-4   #8, 288 yards at Oakmont Country Club, Oakmont, PA

1-5   The Masters Tournament, Augusta National Golf Club, Augusta, GA

1-6   Five; U.S. Amateurs (1924, 1925, 1927, 1928 and 1930), one British Amateur (1930)

1-7   The Claret Jug

1-8   Bobby Jones, 1926 U.S. Open at Scioto Country Club and British Open at Royal Lytham & St. Annes Golf Club

1-9   Julius Boros, 48 years old, 1968 Pecan Valley Golf Club, San Antonio, Texas

1-10   Three, 1962 U.S. Open Championship, 1966 Masters and 1970 British Open Championship

1-11   Harvey Penick, a great golf teacher who passed away a week before the Masters Tournament

1-12   Peter Thomson (1954, 1955 and 1956) also won in 1958 and 1965

1-13   Ken Venturi, one of the major championships most memorable days

1-14   Tom Weiskopf, also finished second in the 1976 U.S. Open Championship

1-15   Scotsman Willie Anderson 1901, 1903, 1904 and 1905

1-16   "Chick" Evans Jr.; Bobby Jones did it later in 1926

1-17   1969 U.S. Open Championship on the Cypress Creek Course at the Champions Golf Club

1-18   1951, Royal Portrush Golf Club (Dunluce Links) in Portrush, Northern Ireland

1-19   1916, Siwanoy Country Club in Eastchester, NY

1-20   Oakland Hills Country Club, Bloomfield Hills, MI

2 QUESTIONS

2-1   How many times did Walter Hagen win the PGA Championship?

2-2   What year was the oldest major championship golf tournament started?

2-3   Who is the oldest player to make the cut in a U.S. Open Championship?

2-4   **T or F**   Chick Evans was an amateur when he won the U.S. Open at the Minikahda Club in 1916.

2-5   What type of ball was used to win the first U.S. Open in 1895 at the Newport Golf Club?

2-6   Which of the four major championships is called "Glory's Last Shot?"

2-7   Who was Jack Nicklaus' biggest rival, all things considered?

2-8   Who were the three leading golf architects in the early 20th century?

2-9   What British Open Championship course is the Pebble Beach of Scotland?

2-10   Which sports writer named the 11th, 12th, and 13th holes at Augusta National, "Amen Corner®?"

2-11   Who hit a 5-iron to two feet from the pin on the 72nd hole at the Atlanta Athletic Club in 1976 to win the U.S. Open Championship?

2-12   During which major championship tournament did the phrase "Arnie's Army" originate?

2-13   Who is the only father/son winner and runner-up in the British Open Championship?

2-14   Who was the club professional that won a Masters Tournament?

2-15   Who is the tallest player to ever win a major championship?

2-16   Who shot the lowest winning aggregate in the British Open Championship?

2-17   What is the longest course in the British Open Championship rotation?

2-18   Which major introduced the Junior Ticket Program for kids ages 8–16 to be admitted FREE with an accredited patron?

2-19   Which of the Masters Tournaments is generally considered the best one in its history?

2-20   Which two groups of two players won five out of six, and seven out of nine Masters Tournaments in consecutive years?

ANSWERS

GROUP
2

2-1   Five times (1921, 1924, 1925, 1926 & 1927), tied with Jack Nicklaus for most wins

2-2   The British Open Championship, October 17, 1860 at Prestwick Golf Club won by Willie Park, Sr.

2-3   Sam Snead, 61 years old, 1973, tied for 29th place

2-4   True; and also won in 1920 as an amateur

2-5   Gutta-percha

2-6   The PGA Championship

2-7   Lee Trevino, especially in 1971 and 1972

2-8   Dr. Alister MacKenzie, Donald J. Ross and A.W. Tillinghast

2-9   Ailsa Course at the Turnberry Resort Golf Club, Turnberry, Scotland

2-10   Herbert Warren Wind, 1958

2-11   Jerry Pate, one of the greatest shots in U.S. Open Championship history

2-12   The Masters Tournament

2-13   Father "Old" Tom Morris, Sr. (runner-up) and son "Young" Tom Morris, Jr. (winner), 1869 at Prestwick Golf Club

2-14   Claude Harmon, 1948

2-15   George Archer, six foot, five and a half inches, 1969 Masters Tournament

2-16   Greg Norman, 1993 at Royal St. George's Golf Club, 267 total

2-17   Carnoustie, 7421 yards, 2007

2-18   The Masters Tournament, 2008. A great idea to introduce and promote golf to young players.

2-19   Jack Nicklaus, 6th win in 1986 at age 46

2-20   Sam Snead (1949, 1952, 1954) and Ben Hogan (1951, 1953) broken by Jimmy Demaret in 1950; Arnold Palmer (1958, 1960, 1962, 1964) and Jack Nicklaus (1963, 1965, 1966) broken by Art Wall in 1959 and Gary Player in 1961

GROUP 3 QUESTIONS

3-1   Who was the first amateur to win the U.S. Open Championship?

3-2   Through 2007, how many times has Oakmont Country Club hosted the U.S. Open Championship?

3-3   What is the only major championship tournament held outside of the United States of America?

3-4   Name the three U.S. Open Championship winners from South Africa.

3-5   Who is the oldest winner of the Masters Tournament?

3-6   What major championship course did Nicklaus and Player call "the hardest course in the world?"

3-7   Who chipped-in on the second hole (#11) of a play-off to win the 1987 Masters Tournament, beating Greg Norman in sudden-death?

3-8   **T or F**   The PGA Championship has always been a stroke play tournament like the other majors.

3-9   What is par and total yardage at Augusta National Golf Club, home of the Masters Tournament?

3-10   Who has had the most consecutive starts in the U.S. Open Championship?

3-11   What is the 1951 movie title about the life of Ben Hogan?

3-12   What former dentist won a Masters Tournament and two U.S. Open Championships?

3-13   Who won two Purple Hearts in WWII, a U.S. Open in 1946 and the Vardon Trophy in 1951 and 1953?

3-14   How many tournaments did Byron Nelson win in the three year period of 1944-1945-1946?

3-15   **T or F** Between 1938 and 1954 the winner of the Masters had at least one round in the 60s.

3-16   How many rounds at par or below were shot in the 2007 U.S. Open Championship at Oakmont?

3-17   Who won the U.S. Open Championship called "The Massacre at Winged Foot?"

3-18   What was Jack Nicklaus' worst finish in the British Open Championship between 1980 and 1996?

3-19   **T or F**   Francis Ouimet, Ted Ray and Harry Vardon were all even after three rounds in the 1913 U.S. Open Championship at the Country Club.

3-20   Who was the "Dean of American Sports Writers" during the "Golden Age of Sports" handling the magazine, *The American Golfer?*

ANSWERS

GROUP
3

3-1   Francis Ouimet, 1913 at The Country Club, Brookline, MA in a play-off with Harry Vardon and Ted Ray

3-2   Eight times, more than any other championship course, Baltusrol Golf Club second at seven times

3-3   The Open Championship (known in the United States as The British Open)

3-4   Retief Goosen (2004, 2001), Ernie Els (1997, 1994), Gary Player (1965)

3-5   Jack Nicklaus, 46 years old, 1986

3-6   Carnoustie, British Open Championship course in Carnoustie, Scotland

3-7   Larry Mize

3-8   False; changed to stroke play in 1958 from match-play

3-9   Par 72, 7445 yards, 2008

3-10   Jack Nicklaus, 44 starts, 1957 to 2000

3-11   "Follow the Sun"

3-12   Cary Middlecoff, the Masters Tournament 1955, U.S. Open Championship 1949 and 1956

3-13   Lloyd Mangrum

3-14   32 tournament wins, including one major championship, the 1945 PGA

3-15   True

3-16   Eight rounds in four days!

3-17   Hale Irwin, 1974, seven over par winning score of 287

3-18   A sixth place finish

3-19   True; then all three players shot 79s in the final round to then play in an 18-hole play-off the next day for the championship

3-20   Mr. Grantland Rice

GROUP

4

QUESTIONS

4-1   Who is the only major winner to dot the "i" in "Script Ohio" at The Ohio State University?

4-2   Name the three players who have won the British Open Championship in three different decades?

4-3   How many golfers played the 36 holes in the first U.S. Open Championship?

4-4   Who shot what is considered the greatest final round ever to win the U.S. Open Championship?

4-5   Who was the first back-to-back winner of the Masters Tournament?

4-6   How many berms are there now in the church pews bunker between the third and fourth fairways at Oakmont Country Club?

4-7   What major championship does not invite amateurs to participate?

4-8   Which one of the three courses at Turnberry is the British Open Championship course?

4-9   Who is considered Europe's most successful golfer of all time?

4-10   Who finished second to Tiger Woods when he shot 270, 18 under par to win the 1997 Masters Tournament by 12 strokes?

4-11   Which Masters Tournament winner was the first to shoot two rounds in the 60s?

4-12   Name the five players who have won the Masters Tournament and the U.S. Open in the same year.

4-13   Who said, "He marked his ball with a dime and the dime slid away?"

4-14   Before Merion was a golf club, what was it?

4-15   Name the only player who has had the best score in all four rounds of the British Open.

4-16   Who won the PGA Championship in 1936 held at Pinehurst #2?

4-17   What classic major championship golf course is known for its "Figure 8" layout?

4-18   Which two players have won the British Open Championship twice at Muirfield?

4-19   What U.S. Open Championship golf course is named after the rarest pine tree in the United States?

4-20   Who was the golf teacher from Carnoustie in Scotland that coached Bobby Jones?

ANSWERS

GROUP 4

4-1   Jack Nicklaus—an easy question—but a great honor for Jack!

4-2   Harry Vardon (1896, 1903, 1911), J.H. Taylor (1894, 1900, 1913), Gary Player (1959, 1968, 1974)

4-3   11 contestants, 1895 at the Newport Golf and Country Club;
       10 pros and one amateur

4-4   Johnny Miller, 63 in 1973 at Oakmont Country Club, Oakmont, PA

4-5   Jack Nicklaus, 1965 and 1966

4-6   12 berms, 102 yards long, 18 yards wide at the narrowest end to 43 yards at the widest end, pews covered in fescue grass

4-7   The PGA Championship

4-8   The Ailsa Course

4-9   Nick Faldo; three British Open Championships and three Masters Tournament wins; also Harry Vardon is arguably in the running

4-10   Tom Kite

4-11   1939 Ralph Guldahl, 72-68-70-69, total 279

4-12   Craig Wood (1941), Ben Hogan (1951 and 1953), Arnold Palmer (1960), Jack Nicklaus (1972) and Tiger Woods (2002)

4-13   Sam Snead talking about Oakmont Country Club's fast greens

4-14   A cricket club

4-15   John Henry "JH" Taylor, never, ever done since in any major championship

4-16   Denny Shute, followed up by winning again in 1937 at Pittsburgh Field Club

4-17   Pebble Beach Golf Links in Pebble Beach, CA

4-18   James Braid (1901 and 1906); Nick Faldo (1987 and 1992)

4-19   Torrey Pines Golf Course, La Jolla, CA

4-20   Stewart Maiden

GROUP 5 QUESTIONS

5-1   What year did the PGA Championship change from match-play to medal-play?

5-2   What is the most northern course used for the British Open Championship?

5-3   Which two players went from being the 1st round leaders in the British Open to missing the cut?

5-4   What years did Walter Hagen win back-to-back PGA Championships?

5-5   What is the historical old nickname for caddies?

5-6   Who is the youngest winner of the British Open Championship?

5-7   Who set the record through 2008 for margin of victory in the PGA Championship of seven strokes?

5-8   Who was the first player to win the Masters Tournament four times?

5-9   Which Masters winner had previously worked the score board at the Augusta National Golf Club?

5-10   Walter Hagen is third with the most major championship wins at 11. Which one did he not win?

5-11   Who was the first player to shoot in the 60s for all four rounds of the U.S. Open Championship?

5-12   How many times did Arnold Palmer three-putt, which cost him the 1962 U.S. Open Championship?

5-13   Who did Ben Hogan beat in an 18-hole play-off to win the 1950 U.S. Open at Merion Golf Club?

5-14   How many U.S. Open Championships has the Olympic Club hosted?

5-15   What is the only major championship golf course to be designated a National Historic Landmark?

5-16   Who is the last man to win the U.S. Open Championship on his first attempt?

5-17   What is the most common name for the 18th hole on British Open Championship golf courses?

5-18   Who are the only two major championship winners on U.S. postage stamps?

5-19   What was the home course of famous golf architect Donald Ross?

5-20   Who are the only players to shoot a 63 in the U.S. Open Championship and not win?

ANSWERS

GROUP 5

5-1   1958

5-2   Carnoustie; Carnoustie, Scotland

5-3   1993, Joey Sindelar and in 1999, Rod Pampling

5-4   1924, 1925, 1926 and 1927, four years straight!

5-5   "The Beast of Burden," for carrying all the golfers' equipment

5-6   "Young" Tom Morris, Jr., 1868, 17 years old

5-7   Jack Nicklaus, 1980 at Oak Hill Country Club (East Course), Rochester, NY, 274 (-6)

5-8   Arnold Palmer, 1958, 1960, 1962 and 1964

5-9   Larry Mize, 1987 winner

5-10   The Masters Tournament, won two U.S. Opens, five PGA Championships and four British Opens

5-11   Lee Trevino, 1968 at Oakhill Country Club (East Course) score of 275 (69-68-69-69)

5-12   Seven times in first 72 holes, three times in play-off with Jack Nicklaus losing 71 to 74

5-13   Lloyd Mangrum (73) and George Fazio (75), Ben Hogan shot a 69

5-14   Four times, 1955, 1966, 1987 and 1998; fifth will be hosted in 2012

5-15   Oakmont Country Club, Oakmont, PA in 1987

5-16   Francis Ouimet, 1913 at the Country Club, Brookline, MA

5-17   "Home"

5-18   Francis Ouimet and Bobby Jones

5-19   Royal Dornoch, Scotland

5-20   Tom Weiskopf at Baltusrol Golf Club 1980 and Vijay Singh at Olympia Fields Country Club 2003

GROUP

6 QUESTIONS

6-1   As an amateur, how many U.S. Open Championships did Bobby Jones win in his career?

6-2   Who is the only player to win the U.S. Junior Amateur, the U.S. Amateur and the U.S. Open?

6-3   Who are the three players to win the Masters on their first attempt in the tournament?

6-4   **T or F** Through 2008, no winner of the Masters Tournament has shot all four rounds in the 60s.

6-5   What does the golf term "Albatross" mean?

6-6   What is "The Home Course" of the British Open Championship?

6-7   What was the nickname of Bobby Jones putter?

6-8   Which famous golf architect was the designer of Augusta National Golf Club?

6-9   Which two players have the highest number of aggregates under par in major championships?

6-10   Which U.S. Open championship winner was in the D-Day invasion June 6, 1944 with the British Navy off Utah Beach?

6-11   Who is the major winner who had his first winless year in 1979, then won the U.S. Open and PGA Championship in 1980?

6-12   What major golf course had the land named after a man who was murdered at his home?

6-13   Who are the three winners of the PGA Championship played at Oakland Hills Country Club?

6-14   What was the original award for the British Open Championship in 1860?

6-15   Which Ohio State Buckeye had a 3-stroke lead with three holes to play in the 1979 Masters to only bogey the last three holes and tie with Tom Watson and Fuzzy Zoeller?

6-16   Who is the only player to win the British Open Championship on five different courses?

6-17   What is the only major championship course with two venues ranked in the Top 100 America's Greatest Golf Courses by *Golf Digest?*

6-18   What year was the 2008 Masters winner Trevor Immelman the "Rookie of the Year?"

6-19   The terms 'Out' Nine and then back 'In' Nine came from what famous major course?

6-20   Which U.S. golf tournament (started in 1899, 3rd oldest) for several decades was regarded as a major championship?

ANSWERS

GROUP
6

6-1   Four times, 1923, 1926, 1929 and 1930

6-2   Tiger Woods

6-3   Horton Smith (1934), Gene Sarazen (1935), and Fuzzy Zoeller (1979)

6-4   True! No winner has four rounds in the 60s yet

6-5   Double-eagle, three strokes under par on a hole

6-6   Prestwick Golf Club, 1860

6-7   "Calamity Jane," after 1926 it was Calamity Jane II

6-8   Dr. Alister MacKenzie

6-9   Jack Nicklaus and Nick Faldo, both 14 times

6-10   Jack Fleck, U.S. Open Championship winner in 1955 over Ben Hogan at Olympic Club

6-11   Jack Nicklaus

6-12   Baltusrol Golf Club (Lower Course), Springfield, NJ named after Mr. Baltus Roll

6-13   Gary Player (1972), David Graham (1979), Padraig Harrington (2008)

6-14   "The Challenge Belt," with silver buckle and emblems

6-15   Ed Sneed

6-16   Tom Watson; Carnoustie (1975), Turnberry (1977), Muirfield (1980), Royal Troon (1982) and Royal Birkdale (1983)

6-17   Winged Foot Golf Club, West is 8th and East is 34th, Mamaroneck, NY

6-18   2006

6-19   Old Course St. Andrews, St. Andrews, Scotland

6-20   The Western Open, now the BMW Championship

QUESTIONS

7-1   Where is the fountain located recognizing Jack Nicklaus at the Masters Tournament?

7-2   How many times was Bobby Jones, Jr. low amateur in the U.S. Open Championship?

7-3   What is "Open Rough?"

7-4   Which two Ohio State Buckeye golfers have won a major championship golf tournament?

7-5   Name the four most popular golf books written by multiple major golf championship winners.

7-6   What year did the rubber-cored golf ball come into play during the major championships?

7-7   State the year each of the four major championships started.

7-8   Which famous World War II General was selected a Captain of the Royal and Ancient?

7-9   Which players have won all four majors at least twice through 2008?

7-10   How many times did Jack Nicklaus win the U.S. Open and the British Open in the same year?

7-11   Who were the modern day golfing "Triumvirate?"

7-12   Who won eight Order of Merit titles, but never won a major championship tournament?

7-13   Who was "the forgotten man of golf" as written by sports writer Jim Murray?

7-14   Which major winner was voted "Athlete of the Decade" for the 1960s?

7-15   How many times did Arnold Palmer win the Vardon Trophy?

7-16   What did winner Sandy Lyle of the 125th British Open Championship receive for his victory?

7-17   What type of planes flew from the Turnberry (Ailsa) air strips during World War II?

7-18   What was the first course outside of Scotland to host the British Open Championship?

7-19   **T or F** From 1940 to 1960 Ben Hogan never finished out of the Top 10 at the U.S. Open Championship except 1949 and 1957, both times because of injuries.

7-20   Who won the 1946 Masters after Ben Hogan missed a 30-inch putt on the 72nd hole?

ANSWERS

GROUP 7

7-1   Between holes #16 and #17, Augusta National Golf Club, Augusta, GA

7-2   Nine times! Most by any amateur, winning four times

7-3   Longer than normal, high cut grass in the rough at the U.S. Open Championship

7-4   Jack Nicklaus (18) and Tom Weiskopf (1)

7-5   *Down the Fairway* by Bobby Jones, *Five Lessons* by Ben Hogan, *Golf My Way* by Jack Nicklaus and *How I Play Golf* by Tiger Woods

7-6   1902, replacing the gutta-percha golf ball

7-7   The Open Championship (British Open) 1860, the U.S. Open Championship 1895, The PGA Championship 1916 and The Masters Tournament 1934

7-8   General Dwight Eisenhower in 1946; also a famous member of the Augusta National Golf Club

7-9   Jack Nicklaus and Tiger Woods

7-10   Never has happened

7-11   Jack Nicklaus, Arnold Palmer and Gary Player (also known as "The Big Three")

7-12   Colin Montgomerie, however five seconds; three U.S. Opens, one British Open and one PGA

7-13   Lloyd Mangrum, one U.S. Open win, major championship runner-up four other times and third in five more championships

7-14   Arnold Palmer

7-15   Four times: 1961, 1962, 1964 and 1967

7-16   A replica of "The Championship Belt," a red Morocco belt with silver clasps

7-17   Spitfires and "B-25 Liberators" flying sorties against German submarines

7-18   Royal St. George, Sandwich, England, 1894

7-19   True, winning four times in 1948, 1950, 1951 and 1953

7-20   Herman Keiser, after both three putted the 72nd hole on Sunday

QUESTIONS

8-1   Who holds the record for the 72-hole low score as an amateur in the U.S. Open Championship?

8-2   What was Ben Hogan's longest streak of Top 10 finishes in major championships?

8-3   Which player has won the most major championships on different golf courses?

8-4   What is the best selling book on golf?

8-5   Who was the first major winner to have a PGA Tour tournament named for him?

8-6   Which two players won U.S. Open Championships with key shots on #17, Par 3 at Pebble Beach?

8-7   Who is the last player to win the U.S. Open Championship back-to-back through 2008?

8-8   What three British Open Championship courses are on the West coast of Scotland?

8-9   **T or F** Through the 2008 Masters, Tiger Woods has never broken 70 in his first round when he went on to win the tournament.

8-10   Which major winner is often mentioned as the "Inventor" of the dog-leg golf hole design?

8-11   Who beat jack Nicklaus and Arnold Palmer in Jack's hometown of Columbus, OH to win the 1964 PGA Championship at Columbus Country Club by 3 strokes?

8-12   How many times has Arnold Palmer finished second in the PGA Championship, the only major he has not won?

8-13   What are the five courses that now make up the rotation for the British Open in Scotland?

8-14   Through 2008, what four California courses have hosted the U.S. Open Championship?

8-15   Which one of the par 3 holes at the Masters has never averaged below par for the tournament?

8-16   What is the largest margin of victory in a major championship?

8-17   Who was the first player to win both the Masters and the U.S. Open in the same year?

8-18   Which two other majors did Arnold Palmer win in 1962 before and after losing the U.S. Open to Jack Nicklaus at Oakmont Country Club?

8-19   **T or F** Sam Parks, Jr., winner of the 1935 U.S. Open at Oakmont, was a member of the club.

8-20   After the 1994 U.S. Open at Oakmont, what was the toughest hole in U.S. Open history?

ANSWERS

GROUP
8

8-1   Jack Nicklaus (282), 1960 at Cherry Hills in Englewood Colorado, runner-up to Arnold Palmer

8-2   18 for Hogan, 15 Hagen, 13 Nicklaus, Palmer and Snead 6

8-3   Jack Nicklaus with 11, Walter Hagen with ten and Ben Hogan with eight

8-4   Harvey's Penick's *Little Red Book.* Author Harvey Penick was a coach and instructor to two major championship winners, Ben Crenshaw and Tom Kite

8-5   Byron Nelson, Byron Nelson Golf Classic renamed in 1968

8-6   Jack Nicklaus in 1972, a one-iron striking the pin for a tap-in birdie and Tom Watson in 1982 with a chip-in out of the rough for a birdie

8-7   Curtis Strange, 1988 and 1989

8-8   Royal Troon Golf Club, Prestwick and Turnberry (Ailsa Course)

8-9   True!

8-10   James Braid

8-11   Bobby Nichols

8-12   Three times!

8-13   Carnoustie, Muirfield, Old Course St. Andrews, Royal Troon Golf Club and Turnberry (Ailsa)

8-14   Riviera Country Club, Olympic Club (Lake Course), Pebble Beach Golf Links and Torrey Pines

8-15   #12 in "Amen Corner®"

8-16   15 strokes, 12 under par, 2000 U.S. Open Championship at Pebble Beach Golf Links by Tiger Woods

8-17   Craig Wood in 1941

8-18   The Masters Tournament and the British Open Championship at Royal Troon Golf Club

8-19   False, however he lived in the area and was a Pro at South Hills Country Club, Pittsburgh, PA

8-20   #10, Par 4, 458 yards at Oakmont Country Club

9 QUESTIONS

9-1　Who is the only winner of the U.S. Open Championship at Winged Foot Golf Club to break par?

9-2　What year and which major championship was called the "Duel in the Sun?"

9-3　Who was the oldest player to win the U.S. Open Championship?

9-4　**T or F**　Ernie Els first American victory and first major win was the U.S. Open in 1994.

9-5　What is known as the "Career Slam?"

9-6　Who did John Daly beat to win the 1995 British Open on the Old Course St. Andrews after his opponent sank a 60-foot putt from the "Valley of Sin?"

9-7　Who won two U.S. Open Championships beating Payne Stewart both times by two strokes?

9-8　Who won four British Open Championships in 1949, 1950, 1952 and 1957?

9-9　How many of the first twelve British Open Championships were won by either "Old" or "Young" Tom Morris?

9-10　Byron Nelson and Ben Hogan were caddies together in the 1920s at what Country Club?

9-11　Who came from 7 strokes down, with 9 holes to play to tie Arnold Palmer and then beat him in the play-off of the 1966 U.S. Open Championship at the Olympic Club, 69 to 73?

9-12　Which two players hold the record for scoring under par (−18) in the PGA Championship?

9-13　Who was the first player to lose all four major championships in extra holes?

9-14　Who won the PGA Championship on both sides of World War I?

9-15　Who is the last champion to win the PGA Championship twice on the same golf course?

9-16　Who won more tournaments between 1964 and 1970 than Nicklaus, Palmer and Player?

9-17　Golf is governed by "34 Rules of Play," how many rules were there originally in 1744?

9-18　Whose sensational play at the British Open Championship is largely responsible for encouraging American players to come back and play in the British Open Championship?

9-19　How many double greens are there on the Old Course at St. Andrews?

9-20　What very famous British Open Championship course is bordered by the Firth of Forth?

ANSWERS

9-1   Fuzzy Zoeller, 1984 (−4) 276

9-2   1977, British Open at Turnberry Ailsa Course won by Tom Watson over Jack Nicklaus by one

9-3   Hal Irwin, 45 years, 15 days old in 1990 at Medinah Country Club #3

9-4   True; winning in a play-off over Colin Montgomerie and Loren Roberts

9-5   Winning all four major championships in a golfing career. Has only done by five players—Sarazen, Hogan, Player, Nicklaus and Woods

9-6   Costantino Rocca, Daly shooting a final round of 71

9-7   Lee Janzen in 1993 Baltusrol-Lower and 1998 Olympic Club-Lake Course

9-8   Bobby Locke from South Africa

9-9   Eight out of 12, four each by father and son

9-10   Glen Garden Golf and Country Club, Fort Worth, TX

9-11   Billy Casper

9-12   Bob May, 2000 and Tiger Woods, 2000 and 2006

9-13   Craig Wood

9-14   Jim Barnes, 1916 and 1919; no championship was held in 1917 and 1918

9-15   Tiger Woods, 1999 and 2006, Medinah Country Club #3, Medinah, IL

9-16   Billy Casper

9-17   "13 Rules of Golf," written by The Honourable Company of Edinburgh Golfers

9-18   Arnold Palmer, "The King," winning at Royal Birkdale Golf Club in 1961

9-19   Seven, only the 1st, 9th, 17th and 18th hole are single greens; (2-16), (3-15), (4-14), (5-13), (6-12), (7-11) and (8-10)

9-20   Muirfield, Gullane, Scotland

"Who Said?"

10-1   "If you have to remind yourself to concentrate during competition, you got no chance to concentrate."

10-2   "I'm not going to let golf interfere with my fishing."

10-3   "Golf is not a game of good shots. It's a game of bad shots."

10-4   "Too many people carry the last shot with them. It is a heavy and useless burden."

10-5   "Golf is a game of days, and I can beat anyone on my day."

10-6   "Confidence is everything. From there, it's a small step to winning."

10-7   "Ben Hogan would rather have a coral snake rolling inside his shirt than hit a hook."

10-8   "Give me a man with big hands, big feet and no brains, and I will make a golfer out of him."

10-9   "Golf is like a chain. You always have to work on the weakest links."

10-10   "If you want to help yourself and the game, don't play slowly, your concentration wanders."

10-11   "When Jack Nicklaus plays well, he wins. When he plays badly, he finishes second. When he plays terribly, he finishes third."

10-12   "Golf, is based on honesty. Where else would you admit to a seven on a par 3."

10-13   "It's like playing in a strait jacket. They just lay you up on the rack and twist on both ends."

10-14   "Golfers find it a very trying matter to turn at the waist, more particularly if they have a lot of waist to turn."

10-15   "Putts get real difficult the day they hand out the money."

10-16   "Work puts a negative connotation on practicing."

10-17   "You can talk to a fade, but a hook won't listen."

10-18   "Golf fairways should be more narrow. Then everybody would have to play from the rough, not just me."

10-19   "What a shame to waste those great shots on the practice tee. I'd be afraid of finding out what I was doing wrong."

10-20   "Golf is deceptively simple and endlessly complicated."

ANSWERS

GROUP

10

"Who Said?"

10-1	Bobby Nichols
10-2	Tiger Woods
10-3	Ben Hogan
10-4	Johnny Miller
10-5	Fuzzy Zoeller
10-6	Craig Stadler
10-7	Claude Harmon
10-8	Walter Hagen
10-9	George Archer
10-10	Gene Sarazen
10-11	Johnny Miller
10-12	Jimmy Demaret
10-13	Ben Crenshaw
10-14	Harry Vardon
10-15	Lee Trevino
10-16	Tom Kite
10-17	Lee Trevino
10-18	Seve Ballesteros
10-19	Walter Hagen
10-20	Arnold Palmer

QUESTIONS

11-1   Who said, "The secret of golf is to turn three shots into two."?

11-2   What did Jack Nicklaus shoot to beat Arnold Palmer in the 1962 U.S. Open play-off?

11-3   What U.S. Open Championship was televised locally for the first time?

11-4   Which U.S. Open winner started sponsoring a college scholarship for qualified caddies?

11-5   **T or F** Sam Snead won the Vardon Trophy in three different decades.

11-6   What course at Oakland Hills Country Club is called "The Monster?"

11-7   Who won the Masters Tournament's first sudden-death play-off?

11-8   What is the lowest single round score in the U.S. Open Championship and the Masters?

11-9   Byron Nelson shot a first round 66 in the 1937 Masters. Who shot a 65 in the first round to break this record?

11-10   Which PGA Championship winner served in the marines, was wounded in the Battle of Iwo Jima and won a purple heart?

11-11   Which course is the most often one used in the British Open Championship rotation?

11-12   Who was the first player to birdie the 72nd hole in a U.S. Open to win the title outright?

11-13   Which major winner was second to S. Davidson Herron in 1916 for the U.S. Amateur at Oakmont Country Club?

11-14   Which two major winners are only missing a British Open Championship to have a Career Grand Slam?

11-15   Which player and golf writer are credited with developing the concept of the "Grand Slam?"

11-16   Which U.S. Open winner was head professional at Chicago Golf Club, America's first course to have 18 holes?

11-17   Who was the first player since Francis Ouimet in the 1913 U.S. Open to win his first major debut?

11-18   What British Open Championship course have produced the two highest aggregate scores (289 and 290) since World War II?

11-19   How many times have players won two consecutive victories in the British Open?

11-20   Which major winner won three consecutive U.S. Amateur Championships?

ANSWERS

11-1   Bobby Jones

11-2   Jack Nicklaus 71, Arnold Palmer 74, at Oakmont Country Club

11-3   1947, St. Louis Country Club

11-4   Chick Evans Jr., 1929, The Evans Scholars Foundation was formed

11-5   True! 1938, 1949, 1950 and 1955

11-6   The South Course

11-7   Fuzzy Zoeller, 1979 over Tom Watson and Ed Sneed

11-8   63

11-9   Raymond Floyd, shooting a 65, 39 years later

11-10   Jay Hebert, 1960 winner at Firestone Country Club, South Course in Akron, OH

11-11   Old Course St. Andrews, 27 times since 1860 and returning in 2010 for 150th Anniversary

11-12   Bobby Jones, 1926 at Scioto Country Club in Columbus, OH (home of Jack Nicklaus).

11-13   Bobby Jones

11-14   Byron Nelson and Raymond Floyd

11-15   Arnold Palmer and his sportswriter buddy, Bob Drum

11-16   James Foulis, winner of the 2nd U.S. Open Championship at Shinnecock Hills Golf Club

11-17   Ben Curtis; 2003 British Open Championship at Royal St. George's, Sandwich, England

11-18   Carnoustie; Carnoustie, Scotland

11-19   17 times from Old Tom Morris, Sr. to Padraig Harrington 2008

11-20   Tiger Woods, only player to ever win three in a row! TPC Sawgrass (1994), Newport Country Club (1995) and Pumpkin Ridge Golf Club (1996)

GROUP

12 QUESTIONS

12-1   Who is the only player to lose three U.S. Open Championships in a play-off?

12-2   What is the lowest final round ever shot by the winner of the British Open Championship?

12-3   What British Open Championship course had gun placements on its Atlantic coastline during World War II?

12-4   Who won the 1972 U.S. Open Championship at Pebble Beach tying Bobby Jones with 13 majors?

12-5   Has the U.S. Open Championship ever ended on a par 3 hole?

12-6   What is the golf governing body outside of the United States and Mexico?

12-7   Who scored the first "Ace," hole-in-one in a major golf championship?

12-8   What were the career earnings of the great Bobby Jones?

12-9   In order, name the Top Five major professional championship tournament winners through 2008.

12-10   How old was Bobby Jones when he retired after "The Impregnable Quadrilateral?"

12-11   What was the first year the Masters Tournament was televised?

12-12   Which two Argentine players have won major championships?

12-13   How many players have won three major championships (since the 1934 Masters) in six major championships or less?

12-14   Who lost the PGA Championship in 1951 to Sam Snead seven and six at Oakmont, but won two years later four and three at Birmingham Country Club?

12-15   Who was the first major championship winner to play in "knickers?"

12-16   **T or F** The winner of the Masters is automatically invited to play in the other three majors for five years and has a lifetime invitation to the Masters Tournament.

12-17   With what debilitating disease was Bobby Jones diagnosed?

12-18   Which winner of the U.S. Open Championship qualified in England to play in the championship?

12-19   Jack Nicklaus won three British Open Championships (1966, 1970 and 1977). How many times was he a runner-up?

12-20   **T or F** Through 2008, Tiger Woods has never missed a cut at the Masters Tournament.

ANSWERS

12-1   Arnold Palmer, 1962 Oakmont Country Club, 1963 The Country Club and 1966 The Olympic Club

12-2   Greg Norman, 64 in 1993 at Royal St. George's Golf Club, Sandwich, England

12-3   Turnberry Ailsa Course to defend against the Germans

12-4   Jack Nicklaus

12-5   Yes, four times: 1896 Shinnecock Hills, 1902 Garden City Golf Club, 1909 Englewood Golf Club and 1997 Congressional Country Club

12-6   Royal and Ancient

12-7   "Young" Tom Morris, Jr. in 1868 at #8 on Prestwick

12-8   Zero, he was an amateur and never accepted any money

12-9   Jack Nicklaus (18), Tiger Woods (14), Walter Hagen (11), Ben Hogan (9) and Gary Player (9)

12-10   28 years old!

12-11   1955

12-12   Roberto DeVicenzo (British Open 1967), Angel Cabrera (U.S. Open 2007)

12-13   Nine: Guldahl, Hogan, Palmer, Nicklaus, Trevino, Watson, Faldo, Woods, Harrington

12-14   Walter Burkemo, also was runner-up the next year four and three to Chick Harbert

12-15   Harry Vardon, also Bobby Jones and Gene Sarazen, but Payne Stewart made them "famous"

12-16   True! plus winning over $1 million and normally numerous endorsements

12-17   Syringomyelia

12-18   Michael Campbell, 2005 at Pinehurst Resort #2

12-19   Seven times

12-20   False; missed cut in 1996 as an amateur

GROUP 13 QUESTIONS

13-1   Who set the record of six-straight sub-par rounds in the U.S. Open Championship?

13-2   What is the oldest golf course in the world?

13-3   What amateur was one stroke off from being in the Ben Hogan and Sam Snead 1954 Masters play-off?

13-4   Which three major golfing legends hit the ceremonial tee shots for the 1998 Masters?

13-5   If a 5-iron is a called "mashie" and a 9-iron is a called "niblick", what is a 7-iron called?

13-6   Since 2002, which major championship has had the largest prize fund?

13-7   How many times did Jack Nicklaus three-putt during the 1962 U.S. Open Championship at Oakmont Country Club over 90 holes?

13-8   What is the name for the award (trophy named after a major winner) for the lowest stroke average for the year/season?

13-9   Who was the first player to win a "Career Grand Slam?"

13-10 How many shots behind Mike Souchak was Arnold Palmer when teeing-off in the final round of the 1960 U.S. Open Championship at Cherry Hills Country Club in Denver, CO?

13-11 Who won the 1956 Masters Tournament and the 1956 PGA Championship?

13-12 Where is the PGA Tour headquarters located?

13-13 Who is the only player to win three straight U.S. Open Championships through 2008?

13-14 Who lost to Francis Ouimet in the 1913 U.S. Open, but won the British Open at Muirfield in 1912 and the U.S. Open Championship at the Inverness Club in 1920?

13-15 Name the two left-handed players who won the same major one year after the other (back-to-back).

13-16 Who lost the last match when the PGA Championship was match-play; but won the first PGA Championship when it was contested in medal-play?

13-17 **T or F** Padraig Harrington lead the 2008 PGA Championship in birdies and putts.

13-18 Who won two PGA Championships in the 70s and tied for second in the Masters and U.S. Open?

13-19 What was the "Spalding Kro-Flite?"

13-20 How many times was Arnold Palmer a runner-up to Jack Nicklaus in major championships?

ANSWERS

13-1   Sam Snead, 1947 and 1948

13-2   The Old Course St. Andrews, 1552 at St. Andrews, Fife, Scotland

13-3   Billy Joe Patton

13-4   Byron Nelson, Gene Sarazen and Sam Snead

13-5   "Mashie-niblick" developed by James Foulis

13-6   The Open Championship, aka British Open in the United States

13-7   One-time! Amazing on Oakmont Country Club's historic "fast" greens

13-8   The Vardon Trophy

13-9   Gene Sarazen, when he won the 1935 Masters Tournament

13-10   Seven shots behind, shoots a 65 (280) to win!

13-11   Jack Burke, Jr.

13-12   100 PGA Tour Blvd., Ponte Vedra Beach, Florida 32082 www.pgatour.com

13-13   Willie Anderson (1903-1904-1905) plus 1901, four out of five years

13-14   English golfer "Ted" Ray

13-15   Mike Weir 2003; Phil Mickelson 2004, Masters Tournament

13-16   Dow Finsterwald, 1957 (match-play), 1958 (medal-play)

13-17   True!

13-18   Dave Stockton, PGAs; 1970 Southern Hills Country Club and
        1976 Congressional Country Club

13-19   The first liquid-center golf ball with wound rubber and balata outer surface, 1930

13-20   Three times, 1962 U.S. Open Championship play-off at Oakmont, 1965 Masters
        Tournament, 1967 U.S. Open Championship at Baltusrol Golf Club.

14-1 How many birdies did Johnny Miller have in his record-setting 63 in the U.S. Open Championship at Oakmont Country Club in 1973?

14-2 Which four players hold the record for the lowest winning score in the U.S. Open at 272?

14-3 Who was the second amateur to win the U.S. Open Championship in 1915 at Baltusrol Golf Club, and also won four U.S. Amateurs?

14-4 Who holed out a greenside bunker shot to win the 1986 PGA Championship at the Inverness Club?

14-5 **T or F** Fuzzy Zoeller won both of his major championships in play-offs.

14-6 On which course did Ben Hogan win his only British Open Championship in 1953?

14-7 What are the only two municipal golf courses used so far for the U.S. Open Championship?

14-8 Besides Gary Player, who is the other player from South Africa to win the Masters Tournament?

14-9 How many club pros out of 156 entries qualify to play in the PGA Championship?

14-10 During World War II, what was Augusta National Golf Club used for?

14-11 Who lost (runner-up) to Ernie Els twice in the U.S. Open Championship?

14-12 What three consecutive years was the winning score (280) the same at the Masters Tournament?

14-13 Which one of the three courses at the Olympic Club is the championship course?

14-14 What two major championships did Hubert Green win?

14-15 What major championship features a four-hole play-off format for all golfers tied after 72 holes?

14-16 Which three winners of the British Open Championship where British born, but U.S. citizens before winning their British Open titles?

14-17 Sam Snead played against Ben Hogan three times in head-to-head play-offs, including one Masters Tournament. What was his record?

14-18 Which major winner led all four majors going into the final round in 1986, but won only once?

14-19 Who finished 20 times in the Top 10 in the major championships, but never won one?

14-20 Who was a runner-up four times to Jack Nicklaus in the majors, one Masters (1972), one U.S. Open (1972), and two PGAs (1973 and 1975)?

ANSWERS

14-1   Nine birdies, one bogey, winning the U.S. Open Championship

14-2   Jack Nicklaus, Lee Janzen, Tiger Woods and Jim Furyk

14-3   Jerome Travers

14-4   Bob Tway, winning by two shots (276) over Greg Norman

14-5   True; 1979 Masters Tournament over Ed Sneed and Tom Watson in sudden-death; 1984 U.S. Open Championship over Greg Norman 67-75.

14-6   Carnoustie, Carnoustie, Scotland

14-7   Bethpage State Park (Black Course) 2002 Bethpage, NY; Torrey Pines (South) 2008 La Jolla, CA

14-8   Trevor Immelman, 2008

14-9   20, from the Club Pro Championship held in July

14-10   A farm, supporting the American war effort

14-11   One stroke in 1997, play-off loss in 1994, 74-78—Colin Montgomerie

14-12   Jimmy Demaret 1940, Wood Craig 1941 and Byron Nelson 1942

14-13   Lakes Course; other two: Ocean Course and Cliffs Course (Par 3)

14-14   1977 U.S. Open Championship at Southern Hills and 1985 PGA Championship at Cherry Hills

14-15   The Open (British Open) Championship

14-16   Jock Hutchinson, Tommy Armour and Jim Barnes

14-17   3-0, never lost a major championship play-off to Ben Hogan

14-18   Greg Norman, winning the British Open Championship at Turnberry Ailsa Course

14-19   Harry Cooper

14-20   Bruce Crampton

GROUP 15 QUESTIONS

15-1   Where are the Hogan and Nelson bridges located at the Augusta National Golf Club?

15-2   Who was the youngest winner of the PGA Championship?

15-3   What two major championships did Nick Price win back-to-back?

15-4   Through 2008, how many times has Tiger Woods won the PGA Championship back-to-back?

15-5   Who was the last amateur to win the British Open Championship?

15-6   Besides Tiger Woods, who was the last player to win two or more majors in the same year?

15-7   Who won two Masters and had two runner-ups in the British Open Championship and is second in career wins on the European Tour?

15-8   What three consecutive years did Tom Watson win the Vardon Trophy?

15-9   Who ended Byron Nelson's streak of 11 straight wins in 1945?

15-10 Who accomplished the best come-from-behind (seven shots) to tie and win the sudden-death play-off in a PGA Championship?

15-11 Which major championship winner was the first to win more than $10 million in a season?

15-12 Who was the first winner of the Masters Tournament to win and wear "The Green Jacket?"

15-13 Who won the first British Open Championship in 1860 and how many more?

15-14 Who was the first international player to win the Masters Tournament?

15-15 What was the first 18-hole course to host the U.S. Open Championship?

15-16 Which two players have the highest number of Top Five finishes in the British Open Championship?

15-17 Since the first telecast of the Masters in 1956, how many times has the winner finished over par?

15-18 How many of each major championship did Lee Trevino win?

15-19 What is the biggest span in years between the first and last win for a player in the British Open?

15-20 When did the string start with more than 100 players entering the U.S. Open Championship?

GROUP
ANSWERS
15

15-1   No. 12, Par 3, 155 yards

15-2   Gene Sarazen, 20 years old in 1922 at Oakmont Country Club, Oakmont, PA

15-3   1994 British Open Championship at Turnberry and the PGA Championship at Southern Hills

15-4   Two times, 1998 and 1999, and 2006 and 2007

15-5   Bobby Jones in 1930 at Royal Liverpool Golf Club, Hoylake, England

15-6   Padraig Harrington, 2008 British Open at Royal Birkdale Golf Club and PGA at Oakland Hills Country Club

15-7   Bernhard Langer

15-8   1977, 1978 and 1979

15-9   Freddie Haas, Jr., an amateur at the Memphis Open

15-10   John Mahaffey, 1978 PGA Championship beating Tom Watson and Jerry Pate at Oakmont Country Club

15-11   Vijay Singh, 2004

15-12   Sam Snead, 1949, one of golf's greatest traditions!

15-13   Willie Park, Sr., three more in 1863, 1866 and 1875

15-14   Gary Player, 1961, 8 under par, 280

15-15   The Chicago Golf Club, 1897, the third U.S. Open Championship

15-16   John Henry "JH" Taylor and Jack Nicklaus, with 16 each

15-17   One time, Zach Johnson, 2007, 1 over par, 289

15-18   Two each U.S. Opens (1968, 1971), British Opens (1971, 1972), PGA Championship (1974, 1984), no Masters Tournament wins

15-19   19 years by John Henry "JH" Taylor, 1894–1913

15-20   1919 with 142 players, no U.S. Open Championship between 1917–1918 during World War I

QUESTIONS

16-1 What is the name of the trophy for winning the PGA Championship?

16-2 What famous shot did Phil Mickelson hit on #18 to win the 2005 PGA Championship at Baltusrol?

16-3 What was the last major championship Gene Sarazen won to complete his "Grand Slam?"

16-4 How many strokes was Johnny Miller behind when he teed-off in the fourth round of the 1973 U.S. Open Championship at Oakmont Country Club?

16-5 What did Jack Nicklaus shoot on his last round at St. Andrews in the 2005 British Open?

16-6 Who was the last match-play era winner of the PGA Championship?

16-7 What is the name of the award given to media members who have covered 40 or more Masters?

16-8 **T or F** Wire-to-wire, Ben Hogan won his fourth U.S. Open Championship by six shots over Sam Snead at Oakmont Country Club in 1953.

16-9 Who was struck by lightning (on a golf course) at the age of 15 to later go on and win two U.S. Open Championship titles?

16-10 Who was the first post-World War II winner of the British Open Championship?

16-11 Who was the fifth and last amateur player to win the U.S. Open Championship?

16-12 Which five players have won wire-to-wire Masters Tournaments through 2008?

16-13 Which British Open Championship winner, actually three time winner, was "Knighted"?

16-14 From a list of the leading major winners as of (2008), how many are still active with five or more?

16-15 Where is the World Golf Hall of Fame located?

16-16 How many times has major winner John Daly won the driving distance crown?

16-17 What tournament is unofficially known as the "Fifth Major?"

16-18 Who did Gene Sarazen beat in the 1922 U.S. Open Championship?

16-19 Who made the most appearances (15) before winning his first Masters?

16-20 How many times has the British Open Championship winner had a hole-in-one?

ANSWERS

GROUP
16

16-1   Wanamaker Trophy, given originally by Rodman Wanamaker a department store magnate

16-2   His trademark "Flop Shot" to two feet for a tap in birdie

16-3   1935 Masters Tournament

16-4   Six shots behind the four co-leaders, Schlee, Palmer, Boros and Heard

16-5   Even par 72, birdied the 18th hole, but missed the cut by three shots shooting 147

16-6   1957, Lionel Hebert over Dow Finsterwald, two and one

16-7   Masters Major Achievement Award, started in 2007

16-8   True! Hogan finished birdie-birdie shooting a 71 to Sam Snead's 76

16-9   Retief Goosen, 2001 at Southern Hills and 2004 at Shinnecock Hills

16-10   Sam Snead, 1946 at the Old Course St. Andrews, St. Andrews, Scotland

16-11   Johnny Goodman 1933; other amateurs Francis Ouimet 1913, Jerome Travers 1915, Chick Evans 1916, and Bobby Jones 1923, 1926, 1929 and 1930

16-12   Craig Wood 1941, Arnold Palmer 1960, Jack Nicklaus 1972, Raymond Floyd 1976, Trevor Immelman 2008

16-13   Sir Henry Cotton, British Open Champion 1934, 1937 and 1948

16-14   One, Tiger Woods with 14 wins, all the others (17) no longer play on the PGA Tour except Gary Player who competed in the 2008 Masters at the age of 72.

16-15   World Golf Hall of Fame, One World Golf Place, St. Augustine, FL 32092 www.wgv.com

16-16   11 times through 2004, eight consecutive times

16-17   The Players Championship, which includes the largest purse of the year

16-18   Bobby Jones by one shot, coming back from a four-shot deficit

16-19   Mark O'Meara, winning the 1998 Masters Tournament

16-20   Three times, Prestwick 1869 (Tom Morris, Jr.) and 1878 (Jamie Anderson) and the Old Course St. Andrews 1921 (Jock Hutchison)

GROUP

17 QUESTIONS

Nicknames of Major Championship Winners

17-1   "The King"

17-2   "Sarge"

17-3   "The Shark"

17-4   "The Merry Mex"

17-5   "Lord Byron"

17-6   "Boom-boom"

17-7   "Gene the Machine"

17-8   "Gentle Ben"

17-9   "Long John"

17-10   "The Golden Bear"

17-11   "The Haig"

17-12   "The Silver Scot"

17-13   "The Big Easy"

17-14   "Tiger"

17-15   "Huckleberry Dillinger"

17-16   "The Hawk"

17-17   "Slammin' Sammy"

17-18   "Fuzzy"

17-19   "The Black Knight"

17-20   "The Squire"

ANSWERS

GROUP **17**

Nicknames of Major Championship Winners

17-1   Arnold Palmer

17-2   Orville Moody

17-3   Greg Norman

17-4   Lee Trevino

17-5   Byron Nelson

17-6   Freddie Couples

17-7   Gene Littler

17-8   Ben Crenshaw

17-9   John Daly

17-10   Jack Nicklaus

17-11   Walter Hagen

17-12   Tommy Armour

17-13   Ernie Els

17-14   Eldrick Woods

17-15   Tom Watson

17-16   Ben Hogan

17-17   Sam Snead

17-18   Frank Urban Zoeller, Jr.

17-19   Gary Player

17-20   Gene Sarazen

18-1   Who were the members of golf's "Great Triumvirate?"

18-2   How many times was Jack Nicklaus second to Lee Trevino in major championships?

18-3   Through 2008, which two players have won the PGA Championship five times?

18-4   Arguably, what is the most difficult finishing hole in the British Open Championship?

18-5   Which British player won the British Open Championship in 1969 for the first time in 18 years?

18-6   Since 1990, how often has St. Andrews been scheduled for hosting the British Open Championship?

18-7   What one major championship did Byron Nelson not win in his career?

18-8   Which one of the British Open Championship golf courses does not have a "Pro Shop?"

18-9   Name the three winners of the Masters with a winning score of plus 1 (289)?

18-10   Name the five players with four runner-up finishes in the U.S. Open Championship?

18-11   Who won one U.S. Open Championship and finished in the Top Ten eight out of nine times?

18-12   On which hole at the Masters Tournament did Arnold Palmer receive a favorable ruling that helped him to his first Masters win in 1958?

18-13   Through 2008, name the four major winners who have won both an NCAA Championship and a U.S. Amateur Championship?

18-14   Which major player won an event, a record eight times, and a PGA Tour event at the age of 52 years, 10 months, 8 days—the oldest player to win a PGA Tour tournament?

18-15   What year did the "Official World Ranking" debut?

18-16   Who reached the semifinals of the PGA Championship in match-play four times, but never won, and finished tied for third?

18-17   Of what fraternity were Payne Stewart, Denny Shute and Jack Nicklaus members?

18-18   **T or F** Curtis Strange won his back-to-back U.S. Open Championships by the same gross score.

18-19   Who did Roberto DeVicenzo beat to win the 1967 British Open Championship?

18-20   Who, on the final day of the 1999 British Open Championship, trailed by 10 shots, but got into the play-off and won?

18-1 British Golfers James Braid, J.H. Taylor and Harry Vardon

18-2 Four times, 1968 and 1971 U.S. Open Championship, 1972 British Open Championship and 1984 PGA Championship

18-3 Walter Hagen: 1921, 1924, 1925, 1926 and 1927; Jack Nicklaus: 1963, 1971, 1973, 1975 and 1980

18-4 The "Home" hole at Carnoustie, Par 4, 444 yards plus the Barry Burn comes into play

18-5 Tony Jacklin

18-6 Every five years, years that end in a "0" or a "5" in the year, 150th Anniversary 2010

18-7 The British Open Championship

18-8 Muirfield in Gullane, Scotland

18-9 Sam Snead 1954, Jack Burke, Jr. 1956 and Zach Johnson 2007

18-10 Bobby Jones, Sam Snead, Arnold Palmer, Jack Nicklaus and Phil Mickelson

18-11 Willie Smith won in 1899, one of the three famous Smith golfing brothers

18-12 Embedded ball on #12 Par 3, 155 yards, credited with a three instead of a five

18-13 Justin Leonard, Phil Mickelson, Jack Nicklaus and Tiger Woods

18-14 Sam Snead winning the Greater Greensboro Open eight times

18-15 1986

18-16 Jimmy Demaret in 1942, 1946, 1948 and 1950

18-17 Phi Gamma Delta ..."Fijis"

18-18 True! 1988, −2 (278) at the Country Club; 1989, −6 (278) at Oak Hill Country Club, East Course

18-19 Jack Nicklaus by two strokes (278) at Royal Liverpool Golf Club

18-20 Scottish Player, Paul Lawrie at Carnoustie

19-1   What was Jack Nicklaus' first professional win?

19-2   Who was the first Canadian ever to win a major championship tournament?

19-3   Who is the only player to make back-to-back eagles at Augusta on the 13th and 14th holes?

19-4   Which one of the courses at Baltusrol Golf Club is used for major championships?

19-5   What were the identical scores Jack Nicklaus and Tom Watson shot for the first three rounds at the British Open Championship "Duel in the Sun" at Turnberry in 1977?

19-6   Who lost to Ben Hogan in the 1950 U.S. Open at Merion Golf Club and later became a notable golf course architect?

19-7   What four courses in England are in the rotation of the British Open Championship?

19-8   Who were the first father and son to play in a PGA Championship?

19-9   Why did King James II ban golf in 1457 at St. Andrews?

19-10   Who made the longest putt (15 feet) in U.S. Open history on the 18th hole (72nd hole) to win?

19-11   **T or F** As of 2008, the tournament record for under par is the same for the Masters and the PGA Championship.

19-12   Who was the first major winner to have won his first event of his professional career?

19-13   Who shot 10 under par over the last 36 holes at Oakmont to beat Tom Watson by one, winning the 1983 U.S. Open Championship?

19-14   Which two major championship winners are also known as outstanding bird hunters?

19-15   Who has the most Top 10 finishes in the U.S. Open Championship?

19-16   Which famous golf architect was fifth in the U.S. Open and eighth in the British Open?

19-17   Who were the "Big Five" in Europe, all winning majors?

19-18   Which major winner designed the British Open Championship course at Royal Birkdale?

19-19   Which two-time winner of the U.S. Open also won the NCAA Division II Golf Championship?

19-20   Who was the first three-time winner of the Masters Tournament?

ANSWERS

19-1   The U.S. Open Championship, 1962 at Oakmont Country Club beating Arnold Palmer in a play-off 71-74. The first of Jack's 18 major championships.

19-2   Mike Weir, the 2003 Masters Tournament 281 (−7)

19-3   Dan Pohl in 1982, later losing to Craig Stadler in a play-off

19-4   The Lower Course, Par 70, 7,392 yards

19-5   68-70-65, final round Jack Nicklaus 66, Tom Watson 65

19-6   George Fazio, uncle to famous course designer Tom Fazio

19-7   Royal St. George's, Royal Birkdale, Royal Lytham & St. Annes and Royal Liverpool Golf Clubs

19-8   1998, The Geibergers, Al (1966 winner) and son Brent

19-9   His archers were playing more golf than practicing their archery for defense of the country

19-10   Payne Stewart beating Phil Mickelson by one shot at the 1999 U.S. Open Championship hosted at Pinehurst Resort #2

19-11   True, 18 under par. British Open is 19 under par and U.S. Open is 12 under par

19-12   Ben Crenshaw in 1973 winning the San Antonio Texas Open

19-13   Larry Nelson; also won the 1981 and 1987 PGA Championships

19-14   Bobby Jones was an avid bird hunter in Georgia, as was Tom Watson in the Plains States

19-15   Jack Nicklaus, 18 times

19-16   Donald Ross, however his brother Alec won the 1907 U.S. Open at the Philadelphia Cricket Club

19-17   Seve Ballesteros, Nick Faldo, Bernhard Langer, Sandy Lyle and Ian Woosnam

19-18   John Henry "J.H." Taylor in 1957

19-19   Lee Janzen, NCAA in 1986 playing for Florida Southern; U.S. Open Championships 1993 Baltusrol Golf Club and 1998 Olympic Club beating Payne Stewart both times

19-20   Jimmy Demaret in 1940, 1947 and 1950, his only major championship wins

GROUP

20 QUESTIONS

20-1 Who was the Oakmont Country Club founder and architect?

20-2 What type of putter did Jack Nicklaus use to win the 1986 Masters Tournament?

20-3 Which amateur played in 18 Masters Tournaments and set the standard?

20-4 What major championship golf course will host its fifth U.S Open in 2010, its 6th major championship overall including the 1977 PGA Championship?

20-5 A #1 wood is called a driver, what is a #2, #3 and #4 wood called?

20-6 The 8th hole, a par 3 at Oakmont replaced what par 3 as the longest one in the U.S. Open history?

20-7 Who went wire-to-wire at Southern Hills to win the 1982 PGA Championship by three strokes?

20-8 What ball was named after Henry Cotton's 65 in the 1934 British Open Championship?

20-9 Who did Tiger Woods beat by one stroke in a three-hole play-off to win his third major in a year to match Ben Hogan's record in 1953?

20-10 Who won two Masters, but had two runner-ups in the British Open, one second in a PGA Championship and a third in a U.S. Open Championship during the 1970s?

20-11 Course logo: A wicker basket (upside down lobster pot)?

20-12 **T or F** "Career Majors" have been the same since the start of the Masters Tournament in 1934.

20-13 Who was the first winner of the Bob Jones Award?

20-14 What major championship has Tom Watson not won to complete a Career Grand Slam?

20-15 Who is the first player from the Republic of Ireland to win a major championship?

20-16 In America we commonly call the tees white, blue and black; what do they call them in Scotland?

20-17 Through 2008, how many times has Tiger Woods been the AP Athlete of the Year?

20-18 What do Ben Crenshaw, Henry Cotton, Julius Boros and Hale Irwin all have in common?

20-19 **T or F** British tradition was to wear red coats to warn others that golfers were coming through.

20-20 Has any player ever eagled the 72nd hole to win a U.S. Open Championship?

ANSWERS

GROUP
20

20-1   Mr. Henry C. Fownes

20-2   Response ZT, manufactured by MacGregor Golf

20-3   Bill Campbell, Former President of USGA and Captain of the Royal & Ancient

20-4   Pebble Beach Golf Links, Pebble Beach, CA

20-5   #2 Brassie, #3 Spoon, #4 Baffy

20-6   Replaced #17 at Interlachen Country Club at 262 yards, 1930 U. S Open Championship

20-7   Raymond Floyd

20-8   Dunlop 65

20-9   Bob May, 2000 PGA Championship at Valhalla Golf Club in Louisville, KY

20-10   Ben Crenshaw

20-11   Merion Golf Club, East Course, Ardmore, PA. Hosted the U.S. Open in 1934, 1950, 1971, 1981 and will host it again in 2013

20-12   False. The current majors started about 1960 with Arnold Palmer's win in the British Open Championship, but Bobby Jones "Grand Slam" included two amateur events, U.S. and British Amateurs

20-13   Francis Ouimet, 1955

20-14   PGA Championship, best finish was 2nd in 1978 at Oakmont to John Mahaffey

20-15   Padraig Harrington, 2007 British Open Championship

20-16   "Short," "Medal" and "Championship"

20-17   Four times, twice more than Byron Nelson in 1944–45

20-18   All had an 11-year gap between major championship wins

20-19   True!

20-20   No! Never has happened through 2008.

GROUP

QUESTIONS

Par + Distance of Major Championship Tournament Courses

HINTS

21-1	Par 71, 6882 Yards	"Walk the path of Legends"
21-2	Par 72, 6828 Yards	Nicklaus won and lost U.S. Open Championships here
21-3	Par 70, 6801 Yards	"Oldest golf course in the world"
21-4	Par 72, 7607 Yards	Fourteenth major championship for Tiger
21-5	Par 70, 7255 Yards	Hogan's last; Jack's first; U.S. Open Championship win
21-6	Par 69, 6440 Yards	"Duel in the Sun"
21-7	Par 71, 6842 Yards	"Giant Killer"
21-8	Par 71, 7366 Yards	Five public golf courses here
21-9	Par 72, 7445 Yards	April Major Championship
21-10	Par 70, 7392 Yards	"Jack is Back"
21-11	Par 72, 7275 Yards	"Old" Tom Morris, "Custodian of the Links"
21-12	Par 70, 7070 Yards	"I've hosted 13 British Open Championships"
21-13	Par 70, 7229 Yards	Bobby Jones won 1929 U.S. Open here
21-14	Par 71, 6941 Yards	Hogan's British Open Championship win
21-15	Par 72, 7258 Yards	2nd leg of Bobby Jones Grand Slam
21-16	Par 72, 6846 Yards	Hogan and Trevino each won a U.S. Open here
21-17	Par 72, 7217 Yards	Donald Ross' BEST!
21-18	Par 71, 7097 Yards	Palmer's win started a trend
21-19	Par 70, 7012 Yards	Bolt and Green each won a U.S. Open Championship here
21-20	Par 71, 7412 yards	Harrington's second British Open Championship win

ANSWERS

Par + Distance of Major Championship Tournament Courses

21-1   Royal Lytham & St. Annes, Lytham St. Annes, England

21-2   Pebble Beach Golf Links, Pebble Beach, CA

21-3   Muirfield, Gullane, Scotland "The Honorary Company of Edinburgh Golfers"

21-4   Torrey Pines (South Course), La Jolla, CA

21-5   Oakmont Country Club, Oakmont (Pittsburgh), PA

21-6   Turnberry (Ailsa Course), Turnberry, Scotland

21-7   The Olympic Club (Lakes Course), San Francisco, CA

21-8   Bethpage State Park Golf Course (Black Course), Farmingdale, Long Island, NY

21-9   Augusta National Golf Club, Augusta, GA

21-10   Baltusrol Golf Club (Lower Course), Springfield, NJ

21-11   Old Course St. Andrews, St. Andrews, Scotland

21-12   Royal St. George's Golf Club, Sandwich, Kent, England

21-13   Winged Foot Golf Club, Mamaroneck, NY

21-14   Carnoustie, Carnoustie, Scotland

21-15   Royal Liverpool Golf Club (Hoylake), Merseyside, England

21-16   Merion Golf Club, Ardmore, PA

21-17   Pinehurst Resort #2, Pinehurst, NC

21-18   Royal Troon Golf Club, Troon, Scotland

21-19   Southern Hills Country Club, Tulsa, OK

21-20   Royal Birkdale Golf Club, Southport, England

GROUP
22 QUESTIONS

22-1   Which three left-handed players have won a major championship?

22-2   Who had a close call in the 1957 British Open with a ruling by the R & A to not impose a penalty when he misreplaced his ball on the #18 green?

22-3   What is the "Winner's Dinner?"

22-4   Which famous golf architect took golf lessons from "Old" Tom Morris?

22-5   What were the three Scottish golf courses to come together to work together and rotate the British Open Championship in 1872?

22-6   **T or F** All of the four majors cancelled their tournaments during WWII from 1942 through 1945.

22-7   What is gorse?

22-8   What four players made a hole-in-one at the 159-yard, Par 3, 6th hole in the U.S. Open at Oak Hill Country club in 1989 during the same round?

22-9   What major tournament was Ben Hogan's greatest win and his greatest loss (upset)?

22-10 How many players made the cut in all four major championships in 2008?

22-11 Who won back-to-back PGA Championships to break Walter Hagen's string of five wins in seven years?

22-12 Named after a major winner, what award is given for "Outstanding and Continuing Contributions to PGA Education?"

22-13 Which winners' tee shot on #12, at the 1992 Masters, hit short on the bank, but did not go into Rae's Creek...saving victory?

22-14 Which two players are tied in fourth place with nine career major championships?

22-15 Which two major winners have been given a ticker-tape parade in New York City?

22-16 Who was the first winner of the PGA Player of the Year?

22-17 Who won three U.S. Open Championships and no other majors?

22-18 **T or F** Raymond Floyd won three out of four of his major championships in a play-off?

22-19 Who did British Open Champion Todd Hamilton beat in his play-off at Royal Troon in 2004?

22-20 How many attempts did it take Phil Mickelson to win his first major championship, the 2004 Masters Tournament?

ANSWERS

GROUP 22

22-1	Bob Charles, Phil Mickelson and Mike Weir
22-2	Bobby Locke, Old Course St. Andrews
22-3	A Tuesday night dinner for all the previous winners of the Masters Tournament
22-4	A.W. Tillinghast
22-5	Prestwick, The Honourable Company of Edinburgh Golfers and The Royal & Ancient Golf Club
22-6	False: Masters 1943-1945; U.S. Open 1942-1945; British Open 1940-1945 and PGA only 1943
22-7	A thorny bush with yellow flowers, common in Western Europe like the Old Course St. Andrews
22-8	Jerry Pate, Nick Price, Doug Weaver and Mark Wiebe
22-9	U.S. Open Championships: Won 1950 "The Comeback;" and lost 1955 "Jack Fleck's upset"
22-10	11 players only
22-11	Gene Sarazen, 1922-1923
22-12	Horton Smith Award
22-13	Fred Couples
22-14	Ben Hogan and Gary Player
22-15	Bobby Jones, Jr. (2) 1926 and 1930; Ben Hogan 1953
22-16	Ben Hogan in 1948; won the award a total of four times
22-17	Hale Irwin, 1974 (Winged Foot), 1979 (Inverness Club) and 1990 (Medinah #3)
22-18	False: He won all four of his major championships in stroke play, 72 holes
22-19	Ernie Els, winning 15 to 16 shots
22-20	47 tries

GROUP 23 QUESTIONS

23-1   In 1945, which major championship winner won 11 tournaments in a row and 18 for the year?

23-2   What was Ben Hogan's trademark?

23-3   What was the yardage in 1903 when Oakmont Country Club opened; and what was it for the 2007 U.S. Open Championship?

23-4   Who finally won his lone major championship at the 1992 U.S. Open at Pebble Beach after having a wonderful golf career?

23-5   **T or F** The British Open Championship winner Ben Curtis was the "Rookie of the Year" in 2003.

23-6   Which major championship player is the career money leader through 2008?

23-7   Who was the first American to win the British Open Championship?

23-8   Who is considered America's first "True" professional golfer and later a multiple major winner?

23-9   **T or F** Sam Snead won his first try at the British Open Championship in 1946.

23-10   Byron Nelson won 18 out of 30 events in 1945; who won 9 out of 20 events?

23-11   Which major winner "whiffed" a two inch "gimme" putt and finished tied for second in the 1983 British Open Championship at Royal Birkdale?

23-12   Who was the first Spaniard to win the British Open Championship?

23-13   Which two players have lost a play-off in all four majors?

23-14   After Bobby Jones retired in 1930, having won the "Grand Slam," who won the U.S. Open Championship the next year in 1931?

23-15   Who won eight majors and led the PGA money list five times in the 1970s–80s?

23-16   What major championship did Raymond Floyd not win to complete a "Career Grand Slam?"

23-17   What is the only British Open Championship course in the rotation that starts with a Par 3?

23-18   What year was the U.S. Open Championship first televised nationally?

23-19   Name the three players with four runner-up finishes in the Masters Tournament.

23-20   Who has had the most Top 25 finishes in the Masters Tournament?

ANSWERS

GROUP
23

23-1   Byron Nelson, still a record! Much like DiMaggio's 56 straight hitting streak in baseball

23-2   His "White Hat"

23-3   6,406 yards when built in 1903; 7,230 yards for the 2007 U.S. Open Championship

23-4   Tom Kite

23-5   True

23-6   Tiger Woods with over $80 million and still going up

23-7   Jock Hutchinson, 1921 at the Old Course St. Andrews

23-8   Walter Hagen, his only job was to play golf

23-9   True, at the Old Course St. Andrews, St. Andrews, Scotland

23-10   Tiger Woods in 2000

23-11   Hale Irwin, the British Open Championship won by Tom Watson

23-12   Seve Ballesteros, 1979 at Royal Lytham & St. Annes Golf Club, Lancashire, England

23-13   Craig Wood and Greg Norman

23-14   Billy Burke at the Inverness Club, Toledo, OH

23-15   Tom Watson, also #1 player between 1978 and 1982

23-16   A British Open Championship, his best finish was second in 1978 at St. Andrews to Jack Nicklaus

23-17   Royal Lytham & St. Annes Golf Club, Lancashire, England

23-18   1954 at Baltusrol Golf Club (Lower Course), won by Ed Furgol

23-19   Ben Hogan (1942, 1946, 1954 and 1955), Jack Nicklaus (1964, 1971, 1977 and 1981) and Tom Weiskopf (1969, 1972, 1974 and 1975)

23-20   Jack Nicklaus with 29 Top 25s out of 45 tournament attempts

QUESTIONS

Colleges & Universities of Major Winners

24-1   Stanford University "Cardinals"

24-2   Arizona State University "Sun Devils"

24-3   Oklahoma State University "Cowboys"

24-4   San Diego State University "Aztecs"

24-5   The Ohio State University "Buckeyes"

24-6   University of Florida "Gators"

24-7   Georgia Institute of Technology, now Georgia Tech "Yellow Jackets"

24-8   University of Colorado "Buffalos"

24-9   Kennesaw Junior College, now Kennesaw State University "Owls"

24-10   Florida Southern College "Moccasins"

24-11   University of Arkansas "Razorbacks"

24-12   Southern Methodist University "Mustangs"

24-13   University of Minnesota "Golden Gophers"

24-14   Fettes College "Bee"

24-15   University of Texas "Longhorns"

24-16   University of Southern California "Trojans"

24-17   Kent State University "Golden Flashes"

24-18   University of North Carolina "Tar Heels"

24-19   Long Beach State University "49ers"

24-20   Wake Forest University "Demon Deacons"

ANSWERS

GROUP
24

Colleges & Universities of Major Winners

24-1   Bob Rosburg, Tom Watson, Tiger Woods

24-2   Phil Mickelson

24-3   Bob Tway

24-4   Gene Littler

24-5   Jack Nicklaus, Tom Weiskopf

24-6   Tommy Aaron, Andy North

24-7   Bobby Jones, Jr.

24-8   Hale Irwin

24-9   Larry Nelson

24-10   Lee Janzen

24-11   John Daly

24-12   Payne Stewart

24-13   Tom Lehman

24-14   Tommy Armour

24-15   Tom Kite, Ben Crenshaw, Justin Leonard

24-16   Dave Stockton, Craig Stadler, Scott Simpson

24-17   Ben Curtis

24-18   Davis Love III, Raymond Floyd

24-19   Mark O'Meara

24-20   Arnold Palmer, Curtis Strange

25-1   Who made the highest score on #12, Par 3 at the Masters with five balls hit into Rae's Creek?

25-2   Which American has the most rounds under par in the British Open Championship?

25-3   What is the longest hole in U.S. Open Championship history?

25-4   Who was the first "owner" of the challenge belt for the British Open Championship?

25-5   **T or F** After the first 36 holes in the 1972 and 2008 PGA Championship at Oakland Hills, there was only one player under par.

25-6   To win the Vardon Trophy, what is the minimum number of rounds one must play to qualify?

25-7   Which major championship winner was first, second or third in 57 out of 72 tournaments over a three-year period?

25-8   Who hit seven shots in a row out of bounds, but still won the 1920 British Open Championship?

25-9   **T or F** In the 1913 U.S. Open Championship, both Walter Hagen, a pro, and Francis Ouimet, an amateur, were 20 years old.

25-10   Before the professional golfer became dominant, what tournament was regarded as a major?

25-11   Which major winner is the only one to captain a Ryder Cup team, but never played in the Masters?

25-12   Which famous sports writer nicknamed Byron Nelson after his 1937 Masters win?

25-13   Who hit (chipped-in) on #17, Par 3 at Pebble Beach in 1982 to win the U.S. Open Championship and beat Jack Nicklaus again?

25-14   Who cancelled a tryout with the Philadelphia Phillips baseball team to play a golf tournament and winning the U.S. Open Championship in 1914?

25-15   Where was the first PGA Championship held?

25-16   Who has the lowest career scoring average in the Masters Tournament with 100 rounds plus?

25-17   What was the first year the British Open Championship was held at the Old Course St. Andrews?

25-18   **T or F** There are only two, five-time winners of the U.S. Open Championship.

25-19   How many club professionals made the cut in the 2008 PGA Championship at Oakland Hills?

25-20   What year and which course did the British Open Championship go to a four-hole play-off system?

ANSWERS

GROUP 25

25-1   Tom Weiskopf in 1980, scoring a 13

25-2   Jack Nicklaus, 61

25-3   #12, Par 5, 667 yards at Oakmont Country Club in 2007 U.S. Open Championship

25-4   Young Tom Morris, Jr., winning for the third consecutive time to take ownership of the belt

25-5   True! "The Monster" still holds on to its reputation

25-6   60 rounds minimum to determine lowest adjusted scoring average

25-7   Byron Nelson 1944–1946

25-8   George Duncan, at the time the penalty was distance only, no stroke penalty

25-9   True, Walter Hagen went on to win 11 major tournaments; Francis Ouimet won one U.S. Open

25-10   The U.S. Amateur Championship

25-11   John Henry "J.H." Taylor, British Captain 1933, British beating the U.S. team winning 6.5 to 5.5

25-12   O.B. Keeler

25-13   Tom Watson, one of the greatest shots in major golf championships

25-14   Walter Hagen, winning 11 major championships in his professional career

25-15   Siwanoy Country Club, Bronxville, NY, 1916

25-16   Jack Nicklaus, 71.98 average per round

25-17   1873

25-18   False, only four, four-time winners, after 108 tournaments!

25-19   Zero!

25-20   1989 at Royal Troon Golf Club, won by Mark Calcavecchia

GROUP

26   QUESTIONS

26-1   What are the holes named after at the Augusta National Golf Club, home of the Masters?

26-2   What is the only water hazard on the Old Course St. Andrews?

26-3   Which three amateurs have finished second at the Masters Tournament?

26-4   What was the common material used for "greens" in many of the original classic golf courses?

26-5   Who was the "Silver Scot" that won the first British Open Championship at Carnoustie in 1931?

26-6   What year was the Masters Tournament officially named?

26-7   On what two courses in Ohio did Jack Nicklaus win two of his five PGA Championships?

26-8   **T or F** Willie Park, Sr. (winner of four British Opens) had a brother and a son who each won a British Open Championship.

26-9   Who was the last rookie to win a major title before John Daly won the 1991 PGA Championship?

26-10   How many years was it between major championship victories by Englishmen starting in 1924 with Cyril Walker and Tony Jacklin?

26-11   Who is the only major championship winner to win the "Vince Lombardi Award for Excellence?"

26-12   Which two brothers have won a U.S. Open Championship?

26-13   By how many shots did Paul Lawrie beat both Justin Leonard and Jean Van de Velde to win the 1999 British Open Championship in a play-off?

26-14   Who did Ralph Guldahl beat to win two of his three major championships?

26-15   On what championship course did Ben Hogan win his first tournament?

26-16   Who developed creeping bent grass for putting greens in 1927?

26-17   Who is the "Course Doctor," a golf architect, who rebuilds courses for major championships?

26-18   What U.S. Open Championship golf course was at one time a 2.7 mile Grand-Prix race track?

26-19   How many players went into the final round at the 2008 U.S. Open even par or better?

26-20   What two other tragedies in history occurred on the same date (different years) as Greg Norman's last round "tragedy" on April 14, 1996 at the Masters Tournament?

ANSWERS

GROUP 26

26-1   Flowering aromatic trees or shrubs

26-2   Swilcan Burn running across #1 and #18 fairways

26-3   Frank Stranahan 1947, Ken Venturi 1956 and Charlie Coe 1961

26-4   Sand, often "oiled" sand was used and the "green" was in a square shape design

26-5   Tommy Armour

26-6   1939, original tournament (1934) was named The Augusta National Invitation Tournament

26-7   1973 Canterbury Golf Club, Beachwood; 1975 Firestone Country Club South Course, Akron

26-8   True; Mongo Park 1874 Mosselburgh Links; Son Willie Park, Jr. 1887 at Prestwick Golf Club

26-9   Jerry Pate won the 1976 U.S. Open Championship at Atlanta Athletic Club, Highlands Course

26-10   46 years, Tony Jacklin winning in 1970 at Hazeltine National Golf Club

26-11   Jack Nicklaus, 2001

26-12   Willie Smith (1899) and Alex Smith (1906 and 1910)

26-13   Three shots in a four-hole play-off format; 15 shots vs. 18 and 18

26-14   Sam Snead, 1937 U.S. Open, 1939 Masters; Guldahl also won 1938 U.S. Open Championship

26-15   Pinehurst #2, Pinehurst, NC

26-16   The U.S. Department of Agriculture

26-17   Rees Jones, seven U.S. Open Championships and six PGA Championships

26-18   Torrey Pines, 1951–1956

26-19   Three players: –1 Mediate, –2 Westwood and –3 Tiger Woods. No one was even par

26-20   President Abraham Lincoln assassinated in 1865 and the RMS Titanic sank 1912

GROUP 27 QUESTIONS

27-1 Which player has had the most consecutive rounds under 70 during the British Open?

27-2 Who won the first "Par 3 Contest" at the Masters?

27-3 Who is the only six-time winner of the British Open Championship?

27-4 What was the first course to host four PGA Championships?

27-5 Who is "The Wee-Ice Man" that won his last major in the British Open Championship?

27-6 How many years did it take to play the British Open Championship in England and not Scotland?

27-7 Between 1960 and 1963, how many times did Arnold Palmer win?

27-8 Who came from 3 shots behind in 1961 to win his only U.S. Open at Oakland Hills Country Club?

27-9 Who shot 65-66 on the last two rounds of the 1975 Masters to still lose to Jack Nicklaus?

27-10 Where was the 1938 U.S. Open Championship held when Ray Ainsley established the record for the highest score on a hole in a major championship?

27-11 Who won the "Career Grand Slam" first—Gary Player or Jack Nicklaus?

27-12 Which player won the British Open twice, but had 8 second place finishes among the four majors?

27-13 What two years did Tom Watson win two major championships?

27-14 How many times did Byron Nelson finish second in match-play in the PGA Championship?

27-15 Who holds the record at 19 for the most consecutive Top 25 finishes in the U.S. Open?

27-16 If you say "20 inches" and "30 inches" in U.S. Open golf history, whom are you referring to?

27-17 What is the longest course in U.S. Open Championship history?

27-18 Name the four courses that have hosted a U.S. Open, PGA, U.S. Amateur Championship and a Ryder Cup.

27-19 Which players have won three U.S. Opens in the same decade?

27-20 **T or F** Rocco Mediate had to qualify at the Columbus, OH sectional the day after the Memorial Tournament for the 2008 U.S. Open Championship.

ANSWERS

GROUP
27

27-1   Ernie Els, seven rounds in 1993 and 1994

27-2   Sam Snead, 1960; played on the Wednesday before the tournament

27-3   Harry Vardon, 1896, 1898, 1899, 1903, 1911 and 1914

27-4   Southern Hills Country Club, Tulsa, OK, 1970, 1982, 1994 and 2007

27-5   Ben Hogan, his ninth major, in 1953 at Carnoustie, Carnoustie, Scotland

27-6   1860 until 1894 – 34 years; then played at Royal St. George's Golf Club won by J.H. Taylor

27-7   29 tournaments, including five majors; one U.S. Open, two British Opens and two Masters

27-8   Gene Littler

27-9   Johnny Miller

27-10   Cherry Hills Country Club, Denver, CO, #16, Par 4, 397 yards shooting a 19

27-11   Gary Player 1965, Jack Nicklaus 1966

27-12   Greg Norman

27-13   1977 (Masters Tournament and British Open); 1982 (U.S. Open and British Open)

27-14   Three times second: 1939, 1941 and 1944; winning twice in 1940 and 1945

27-15   Walter Hagen

27-16   Missed Putts: Jack Nicklaus 1960 at Cherry Hills Country Club; Sam Snead 1947 at St. Louis Country Club

27-17   Torrey Pines, 2008, 7643 yards, par 71, La Jolla, CA

27-18   Scioto Country Club, Oakland Hills Country Club, Oakhill Country Club and Pinehurst Resort #2

27-19   Willie Anderson 1901, 1903, 1904, 1905; Bobby Jones 1923, 1926, 1929 (1930); Ben Hogan (1948) 1950, 1951, 1953; Tiger Woods 2000, 2002, 2008

27-20   True; played at the Ohio State University Scarlet Golf Club and Brookside Country Club

28-1   What British Open Championship course in the rotation is considered the toughest?

28-2   At the Masters Tournament, the caddy wearing number 1 signifies what?

28-3   **T or F** American players have won six straight of the last eight British Open Championships held at Royal Troon, Troon, Scotland.

28-4   Who was the first major winner to pass the $1 million dollar mark in career earnings?

28-5   Who was the first wire-to-wire winner of the Masters Tournament?

28-6   What years did "The Big Three" win eight out of nine Masters Tournaments?

28-7   What is the only major that "The Silver Scot" did not win?

28-8   Which major winner held the 54-hole leaad for three years running (1995–1997), but failed to win a single U.S. Open Championship?

28-9   How old was Ben Hogan before he won his first of four U.S. Open Championships?

28-10   What championships were the "original" majors?

28-11   Which two TV commentators both won a PGA Championship?

28-12   Who is the youngest player to win a "Career Grand Slam?"

28-13   Which major winner was the first to add a third wedge in his bag?

28-14   Which player's name was the first one to be engraved on the Claret Jug?

28-15   What hole at Carnoustie is called "Hogan's Alley?"

28-16   Who was the first major winner to start a golf equipment company under his own name?

28-17   What is the highest score shot by the winner of the U.S. Open Championship in the first round?

28-18   Who are the only two professional players to have a "Career Grand Slam" three times?

28-19   Who was the first player to break par in all four rounds of the Masters Tournament?

28-20   Who was the last winner of the U.S. Open Championship after going through local and sectional qualifying?

ANSWERS

28-1   Carnoustie "Car-Nasty"

28-2   The defending champion

28-3   True; Palmer (1962), Weiskopf (1973), Watson (1982), Calcavecchia (1989),
        Leonard (1997), Hamilton (2004)

28-4   Arnold Palmer, 1968

28-5   Craig Wood (1941), 66-71-71-72 = 280, beating Byron Nelson by three shots

28-6   Palmer (1958, 1960, 1962 and 1964), Player (1961) and Nicklaus (1963, 1965 and 1966)

28-7   A Masters Tournament

28-8   Tom Lehman

28-9   36 years old in 1948, won again in 1950, 1951 and 1953

28-10   The Open (British) Championship, British Amateur, U.S. Open Championship and
        U.S. Amateur

28-11   Dave Marr and Bob Rosburg

28-12   Tiger Woods (age 24), after winning the 2000 British Open Championship at the
        Old Course St. Andrews

28-13   Tom Kite

28-14   "Young" Tom Morris, Jr., 1872

28-15   #6, Par 5, 575 yards; Ben Hogan won the 1953 British Open Championship by four shots

28-16   Walter Hagen in 1922

28-17   91 shot by Horace Rawlins in the 1st U.S. Open Championship 1895 at Newport Golf Club

28-18   Jack Nicklaus and Tiger Woods

28-19   Jimmy Demaret, 1947, 69-71-70-71 = 281 (−7)

28-20   Orville Moody, 1969, at Champions Golf Club, Houston, TX

29 QUESTIONS

29-1   What year did Augusta National discontinue the club-caddies only policy during the Masters Tournament?

29-2   Who was the first African-American to play in the U.S. Open Championship?

29-3   Oakland Hills has hosted how many U.S. Open and PGA Championships through 2008?

29-4   **T or F** Tom Weiskopf and Ben Hogan both finished second at the Masters four times.

29-5   Who was the first foreign player since Alex Smith (1906–1910) to win two U.S. Opens?

29-6   Which winner of the Masters shot a round with four pars, seven bogeys and seven birdies for an even par round of 72?

29-7   What streak do Ben Hogan (1953) and Tiger Woods (2000) have in common?

29-8   Where and what score did Bobby Jones shoot to represent his worst score in a U.S. Open?

29-9   Who was the first left-hander to win the British Open Championship?

29-10   What five golf courses (delegates) started the United States Golf Association (USGA)?

29-11   Which two major players played together in college at the University of Texas and tied in winning the 1972 NCAA Individual Championship?

29-12   **T or F** Walter Hagen won all of his majors out-right and never needed to win a play-off.

29-13   Who was the last Briton to win the U.S. Open Championship?

29-14   Who was the first player to win both the U.S. Open and the British Open Championships?

29-15   Since WWII, what is the highest score shot by the winner of the U.S. Open in the fourth round?

29-16   How many shots did Justin Leonard come back from to beat Jesper Parnevik in the 1997 British Open Championship at Royal Troon?

29-17   What one thing caused the birth of the golf course architect?

29-18   What is the only major championship Davis Love III has won?

29-19   Who became the oldest player to win two major championships in the same year?

29-20   Who was the first American to be elected Captain of the Royal & Ancient Golf Club in Scotland?

ANSWERS

GROUP 29

29-1 1983

29-2 John Shippen, 1896 at Shinnecock Hills Golf club

29-3 Six U.S. Opens 1924, 1937, 1951, 1961, 1985, 1996; three PGAs 1972, 1979, 2008

29-4 True; Jack Nicklaus also had four seconds, but six wins, Hogan had two, Weiskopf no wins

29-5 Ernie Els, 1994 Oakmont Country Club and 1997 Congressional Country Club

29-6 Bernard Langer winning his second Masters Tournament 1993

29-7 Both won three majors in one year; Hogan 1953 (Masters, U.S. Open and British Open), 2000 Tiger Woods 2000 (U.S. Open, British Open and PGA Championship)

29-8 79 at Scioto Country Club, Columbus, OH in 1926, but he still won by one, birding #18 (72nd)

29-9 Bob Charles from New Zealand in 1963 at Royal Lytham & St. Annes Golf Club

29-10 Newport Country Club, Shinnecock Hills Golf Club, Chicago Golf Club, The Country Club all major tournament golf courses and the fifth one, St. Andrews (NY)

29-11 Ben Crenshaw and Tom Kite

29-12 False; he won 10 out of 11, but had to beat Mike Brady in a play-off 77 to 78 to win the 1919 U.S. Open Championship at Brae Burn Country Club in West Newton, MA

29-13 Tony Jacklin, 1970 at Hazeltine National Golf Club, wire-to-wire, winning by seven shots

29-14 Harry Vardon; British Open 1896 at Muirfield, U.S. Open 1900 at the Chicago Golf Club

29-15 75 (four-over), Cary Middlecoff 1949 at Medinah #3; Hale Irwin 1979 at Inverness Club

29-16 Six shots

29-17 The Gutta-Percha ball, replacing the Feathery Ball

29-18 1997 PGA Championship at Winged Foot Golf Club, Mamaroneck, NY

29-19 Mark O'Meara (age 41), 1998 Masters Tournament and British Open at Royal Birkdale Golf Club

29-20 Amateur, Francis Ouimet, 1951; 1913 U.S. Open Champion

QUESTIONS

Major Golf Course Features located where?

30-1   Amen Corner®

30-2   The Road Hole

30-3   R.A.F. Memorial

30-4   The Lighthouse

30-5   Spectacles Bunker

30-6   Postage Stamp

30-7   White Faces of Merion

30-8   Furrowed Bunkers

30-9   Valley of Sin

30-10 Hell Bunker

30-11 Church Pews

30-12 Suez Canal

30-13 The Sahara

30-14 Big Mouth Bunker

30-15 Swilcan Bridge

30-16 "The Alps"

30-17 The Big Oak Tree

30-18 TILT

30-19 Wicker Baskets

30-20 Principal's Nose

ANSWERS

Major Golf Course
Features located where?

30-1 Holes #11, Par 4; #12, Par 3; and #13, Par 5 Augusta National Golf Club, Augusta, GA

30-2 #17, Par 4, 461 yards, Old Course St. Andrews, St. Andrews, Scotland

30-3 Royal Air Force Memorial, Turnberry by hole #12, Par 4, 446 yards, Turnberry, Scotland

30-4 #10, Par 4, 452 yards, Turnberry (Ailsa Course), Turnberry, Scotland

30-5 #14, Par 5, 482 yards, Carnoustie, Carnoustie, Scotland

30-6 #8, Par 3, 126 yards, Royal Troon, Troon, Scotland "Shortest Hole in the Open Championship"

30-7 Scottish-Style Bunkers, Merion Golf Club, Ardmore, PA

30-8 Oakmont Country Club's famous bunkers, created by the use of "Toothy Rakes," Oakmont, PA

30-9 #18, Par 4, 357 yards; in front of the green on Old Course St. Andrews, St. Andrews, Scotland

30-10 #14, Par 5, 567 yards, Old Course St. Andrews, St. Andrews, Scotland

30-11 Sand Trap(s) between holes #3 and #4, Oakmont Country Club, Oakmont, PA

30-12 Stream, Royal St. George's Golf Club, #14, Par 5, 551 yards, Sandwich, Kent, England

30-13 Bunker # 17, Par 5, 630 yards, Baltusrol Golf Club (Lower), Springfield, NJ

30-14 Right-side, green side bunker, #17, Par 4 , 319 yards, Oakmont Country Club, Oakmont, PA

30-15 #18, Par 4, 357 yards, bridge over the Swilcan Burn, Old Course St. Andrews, St. Andrews, Scotland

30-16 #17 at Prestwick (originally #2), a ridge over sand hills…a blind shot!

30-17 Augusta National Golf Club, by the clubhouse, home of the Masters Tournament, Augusta, GA

30-18 Oakmont's greens, their pitch away from the fairways on #1, #3, #10 and #12, Oakmont, PA

30-19 Pins are topped with wicker baskets (actually they are lobster pots) instead of flags, Merion Golf Club, Ardmore, PA

30-20 A three bunker group, #16, Par 4, 382 yards, Old Course St. Andrews, St. Andrews, Scotland

QUESTIONS

31-1   Who took a triple-bogey seven on the 72nd hole in the British Open Championship to tie and later lose in a play-off?

31-2   In how many Masters Tournaments did founder Bobby Jones participate?

31-3   What was Ben Curtis' world ranking when he won the 2003 British Open at Royal St. George's?

31-4   Which three leading major winners were born within six months of each other in 1912?

31-5   What river adjoins Oakmont Country Club and meets the Monongahela River to form the Ohio River?

31-6   What was the last major championship win for Arnold Palmer?

31-7   Harry Vardon, winner of the most British Open Championships is from what country?

31-8   What five years straight did Jack Nicklaus and Arnold Palmer trade back and forth the "Green Jacket" at the Masters Tournament?

31-9   Walter Hagen won four PGA Championships straight (1924–1927). When did he win two straight British Open Championships?

31-10   How many coins does Jack Nicklaus carry in his pocket when he plays golf?

31-11   Who was the first real "Dark Horse" to win the U.S. Open Championship?

31-12   Which major winner's book, *Every Shot I Took,* honors his father's lessons on life and golf?

31-13   **T or F** With Tom Watson's win at Turnberry (Ailsa Course) in 1977, his aggregate score of 268 was a record beating the previous record by eight strokes.

31-14   Who follows Harry Cooper with the most wins without winning a single major championship?

31-15   Which famous golf architect did the make-over design for the 2008 U.S. Open Championship at Torrey Pines?

31-16   Which multiply major winner was born on a military base?

31-17   Who is the only player to win the British Open twice at Royal Lytham & St. Annes Golf Club?

31-18   Which player broke the string of American players winning the U.S. Open from 1926 on?

31-19   Who shot what score to set the U.S. Open 18-hole record with a Gutta Perch golf ball?

31-20   Who holds the record for the lowest 18-hole score as an amateur in a Masters Tournament?

ANSWERS

31-1   Jean Van de Velde in 1999 at Carnoustie, winner in play-off was Paul Lawrie

31-2   Bobby Jones played in 12 Masters Tournaments, best finish was 13th in his first Masters, 1934

31-3   396th ranking; first player since Ouimet in 1913 to win first attempt at a major championship

31-4   Ben Hogan, Byron Nelson and Sam Snead

31-5   The Allegheny River, a little geography lesson just for some fun

31-6   The 1964 Masters Tournament, Arnold's seventh major championship

31-7   He is English, born in Grouville, Jersey Channel Islands

31-8   1962 to 1966, Jack Nicklaus won 1963, 1965 and 1966; Arnold Palmer won 1962 and 1964

31-9   1928 at Royal St. George's Golf Club; 1929 at Muirfield

31-10   Three coins, one for him, one for his playing partner and one in case another coin is lost

31-11   Sam Parks, Jr., 1935 U.S. Open Championship at Oakmont Country Club, 11 shots over par, 299

31-12   Davis Love III

31-13   True; Jack Nicklaus was one shot behind Tom Watson; Hubert Green was third— 11 shots back

31-14   MacDonald Smith

31-15   Rees Jones

31-16   Raymond Floyd, September 4, 1942 at Fort Bragg, NC

31-17   Seve Ballesteros, 1979 and 1988

31-18   Gary Player in 1965 at Bellerive Country Club in St. Louis, MO

31-19   James Foulis, shot a 74 in 1896 at Shinnecock Hill Golf Club, Shinnecock Hills, NY

31-20   Ken Venturi shot a 66 in the first round, 1956

GROUP

QUESTIONS

32-1   What course has hosted the U.S. Open Championship four times in three different centuries?

32-2   Which two major championship tournaments did the Hebert brothers win?

32-3   Since 1961, who are the only players to win back-to-back British Open Championships?

32-4   What is the major championship record for the lowest score in relation to being under par?

32-5   **T or F** Gary Player, in the 1990 British Open Championship at Royal Birkdale, got up and down eight out of nine times from the bunkers; the other time he holed out the shot.

32-6   Which major championship winner conceived the sand wedge?

32-7   **T or F** The 1913 U.S. Open was delayed from June to September to allow Harry Vardon and Ted Ray to complete an exhibition schedule.

32-8   Who was the first winner of the Vardon Trophy in 1937?

32-9   Which two major winners hosted the popular TV show "Shell's Wonderful World of Golf?"

32-10   Which major winner three-putted from 20 feet to lose the 1946 Masters to Herman Keiser?

32-11   Who holds the record for the most British Open Championship wins by an amateur?

32-12   On which two courses did Andy North win his U.S. Open Championships?

32-13   Which major winner was second to Tiger Woods by 12 strokes in the 1997 Masters Tournament?

32-14   **T or F** Ben Hogan was left-handed, played right-handed and did not wear a golf glove.

32-15   Who won the 2007 British Open in a play-off by one stroke over Sergio Garcia?

32-16   Which major winner almost won a major in four decades but lost the Masters in 1990 in a play-off to Nick Faldo?

32-17   Which major winner through 2007 has won the Vardon Trophy the most times?

32-18   What hole on the British Open Championship rotation is named after Bobby Jones?

32-19   What year did the U.S. Open Championship start international qualifying sites?

32-20   The "Ross Room," a room dedicated to architect Donald Ross, is located at which famous major championship golf course?

ANSWERS

32-1   Shinnecock Hills Golf Club, 1896, 1986, 1995 and 2004

32-2   Lionel, 1957 PGA Championship (match-play) at Miami Valley Country Club, Dayton, OH; Jay, 1960 PGA Championship (medal-play) at Firestone Country Club, Akron, OH

32-3   Arnold Palmer 1961–1962, Lee Trevino 1971–1972, Tom Watson 1982–1983, Tiger Woods 2005–2006 and Padraig Harrington 2007–2008

32-4   19 under par (269) by Tiger Woods at the Old Course St. Andrews in 2000

32-5   True; Gary Player was a great bunker player!

32-6   Gene Sarazen, won the British Open Championship that year in 1932 at Prince's Golf Club

32-7   True; then Francis Ouimet beat them both in the play-off for the U.S. Open Championship

32-8   Harry Cooper, but he never won a major championship

32-9   Jimmy Demaret and Gene Sarazen

32-10   Ben Hogan

32-11   Bobby Jones three times 1926, 1927 and 1930

32-12   1978 Cherry Hills, Denver, CO; 1985 Oakland Hills, Bloomfield Hills, MI

32-13   Tom Kite

32-14   True

32-15   Padraig Harrington, Sergio Garcia was also runner-up in the 2008 PGA Championship

32-16   Raymond Floyd, PGA 1969 and 1982, Masters 1976 and U.S. Open 1986

32-17   Tiger Woods, seven times, 1999, 2000, 2001, 2002, 2003, 2005, 2007

32-18   #10, Par 4, 380 yards, the Old Course St. Andrews, St. Andrews, Scotland

32-19   2005 and it is a very successful program

32-20   Scioto Country Club, Columbus, OH "Home of Jack Nicklaus"

QUESTIONS

GROUP 33

33-1   What course is responsible for the standard in golf being 18 holes?

33-2   What year did Ernie Els have three runner-up finishes at the Masters, the U.S. Open Championship and the British Open Championship?

33-3   What famous hole has a tree in the middle of the fairway and a 100-yard long sand trap along the ocean?

33-4   What was the first year the British Open Championship went from 36 holes to 72 holes?

33-5   Who was 13 strokes behind in the fourth round of the 1920 British Open but came back to win?

33-6   How many foreign-born players have won the U.S. Open Championship through 2008?

33-7   Who broke the British Open Championship scoring record by seven shots and still lost by one?

33-8   In the 1995 Masters, how many three-putt greens did winner Ben Crenshaw record for the entire tournament?

33-9   Who has the longest run as Honorary Starter at the Masters Tournament?

33-10   Who is the leading major winner with the most covers in *Sports Illustrated* for golfers?

33-11   At which major championship course is the Himalayas putting course located near?

33-12   Which two Americans have won the British Open Championship twice at "The Home of Golf?"

33-13   **T or F** The winner of the Par 3 Contest at the Masters has gone on to win the tournament.

33-14   Who holds the British Open Championship record for the lowest 72-hole score?

33-15   **T or F** From 1860 to 1889, a Scotsman won every British Open Championship.

33-16   What shot cost Ben Hogan his fifth U.S. Open Championship?

33-17   What was the name of the Army base located at Torrey Pines during World War II?

33-18   Name the three golfers who won a tournament event and then later in the same year won a U.S. Open Championship on the same course.

33-19   When was the first time Jack Nicklaus and Arnold Palmer played golf against each other?

33-20   What was the number one (first job) for many major championship winners?

ANSWERS

GROUP

33

33-1   The Old Course St. Andrews, established 18 holes in 1764

33-2   2000

33-3   #18, Par 5, 550 yards, Pebble Beach Golf Links, Pebble Beach, CA

33-4   1892 at Muirfield, Gullane, Scotland, won by Harold Hilton, an amateur

33-5   George Duncan at Royal Cinque Ports Golf Club, Deal, England

33-6   26 different players, 31 victories out of 108 championships or a winning percentage of (.287%)

33-7   Jack Nicklaus, 1977 at Turnberry (Ailsa Course) "Duel in the Sun," losing to Tom Watson

33-8   None! WOW!

33-9   Byron Nelson, 1981–2001

33-10   Tiger Woods is second to Jack Nicklaus' 22 covers (but time will tell the all-time leader)

33-11   Old Course St. Andrews, beside the Link Clubhouse, St. Andrews, Scotland

33-12   Jack Nicklaus 1970 and 1978; Tiger Woods 2000 and 2005; Old Course St. Andrews

33-13   False; never has happened through 2008

33-14   Record held by Greg Norman, 1993 at Royal St. George's Golf Club, 66-68-69-64 = 267

33-15   True; except in 1871, when no British Open Tournament was held because of a dispute

33-16   A wedge shot that backed-up off the green into the creek at #17 Cherry Hills, 1960

33-17   Camp Callan, an artillery training base

33-18   Ben Hogan, 1948, Riviera; Jack Nicklaus, 1972, Pebble Beach; and Tiger Woods, 2008, Torrey Pines

33-19   September 1958, Jack was 15 years old and Palmer 29. A nine-hole golf course at Ohio University, Athens Country Club, a day honoring PGA Champion Dow Finsterwald

33-20   Caddying—Nelson, Hogan, Sarazen, Snead…Cabrera and many, many more

34 QUESTIONS

34-1   When was the first time Tiger Woods finished second in the Masters Tournament?

34-2   The home course of Jack Nicklaus, Scioto Country Club, has hosted which two majors?

34-3   What four players have made an eagle (2) on #11, a Par 4 at the Masters Tournament?

34-4   What major championship was the last one won by Sam Snead?

34-5   In the 1920s, how many times did Walter Hagen win the British Open Championship?

34-6   Who broke the color line by being the first African-American to play in the 1975 Masters?

34-7   What was major winner Tom Kite's best year on tour?

34-8   Who won two U.S. Opens, lost one in a play-off, won one Masters and was runner-up twice?

34-9   Who broke Walter Hagen's win streak at four straight PGA Championships?

34-10   In what year and in which major championships did Jack Nicklaus finish second three times?

34-11   Course logo: A pioneering golfer in knickers and a bright red coat?

34-12   How many times did John Henry "J.H." Taylor win the British Open Championship?

34-13   Which British Open Championship course is two nine-hole loops; one clockwise and the other counter-clockwise?

34-14   When sportswriter Mr. Grantland Rice wrote, "His legs weren't strong enough to carry his heart around." Who was he writing about?

34-15   **T or F** Golf course designer Dr. Alister MacKenzie died before the first Masters Tournament in 1934.

34-16   In 1995, who did John Daly beat in a play-off to win the British Open Championship at the Old Course St. Andrews?

34-17   Through 2008, how many defending U.S. Open Champions missed the cut the following year?

34-18   Who was the first champion to break 280 in the British Open Championship?

34-19   Who was the first player to win both the U.S. Open and PGA Championship in the same year?

34-20   Which major winner was the youngest player ever to qualify and play in the U.S. Amateur Championship?

ANSWERS

GROUP
34

34-1   2008, second by three shots to Trevor Immelman

34-2   1926 U.S. Open (winner Bobby Jones); 1950 PGA Championship (winner Chandler Harper)

34-3   Jerry Barber (1962), Brad Faxon (2002), K.J. Choi (2004) and Rory Sabbatini (2006)

34-4   1954 Masters Tournament

34-5   Four times: 1922 and 1928, Royal St. George's Golf Club; 1924, Royal Liverpool Golf Club; and 1929, Muirfield

34-6   Lee Elder

34-7   1981, 21 Top 10 finishes out of 26 starts and #1 on the money list

34-8   Cary Middlecoff won 1949 and 1956 U.S. Opens, lost play-off in 1957, won Masters in 1955, runner-up in 1948 and 1959, was second in PGA 1955

34-9   Leo Diegel in 1928; also won in 1929

34-10   1964, Masters Tournament, British Open Championship and PGA Championship tied for second

34-11   Muirfield, Gullane, East Lothian, Scotland

34-12   Five times, 1894, 1895, 1900, 1909 and 1913; One of the "Great Triumvirate"

34-13   Muirfield, a unique layout!

34-14   Ben Hogan, after losing a play-off to Sam Snead at Riviera in 1950

34-15   True

34-16   Italian, Costantino Rocca

34-17   It has happened seven times

34-18   Bobby Locke, 279, 1950 at Royal Troon Golf Club

34-19   Gene Sarazen, 1922; he was only 20 years old at the time

34-20   Bobby Jones (age 14) in 1916, losing out in the third round

GROUP

QUESTIONS

35-1   Where is the largest golf complex located in Europe?

35-2   **T or F** The British Open was played at three courses in rotation for the first 12 championships.

35-3   Who was the first wire-to-wire winner of the PGA Championship after it switched from match-play to stroke (medal) play?

35-4   What was the last major championship won by Bobby Jones?

35-5   What is the only state to host back-to-back U.S. Open Championships?

35-6   Which major championship winner was known as "Mr. 59?"

35-7   How many under par (a record), at the 2000 British Open Championship, hosted by the Old Course St. Andrews, was Tiger Woods?

35-8   Who was the first Scotsman to win a "Green Jacket?" He won with a great sand shot on the 72nd hole in 1988.

35-9   Who hit a seven-iron, 175-yards, two inches from the cup, to win the 2003 PGA Championship over Chad Campbell?

35-10   What is the only major championship that has never had a winner shoot four rounds in the 60s?

35-11   Who won two NCAA Division I Individual Championships and one U.S. Open Championship?

35-12   During "The Golden Age of Sports," Bobby Jones represented golf; who represented baseball, boxing, football and tennis?

35-13   Which course is the oldest "Golf *Club*" and which one is the oldest "Golf *Course*" in the world?

35-14   Which years did Scottish golfers win the U.S. Open Championship eight years straight?

35-15   What was the first major play-off that Byron Nelson and Ben Hogan played against each other?

35-16   Who was the first golfer to win the Associated Press Athlete of the Year award?

35-17   Who did Rich Beem beat for the 2002 PGA Championship title?

35-18   How many times has the U.S. Open been held in California? Name the courses.

35-19   In 1970, which British player was the first one to hold both the U.S. and British Open Championship titles at the same time?

35-20   Who won two U.S. Open Championships with Payne Stewart in the runner-up position?

ANSWERS

35-1   St. Andrews, 99 holes, St. Andrews, Scotland

35-2   False; first 12 were played at Prestwick Golf Club

35-3   Bobby Nichols, 1964 at Columbus Country Club, Columbus, OH

35-4   1930 British Open Championship at Royal Liverpool Golf Club, establishing the Grand Slam

35-5   Pennsylvania; 1934 Merion Golf Club East and 1935 Oakmont Country Club

35-6   Al Geiberger, shooting a 59 at the Danny Thomas Memphis Classic, June 10, 1977

35-7   19 under par, winning by eight shots

35-8   Sandy Lyle, −7, winner by one shot

35-9   Shaun Micheel at Oak Hill Country Club, East Course, Rochester, NY, 276 (4 under par)

35-10   The Masters Tournament

35-11   Scott Simpson, 1976 and 1977 NCAA Champion, 1987 U.S. Open Champion at Olympic Club

35-12   Babe Ruth (baseball), Jack Dempsey (boxing), Red Grange (football) and Bill Tilden (tennis)

35-13   Oldest "Golf *Club*" is Muirfield, Gullane, Scotland; Oldest "Golf *Course*" is the Old Course St. Andrews, St. Andrews, Scotland

35-14   1901 through 1908, Willie Anderson winning four times

35-15   1942 Masters Tournament, Byron Nelson beating Ben Hogan 69-70

35-16   Gene Sarazen, 1932

35-17   Tiger Woods by one shot. Championship played at Hazeltine National Golf Club

35-18   Nine times: Riviera (one), Olympic Club (three), Pebble Beach (four), Torrey Pines (one)

35-19   Tony Jacklin, first time in 70 years; Jacklin won the 1969 British Open at Royal Lytham & St. Annes Golf Club and the 1970 U.S. Open at Hazeltine National Golf Club

35-20   Lee Janzen, 1993, at Baltusrol Golf Club 272-274; 1998, Olympic Club 280-281

36-1   Which course has the distinction of having the longest and shortest holes in the British Open?

36-2   Which major winner was known for his green-keeping skills and golf course management?

36-3   Who is the last major winner of the British Open Championship to win by going wire-to-wire?

36-4   Whose record did Tiger Woods beat when he shot 18 under par, 270 at the 1997 Masters?

36-5   Which state has hosted the most major championships?

36-6   Which player was the first to win the first two major championships in a year?

36-7   Name the five gentlemen who succeeded Clifford Roberts as Chairman of Augusta National.

36-8   Who won the "Centenary" British Open Championship at St. Andrews Old Course in 1960?

36-9   How many shots was Ben Hogan better in 1953 at Oakmont than Sam Parks, Jr. in 1935?

36-10   What was the first year Jack Nicklaus won two major championships in a single year?

36-11   **T or F** The first professional golfers were caddies in Scotland.

36-12   Which three major winners have won the NCAA Individual Championship and U.S. Amateur in the same year?

36-13   Who won three PGA Championships, three Masters, one British Open, and was second four times in the U.S. Open Championship?

36-14   Which professional golfer broke the "social ostracism" against pro golfers?

36-15   Who was the first Englishman to win the British Open Championship in England?

36-16   Which player has led the U.S. Open Championship the most times after 18, 36 and 54 holes?

36-17   **T or F** Tiger Woods, in the 2000 British Open at the Old Course St. Andrews, never hit into a single sand trap in four rounds.

36-18   Which two major winners have the most rounds under 70 in the British Open Championship?

36-19   During which U.S. Open Championship were steel-shafted putters allowed for the first time?

36-20   What is often considered the perfectly balanced round of golf?

ANSWERS

36-1   Royal Troon Golf Club, #6, Par 5, 599 yards; #8 "Postage Stamp" Par 3, 123 yards

36-2   "Old" Tom Morris, Sr.

36-3   Tom Weiskopf, 1973 at Royal Troon Golf Club, 12 under par, 276, Troon, Scotland

36-4   Jack Nicklaus (1965) and Raymond Floyd (1976)

36-5   Georgia, because of the Masters, but New York is second, with Pennsylvania a very close third

36-6   Craig Wood in 1941, the Masters Tournament and U.S. Open Championship

36-7   William Lane, Hord Hardin, Jackson Stephens, "Hootie" Johnson and William "Billy" Payne

36-8   Ken Nagle

36-9   16 shots, 283 vs. 299

36-10   1963: The Masters Tournament and the PGA Championship in his 2nd year on the tour

36-11   True; the first invitations to play in the British Open read, "The player should be a known and respectable caddy"

36-12   Jack Nicklaus (1961), Phil Mickelson (1990) and Tiger Woods (1996)

36-13   "Slammin' Sammy" Sam Snead

36-14   Walter Hagen—Professional golfers owe Walter a lot for where the game is today!

36-15   John Henry "J.H." Taylor, 1894

36-16   11 times by Payne Stewart, winning 1991 and 1999

36-17   True! Pretty amazing shot-making on that championship golf course

36-18   Jack Nicklaus and Nick Faldo; tied at 35 rounds

36-19   1924, Oakland Hill Country Club, Bloomfield Hills, MI

36-20   33 on the front nine, 33 on the back nine (66), 33 strokes, 33 putts and no 5s on the card

QUESTIONS

37-1   Who is the youngest winner of the Masters Tournament?

37-2   How much did Jack Nicklaus win in the first tournament he entered as a professional?

37-3   Who, in his first appearance, was the last major winner of the British Open Championship?

37-4   How many holes did Prestwick have in 1860 for the first British Open Championship?

37-5   Who are the three players that won the British Open Championship in three different decades?

37-6   How many times did Walter Hagen beat Bobby Jones in match-play during the PGA Championships?

37-7   Which major championship concludes on Sunday, "Father's Day?"

37-8   Which major championship golf courses did Jack Nicklaus design?

37-9   **T or F** The first U.S. Open Championship and U.S. Amateur Championship were both played at Newport Country Club.

37-10 Who was the first player to win all four of the major championships twice?

37-11 Which major championship winner is the all-time Champions' Tour money list leader?

37-12 **T or F** James Braid, winner of five British Open Championships, won all by three strokes or more.

37-13 Who has the biggest fourth round come back in U.S. Open history to win by two shots?

37-14 **T or F** Between 1921 and 1927 Walter Hagen and Gene Sarazen won every PGA Championship.

37-15 Who was the first major winner to break 300 in a golf tournament held in the United States?

37-16 **T or F** Through 2008, the last five PGA Champions have been won by players ranked on the World Rankings top four positions.

37-17 Who was the first player to take Tiger Woods to a tie and force a play-off in a major championship after Tiger had the 54-hole lead?

37-18 Through 1932, whose 66 was the lowest round in U.S. Open Championship history?

37-19 Through 2008, how many times has the U.S. Open Championship ended with a play-off?

37-20 Who is the "Parking-Lot Champion?"

ANSWERS

GROUP
37

37-1   Tiger Woods, 21 years, 104 days old in 1977

37-2 $33.33

37-3   Ben Curtis, 2003, at Royal St. George's Golf Club, Sandwich, England

37-4   12 holes, played three times for the British Open Championship in one day

37-5   Harry Vardon (1896, 1903, 1911), J.H. Taylor (1894, 1900, 1913) Gary Player (1959, 1968, 1974)

37-6   Never. Bobby Jones was an amateur and never played in the PGA Championship

37-7   U.S. Open Championship

37-8   Valhalla Golf Club, Louisville, KY and Shoal Creek, Birmingham, AL

37-9   True; in 1895

37-10   Jack Nicklaus

37-11   Hale Irwin with over $23 million

37-12   False; he won by 3, 4, 5 and 8 strokes and won by 1 stroke in 1906

37-13   Arnold Palmer, 1960 at Cherry Hills, his 65 beat amateur Jack Nicklaus by two shots

37-14   True! Walter Hagen 5 times (1921, 1924, 1925, 1926, 1927); Gene Sarazen twice (1922, 1923)

37-15   Willie Anderson, 1902, Western Open—considered a major tournament at the time

37-16   True. 2004, No. 3, Singh; 2005, No.4, Mickelson; 2006–2007, No. 1, Woods; 2008, No.3, Harrington

37-17   Rocco Mediate, 2008 at Torrey Pines, 71-73

37-18   Gene Sarazen, 1932, at Fresh Meadow Country Club, Flushing, NY

37-19   33 times, first in 1901 (Myopia Hunt Club), and last time 2008 (Torrey Pines)

37-20   Seve Ballesteros, 1979 British Open Championship. A shot from a parking lot at the 16th hole at Royal Lytham & St. Annes Golf Club, Lancashire, England

38-1   Who beat Sam Snead 8 and 7 in 1938 to win the PGA Championship at Shawnee
Golf Resort?

38-2   Who lost two consecutive majors by a final-hole sand shot and a play-off chip-in?

38-3   How many amateurs have won the Masters Tournament?

38-4   Who was the first player to win the first two major championships after Arnold Palmer
in 1960?

38-5   What major championship did Lee Trevino not win?

38-6   Who proudly wears his kilt with his "Green Jacket?"

38-7   What three scores did Padraig Harrington shoot in each of his last rounds to win his first
three major championships?

38-8   **T or F** The British Open Championship was cancelled in its eleventh year (1871) because
of disagreement among various golf clubs.

38-9   Which three-time U.S. Open Championship winner was an All-Big Eight DB in football and
an Academic All-American at Colorado?

38-10   **T or F** Two Welshmen have won the British Open Championship.

38-11   What was Walter Hagen's match-play record for his record five wins in the PGA
Championship?

38-12   How many extra play-off holes were required to determine the 1931 U.S. Open Champion,
Billy Burke?

38-13   Name the first 11 members, all major winners, to be inducted in the World Golf Hall
of Fame.

38-14   What type of ball did Sandy Herd use to win the 1902 British Open Championship?

38-15   Name the four-straight international winners of the Masters Tournament from 1988–1991?

38-16   Who made the famous 12-foot putt on the 18th hole to set up victory at Winged Foot in the
1929 U.S. Open Championship?

38-17   How many times did Alex Smith finish runner-up before he won his first U.S. Open
Championship?

38-18   Who was the last Frenchman to win the British Open Championship?

38-19   Who birded #17 and #18 in rounds 1, 2 and 4 at Pebble Beach during the 1982 U.S. Open?

38-20   Who was the last player to win the British Open Championship in three consecutive years?

ANSWERS

38-1   Paul Runyan, winning by the largest margin in the Match-Play Era.

38-2   Greg Norman, PGA Championship 1986 to Bob Tway; Masters, to Larry Mize in 1987

38-3   None through 2008

38-4   Jack Nicklaus, the 1972 Masters Tournament and the U.S. Open Championship at Pebble Beach

38-5   The Masters Tournament

38-6   Scotsman Sandy Lyle, the Masters Champion, 1988

38-7   2007 (67) at Carnoustie; 2008 (69) at Royal Birkdale; and 2008 (66) at Oakland Hills (PGA Championship)

38-8   True; however it started up again the next year, in 1872

38-9   Hale Irwin

38-10   False; no Welshmen have ever won. Two Irishmen have, Fred Daly in 1947 and Padraig Harrington in 2007.

38-11   22 straight match-play victories between 1924 and 1927

38-12   First 36 holes still tied at 149, Billy Burke won by one shot over George Von Elm, 148 to 149 on the second 36-hole play-off.

38-13   Hagen, Hogan, Jones, Nelson, Nicklaus, Ouimet, Palmer, Player, Sarazen, Snead and Vardon

38-14   The Haskell Ball—a rubber-core ball was the new craze in golf

38-15   Sandy Lyle (1988), Nick Faldo (1989–1990), Ian Woosnam (1991), all from the United Kingdom

38-16   Bobby Jones

38-17   Three times; 1898, 1901 and 1905, winning in 1906 and 1910

38-18   Arnavo Massy, 1907 at Royal Liverpool Golf Club, Hoylake, England

38-19   Winner, Tom Watson

38-20   Australian Peter Thomson (1954, 1955 and 1956), plus 1958 and 1965

QUESTIONS

"Who Said?"

39-1   "It's the toughest short Par 3 ever."

39-2   "If you want to test yourself, to see if you are not a golfer but a player, this is where you come."

39-3   "Acre for acre, it may be the best test of golf in the world."

39-4   "Close, Hell, I'm going to make it."

39-5   "Should have won by 10 shots."

39-6   "The Greatest Game."

39-7   "I never wanted to be a millionaire, I just wanted to live like one..."

39-8   "This is the greatest thrill of my life, bar none."

39-9   "You drive for show, but putt for dough."

39-10   "I saw Nicklaus watch Hogan practice, but I never saw Hogan watch Nicklaus."

39-11   "An angry golfer is a loser. If he can't control himself, he can't control his shots."

39-12   "The shot of my life."

39-13   "I always out-worked everybody."

39-14   "My God, that's the greatest shot of my life."

39-15   "If not for you, Walter, this dinner tonight would be downstairs in the pro shop, not in the ballroom."

39-16   "I'm only scared of three things: Lightning, a side hill putt and Ben Hogan."

39-17   "Golf is not a game of great shots. It's a game of the most accurate misses. The people who win make the smallest mistakes."

39-18   "He's playing a game with which I'm not familiar."

39-19   "My God, I won the Open!"

39-20   "Fear ruins more golf shots, for duffer and star, than any other factor."

ANSWERS

GROUP 39

"Who Said?"

39-1   Gary Player, 1996, regarding #12 at August National Golf Club, host of the Masters

39-2   Johnny Miller, 1973, U.S. Open Champion speaking about Oakmont Country Club

39-3   Jack Nicklaus speaking about Merion Golf Club East

39-4   Tom Watson, 1982, U.S. Open Champion, chipping in for a birdie on #17 to win

39-5   Ben Hogan talking about Jack Nicklaus in the 1960 U.S. Open at Cherry Hills

39-6   Bobby Jones

39-7   Walter Hagen

39-8   Arnold Palmer, upon winning his first Masters, in 1958

39-9   Bobby Locke, four-time winner of the British Open Championship

39-10   Tommy Bolt, 1958 U.S. Open Champion

39-11   Sam Snead

39-12   Gary Player, winning the 1968 British Open Championship at Carnoustie, Carnoustie, Scotland

39-13   Ben Hogan speaking about his practice work ethic

39-14   Doug Ford's sand shot in the 1957 Masters—holing-out to beat Sam Snead

39-15   Arnold Palmer honoring golf's greatest showman, Walter Hagen

39-16   Sam Snead talking about his good friend and competitor

39-17   Gene Littler, 1961 U.S. Open Champion

39-18   Bobby Jones speaking about Jack Nicklaus at the Masters Tournament

39-19   Ken Venturi, on making his final putt in the 1964 U.S. Open Championship at the Congressional Country Club, Bethesda, MD

39-20   Tommy Armour, "The Silver Scot," winner of the 1927 U.S. Open, 1930 PGA and 1931 British Open Championships

GROUP 40 QUESTIONS

40-1   Amen Corner® at Augusta National Golf Club, was named by golf writer Herbert Warren Wind, after what Jazz tune?

40-2   Who was the first American-born player to win the British Open Championship?

40-3   How many U.S. Open Championships has Baltusrol Golf Club hosted?

40-4   When did the Masters use a sudden-death play-off format to determine the winner for the first time?

40-5   Who broke the low score record (271) in the PGA Championship held by Bobby Nichols for 30 years?

40-6   Who was the first post-World War II winner of the PGA Championship in 1946?

40-7   Between 1949 and 1958, which two players won eight out of 10 British Open Championships?

40-8   Did Horton Smith break 70 in his one shot victory in the first (1934) Augusta National Invitational (later the Masters Tournament)?

40-9   Who was the ninth alternate, but got in and won, the 1991 PGA Championship at Crooked Stick Golf Club in Carmel, IN?

40-10   **T or F** The PGA Tour manages all four of the major championships.

40-11   Who did Tony Manero beat by two shots in the 1936 U.S. Open Championship?

40-12   Who does the defending Masters Champion play with in the first two rounds?

40-13   How old was Jack Nicklaus when he qualified for his first U.S. Open Championship?

40-14   How many Masters (setting the record) has Gary Player teed-off in through 2008?

40-15   In which British Open did the entire U.S. Ryder Cup Team play together for the first time?

40-16   Who is the oldest major winner to make the cut in the U.S. Open Championship?

40-17   Who called the Columbus *Citizen Journal* newspaper to report on Jack Nicklaus during his great playing in the 1960 U.S. Open Championship at Cherry Hill in Denver?

40-18   Where is the longest Par 4 in U.S. Open Championship history?

40-19   On what course did Bobby Jones win his first (1924) and last (1930) U.S. Amateur Championships?

40-20   Who made 18 consecutive pars at Muirfield in 1987, to beat Paul Azinger and win the British Open Championship?

ANSWERS

40-1   "Shootin' in that Amen Corner®"

40-2   Walter Hagen in 1922 at Royal St. George's Golf Club, Sandwich, England

40-3   Seven U.S. Opens, 1903, 1915, 1936, 1954, 1967, 1980 and 1993; one PGA 2005

40-4   1979, Fuzzy Zoeller winning over Ed Snead and Tom Watson

40-5   Nick Price 269 (11 under) in 1994 at Southern Hills Country Club, Tulsa, OK

40-6   Ben Hogan in 1946, winning his first of nine major championships, but Bob Hamilton (1944) and Byron Nelson (1945) won during World War II. No PGA Championship in 1943

40-7   Four times each: Bobby Locke (1949, 1950, 1952 and 1957); Peter Thomson (1955, 1955, 1956 and 1958)

40-8   NO! He Shot 70-72-70-72 (284). He won again in 1936 with a total score of 283

40-9   John Daly

40-10 False; Masters (Invitational), U.S. Open (USGA), British Open (R & A), PGA Championship (PGA of America)

40-11 "Hard Luck" Harry Copper, who also lost the Masters that same year by one shot to Horton Smith

40-12 The current U.S. Amateur Champion

40-13 17 years old, Jack's birthday is January 21, 1940

40-14 51 times!

40-15 1937 at Carnoustie, Carnoustie, Scotland

40-16 Sam Snead at age 61 in 1973, tied for 29th place at Oakmont Country Club, Oakmont, PA

40-17 The Ohio State University Head Football Coach Wayne Woodrow "Woody" Hayes

40-18 #12 at Torrey Pines, 504 yards during the 2008 U.S. Open Championship

40-19 Merion Cricket Club, Renamed Merion Golf Club, East Course, Ardmore, PA

40-20 Nick Faldo

GROUP

QUESTIONS

41-1   What is the most popular sandwich served during the Masters Tournament?

41-2   Which two major championship winners have won the Ohio Amateur in consecutive years?

41-3   Has the British Open Championship ever been played in Wales?

41-4   In 1971, in which three tournaments (two majors) did Lee Trevino win in a three-week period?

41-5   Members complained about the Par 3, #4 at Baltusrol (the host of the 1954 U.S. Open Championship). What were they complaining about?

41-6   What year did major championship winner Johnny Miller win eight regular tournaments (no-majors) setting a season money winning record?

41-7   Which major winner has had the longest-running endorsement deal in all of professional sports?

41-8   How many tries did it take Sam Snead and Ben Hogan to win their first Masters Tournament?

41-9   Who played in a record 154 consecutive major championships?

41-10   Which course has the Putter Boy, a 1912 sculpture by Lucy Richards, titled "Sundial Boy," as its logo?

41-11   Which two Masters' winners hold the record for the highest score in the final round, but still won?

41-12   Who was known to have a swing that only got better when you put on more pressure?

41-13   Between the World Wars, which two players won two consecutive U.S. Open Championships?

41-14   What was the "Original" award/prize for winning the British Open Championship?

41-15   "The Pyramids" also known as "Chocolate Drops," are what kind of golf course feature?

41-16   Which major winners laid-out Muirfield in Scotland and Muirfield Village in Dublin, OH?

41-17   Who was the first player to win $200,000.00 and then $300,000.00 in a single season?

41-18   Who won his first tournament (the 1976 U.S. Open Championship) after turning pro?

41-19   **T or F** Tiger Woods has held the lead or been tied after 54 holes in his first 14 major wins.

41-20   Who waved a white towel in mock surrender to then tie, and win, the 1984 U.S. Open Championship in a play-off?

ANSWERS

41-1   The pimento cheese sandwich, very famous in the South!

41-2   Arnold Palmer (1953 and 1954); Ben Curtis (1999 and 2000)

41-3   No, nor in seven of the other nine regions in England

41-4   The U.S. Open Championship, the Canadian Open and the British Open Championship…WOW!

41-5   Architect Robert Trent Jones went out and made a hole-in-one! Not that difficult!

41-6   1974, $353,201

41-7   Gene Sarazen, 75 years, with Wilson Sporting Goods

41-8   Both took 10 tries, and then both won several times thereafter

41-9   Jack Nicklaus, from 1957 to 1998, U.S. Open Championships

41-10   Pinehurst Resort #2, Pinehurst, NC

41-11   Arnold Palmer (1962); Trevor Immelman (2008); both shot a 75 in the final round

41-12   Ben Hogan—a legendary striker of the ball!

41-13   Bobby Jones (1929 and 1930), Ralph Guldahl (1937 and 1938)

41-14   "The Championship Belt"

41-15   Conical mounds of dirt, a common hazard in the early 20th century

41-16   "Old" Tom Morris, Sr., circa 1891; Jack Nicklaus, circa 1972

41-17   Jack Nicklaus, 1971 and 1972

41-18   Jerry Pate

41-19   True! Through 2008 U.S. Open Championship at Torrey Pines, San Diego, CA

41-20   Fuzzy Zoeller, then he beat Greg Norman 67 to 75 in the play-off

42-1   What major championship course was the first one used to host a U.S. Open on the Pacific Coast?

42-2   Who is the only U.S. Open winner to finish under par in three consecutive U.S. Opens?

42-3   Who is the only American to win the British Open Championship between Sam Snead in 1946 and Arnold Palmer in 1961?

42-4   **T or F** In the current course rotation of the British Open Championship, it will be played six times in Scotland and four times in England.

42-5   Who was the first winner of a major championship tournament to use steel-shafted golf clubs?

42-6   **T or F** The Old Course St. Andrews is an 18-hole palindrome.

42-7   What was the land used for at Augusta National before the construction of the golf course?

42-8   From 1934 until 1980, the 44th Masters, how many international players won the Masters?

42-9   What is the highest winning score at the Masters Tournament?

42-10 Between 1913 and 1933, how many amateurs have won the U.S. Open Championship?

42-11 **T or F** The British Open Championship is always played on a "links" course.

42-12 Which major is considered by many as the best one-on-one battle between two major winners?

42-13 **T or F** The USGA and the R & A have always played by "The Rules of Golf."

42-14 When Lee Trevino chipped in on #17 at Muirfield during the 1972 British Open, who was his playing partner that he beat?

42-15 Who won the first unofficial U.S. Open Championship (match-play) in 1894 at the St. Andrews Club in Yonkers, New York?

42-16 Since 1930, what has been the highest score in the fourth round, still good enough to win a U.S. Open Championship?

42-17 Who survived a sudden-death play-off to qualify for the 2008 U.S. Open at Torrey Pines, to finish tied with Tiger Woods after 72 holes?

42-18 What is meant by "The Field?"

42-19 Who was the first player to break 70 in the British Open Championship?

42-20 Which major winner was scheduled for the maiden transatlantic voyage on the Titanic, but cancelled due to an illness?

ANSWERS

GROUP 42

42-1   Riviera Country Club 1948. Ben Hogan set the 72-hole scoring record of 276

42-2   Curtis Strange, 1988, 1989, 1990

42-3   Ben Hogan in 1953 at Carnoustie, Carnoustie, Scotland

42-4   True, in years ending in 0, 2, 4, 5, 7 and 9 in Scotland, and 1, 3, 6 and 8 in England

42-5   Billy Burke, 1931 U.S. Open Championship at Inverness Club in Toledo, OH

42-6   True, the holes' par is the same forward or backwards: 444 454 434—434 454 444

42-7   A nursery owned by the Berckman family

42-8   One: Gary Player (1961, 1974, 1978); Seve Ballesteros won in 1980

42-9   289 plus one: Snead in 1954, Burke in 1956 and Johnson in 2007

42-10   Eight times in 19 years

42-11   True; coastal course, front nine "Outward" and back nine "Inward"

42-12   1977 British Open at Turnberry (Ailsa Course), Jack Nicklaus finished 65-66, Tom Watson 65-65

42-13   False! There has been disagreement for decades

42-14   Tony Jacklin

42-15   Noted golf course designer, Willie Dunn, Jr.

42-16   76, 1933 by Johnny Goodman (North Shore Country Club) and Sam Parks (Oakmont) in 1935

42-17   Rocco Mediate, ranked 158th, lost to Tiger Woods, one down after 19 holes in a play-off

42-18   A group of players who might have a legitimate chance to win a major championship... common in Las Vegas betting circles

42-19   John Henry "J.H." Taylor (68) at Royal St. George's Golf Club, Sandwich, England

42-20   Harry Vardon, The RMS Titanic sank April 14, 1912

QUESTIONS

GROUP 43

43-1   What is considered the most amazing shot by Tiger Woods to help him win a Masters Tournament?

43-2   Which two majors held in the United States cancelled tournament play during WW I in 1917–18?

43-3   What was the last major championship tournament won by Nick Faldo?

43-4   How old was Francis Ouimet's famous caddy in the 1913 U.S. Open Championship?

43-5   **T or F** The first U.S. Open Championship in 1895 was played following the first U.S. Amateur championship on the same golf course.

43-6   Whose winning margin of nine strokes in the U.S. Open Championship of 1921 was upheld until Tiger Woods broke it in 2000 with a 15-stroke victory?

43-7   **T or F** The "Golden Bear" Jack Nicklaus was third or better in 41 of 76 major championships between 1962 and 1980.

43-8   Jack Nicklaus, the "Golden Bear" was known as "___ ____" early on in his career.

43-9   What is the only major where the yardage is in increments of five yards?

43-10   What is the name of the first golf course Tiger Woods designed in the United States?

43-11   Who was the second player to win all four of the "Modern Day Majors?"

43-12   How many times was Bobby Jones, Jr. low amateur in the U.S. Open Championship?

43-13   How many sixes did Ben Hogan have in his 1953 British Open Championship win at Carnoustie?

43-14   The Golf Coaches Association of America annually awards the Jack Nicklaus Award. How many times did collegiate player Phil Mickelson win the award?

43-15   At what course did the PGA celebrate 50 years of stroke play in their PGA Championship?

43-16   **T or F** Tiger Woods has won back-to-back PGA Championships.

43-17   Who is the only major winner to have shot the best score in all four rounds of the British Open?

43-18   Which two players broke the U.S. Open record of 286 held by Gene Sarazen and Chick Evans in the 1936 U.S. Open at Baltusrol (Upper)?

43-19   Who said, "A shot poorly played should be a short irrevocably lost?"

43-20   Byron Nelson might have won the 1946 U.S. Open Championship at Canterbury Golf Club if not for what occurred. What happened?

ANSWERS

GROUP 43

43-1   His chip-in on the Par 3, #16 during the final round, then won the play-off over Chris Di Marco

43-2   U.S. Open and PGA Championships, Masters not yet founded and the British Open Championship was cancelled 1915–1919

43-3   The 1966 Masters Tournament, his 6th major championship

43-4   Eddie Lowery was 10 years old. Some sources say he was 11, but no matter he was very young.

43-5   True, both championships played on the Newport Golf Club, Newport, RI

43-6   Jim Barnes

43-7   True, an amazing record for 19 years!

43-8   "Fat Jack" but that nickname changed quickly after the 1962 U.S. Open Championship win over Arnold Palmer at the Oakmont Country Club

43-9   Augusta National Golf Club, home of the Masters Tournament

43-10   The Cliffs at High Carolina, near Asheville, NC (one of eight current golf courses in the Cliffs Communities).

43-11   Ben Hogan was second in 1953; Gene Sarazen was the first when he won the 1935 Masters

43-12   Nine times, winning four times

43-13   One time, on #17 during the third round

43-14   Three times 1990, 1991 and 1992 as a player for Arizona State University in Phoenix, AZ

43-15   2008 at Oakland Hills South Course, Bloomfield Hills, MI

43-16   True, two times; in 2006–2007 and in 1999–2000; also done by Denny Shute in 1936–1937

43-17   John Henry "J.H." Taylor in 1900 at the Old Course St. Andrews

43-18   Winner Tony Manero (282); Tommy Armour (284) runner-up

43-19   Henry C. Fownes, Oakmont Country Club's founder and golf course designer

43-20   His caddy accidentally kicked his ball causing a one-stroke penalty

GROUP
44 QUESTIONS

44-1 **T or F** Arnold Palmer lost the U.S. Open Championship two consecutive years.

44-2 Which major winner was Europe's most successful Ryder Cup Captain?

44-3 Who was ranked No. 1 when the inaugural official World Golf Rankings started in 1986?

44-4 Nicklaus established himself in 1962 with the "Changing of the Guard" with Arnold Palmer. What year and who "Changed the Guard" with Jack Nicklaus?

44-5 What state has the most Masters champions?

44-6 Course logo: Lighthouse with a beacon of light?

44-7 What is the title of the famous photo of Ben Hogan's 18th hole tee shot in the 1950 U.S. Open?

44-8 How many players have won both the U.S. Open and the U.S. Amateur Championships?

44-9 Which golf architect is famous for his "sensitivity to the nature of the site?"

44-10 Name the four, 4-time winners of the U.S. Open Championship through 2008?

44-11 What year did the U.S. Open Championship change from a 36-hole final day to the current format of 18 holes over four rounds?

44-12 Who was the last man to beat Bobby Jones before he retired in 1930?

44-13 Who was the only player under par in the 1986 U.S. Open Championship at Shinnecock Hills?

44-14 Who was the first winner of the NCAA Division 1 Championship to win a major championship?

44-15 Of his seven major championship wins, how many did Sam Snead win in a play-off?

44-16 What is the honor given by the USGA in recognition of "Distinguished Sportsmanship in Golf?"

44-17 Who won both the U.S. Open Championship and the PGA Championship at the age of 20?

44-18 What is considered by many golf fans as the greatest twosome in the 4th round of the U.S Open?

44-19 What major championship is included in Byron Nelson's record of 11 consecutive wins in 1945?

44-20 Which major championship winner had the longest tenure as a broadcaster for televised golf?

ANSWERS

44-1   True, twice in 1962 and 1963; 1966 and 1967

44-2   Tony Jacklin, winning four times from 1983 to 1989

44-3   Bernhard Langer, Greg Norman finished #1 at year end

44-4   Tom Watson, 1977 at the Masters and the British Open Championship

44-5   Texas: Hogan, Nelson, Crenshaw, and Demaret (to name a few)

44-6   Turnberry Resort, (Ailsa Course), Turnberry, Ayrshire, Scotland

44-7   "The One Iron"

44-8   Through 2008, 11 players: Evans, Goodman, Jones, Little, Littler, Nicklaus, Ouimet, Palmer, Pate, Travers, Woods

44-9   Dr. Alister MacKenzie

44-10   Willie Anderson, Bobby Jones, Ben Hogan and Jack Nicklaus

44-11   1965 at Bellerive Country Club, St. Louis, MO, won by Gary Player

44-12   Horton Smith, he also won Bobby Jones' 1st and 3rd Masters Tournaments

44-13   Raymond Floyd, winning by two strokes

44-14   Jack Nicklaus, 1961 NCAA Champion for Ohio State; 1962 U.S. Open Champion at Oakmont

44-15   One, the 1954 Masters Tournament. He beat his great competitor Ben Hogan 70-71

44-16   Bob Jones Award

44-17   Gene Sarazen in 1922; U.S. Open at Skokie Country Club; PGA at Oakmont Country Club

44-18   1960 Cherry Hills Country Club, Jack Nicklaus (Amateur) and Ben Hogan

44-19   The PGA Championship at Moraine Country Club in Dayton, OH, winning 4 and 3 over Sam Byrd

44-20   Ken Venturi with CBS for 35 years

GROUP

QUESTIONS

45-1   On what date did Tiger Woods hold all four major championships at the same time?

45-2   How many bunkers were re-built for the 2007 U.S. Open Championship at Oakmont?

45-3   Name the three players from South Africa who have won the U.S. Open Championship?

45-4   Through 2008, who is the only European player since WWII to win the U.S. Open Championship?

45-5   **T or F** "The Triumvirate"—Harry Vardon, J.H. Taylor and James Braid—won 16 British Open Championships and had 12 runner-ups between 1894 and 1914.

45-6   **T or F** Arnold Palmer, after losing the 1962 U.S. Open in a play-off, also lost the 1963 U.S. Open Championship in a play-off.

45-7   Which three-time major winner won 51 PGA Tour events including two U.S. Opens and one Masters?

45-8   What was Jack Nicklaus' highest winning score from all of his six Masters victories?

45-9   What is the lowest score shot in any one round in any of the four majors?

45-10   Which major championship held the first ever sudden-death play-off?

45-11   Which major championship winner is "Golf's Greatest Ambassador?"

45-12   Who was the only other player, before Tiger Woods matched the record in 2000, to win three major championships in a season?

45-13   In what decade did Jack Nicklaus and Arnold Palmer lead the PGA Tour in earnings three times each?

45-14   Who was the first major championship winner to win $6 million, then $7 million, $8 million and $9 million in career winnings?

45-15   How many major championships did Walter Hagen win in the 1920s?

45-16   **T or F** CBS TV rankings for 2008 vs. 2007 were approximately the same, even with Tiger Woods on the sidelines during the PGA Championship.

45-17   **T or F** Golf architect great Donald Ross was an apprentice under "Old" Tom Morris at the Old Course St. Andrews.

45-18   Who won the only U.S. Open Championship held at Riviera Country Club in Los Angeles, CA?

45-19   How many times has a player been the outright leader after every round in the British Open?

45-20   If a wedge is called a "jigger," what are the "historical" names for a putter and a driver?

ANSWERS

45-1   Sunday, April 8, 2001, "The Tiger Slam"

45-2   189

45-3   Ernie Els 1997 and 1994, Gary Player 1965 and Retief Goosen 2001 and 2004

45-4   Tony Jacklin

45-5   True

45-6   True, losing to Julius Boros at The Country Club, Brookline, MA

45-7   Billy Casper

45-8   Even Par 288, 1966 winning in a play-off over Tommy Jacobs and Gay Brewer

45-9   63, done several times over the years

45-10 1977 PGA Championship, Lanny Wadkins beating Gene Littler

45-11 Arnold Palmer

45-12 Ben Hogan in 1953; Masters, U.S. and British Open Championships

45-13 The 1960s; Palmer 1960, 1962 and 1963; Nicklaus 1964, 1965 and 1967

45-14 Tom Kite

45-15 Nine of his 11 majors; five PGA Championships and four British Open Championships

45-16 False, off over 60%. A 2008 share of 6 vs. 2007 share of 15

45-17 True, a great beginning

45-18 Ben Hogan, his first of four U.S. Open Championship wins in 1948

45-19 Six times: Ted Ray (1912), Bobby Jones (1927), Gene Sarazen (1932), Henry Cotton (1934), Tom Weiskopf (1973) and Tiger Woods (2005)

45-20 Putter is a "blank" and driver "play club"

GROUP 46 QUESTIONS

46-1   Who made the first hole-in-one on #12, a Par 3, 155 yards long at the Masters Tournament?

46-2   How many times did Byron Nelson finish second the year he won 11 straight and 18 tournaments over all?

46-3   In what direction do the players play when the British Open is hosted at Old Course, St. Andrews?

46-4   Which U.S. Open Championship winner invented the "Bramble" pattering for the new rubber-cored ball developed by Coburn Haskell?

46-5   Which British Open Championship winner was the first inductee into the World Golf Hall of Fame (1977) who was not from the United States or the United Kingdom?

46-6   When did Gene Sarazen beat Walter Hagen on the second extra hole after being tied in the 36-hole match final?

46-7   Who was the first winner of the U.S. Open Championship to shoot double digits under par?

46-8   Which two major championship winners have been the head club pro at Winged Foot Golf Club?

46-9   What is the lowest-round shot in the U.S. Open Championship?

46-10 Course logo: Winged "O"?

46-11 In what year, and in which major, did Jack Nicklaus win to break Bobby Jones record of 13 majors?

46-12 Which British Open course "hotel" has the largest "single malt" scotch bar in the world?

46-13 For the first five years, what was the Masters Tournament called?

46-14 When Prestwick Golf Club was dropped from the British Open Championship rotation, how many times had it hosted the British Open Championship?

46-15 What did Tiger Woods shoot on the back-side during the Friday round of the 2008 U.S. Open Championship held at Torrey Pines?

46-16 Which U.S. Open Championship had three sets of brothers competing?

46-17 Which member of the "Great Triumvirate" won five British Opens and was second six times?

46-18 What is the single most important major win to establish golf as a popular sport in America?

46-19 In what year was the first U.S. Open Championship to play over 7,000 yards?

46-20 Which major winner has won the most U.S. Amateur Championships?

ANSWERS

46-1   Claude Harmon, 1947, seven iron

46-2   Seven times!

46-3   Counter-clockwise, OUT and then back IN

46-4   James Foulis

46-5   Bobby Locke

46-6   1923 PGA Championship hosted at the Pelham Country Club, Pelham Manor, NY

46-7   Tiger Woods at Pebble Beach Golf Links, 2000, 12 under par, 276

46-8   Craig Wood 1939–1945; Claude Harmon 1945–1978

46-9   63 by Jack Nicklaus, Tom Weiskopf, Johnny Miller and Vijay Singh

46-10   The Olympic Club, Daly City, San Francisco, CA

46-11   1973 PGA Championship at Canterbury Golf Club, Cleveland, OH

46-12   The Old Course Hotel on #17, "The Road Hole" at the Old Course St. Andrews

46-13   Augusta National Invitation Tournament, 1934–1938, then renamed the Masters Tournament

46-14   24 times when dropped in 1925

46-15   A 30 to get back in the championship and eventually win in a 19-hole sudden-death play-off.

46-16   1932, Dutras (Olin and Mortie), Espinosas (Abe and Al) and Turnesa (Joe, Mike and Phil)

46-17   J.H. Taylor won 1894, 1895, 1900, 1909, 1913; second 1896, 1904, 1905, 1906, 1907 and 1914

46-18   Francis Ouimet winning the 1913 U.S. Open play-off over heavily favored British golfers Ted Ray and Harry Vardon. Called by golf experts "The Greatest Game Ever Played."

46-19   1937, Oakland Hills Country Club (South Course), Bloomfield Hills, MI, 7037 yards long

46-20   Bobby Jones, five times; Tiger Woods, second with three victories

47 QUESTIONS

47-1   Where do amateurs stay during the Masters Tournament?

47-2   Name the four other courses associated with the Old Course St. Andrews at the Royal & Ancient Golf Club.

47-3   Where is the "Home of Golf" located?

47-4   Name the three players who performed amazing upsets in the U.S. Open, British Open and PGA?

47-5   What was the last major championship won by Gary Player?

47-6   During Byron Nelson's 11-event win streak in 1945, for 38 rounds, how much was he under par?

47-7   What year was the U.S. Open Championship televised nationally?

47-8   Which two-time major winner had four second places and three play-off losses in a two-year span?

47-9   What was known as the "Biggest Swing" in the Masters during the final round of 1937?

47-10   Where is the Jack Nicklaus Museum located?

47-11   What major tournament has the highest TV rating for worldwide golf broadcast?

47-12   Name the two major winners who have also won three NCAA Division 1 Championships.

47-13   Who was the last major championship winner (through 2008) to win 11 events in a year?

47-14   Who won the 1994 British Open Championship and 1994 PGA Championship... back-to-back?

47-15   Who hit the pin six times during the 1939 U.S. Open Championship and eventually won in a play-off?

47-16   Who was the first player (a major championship winner) to win a million dollars a year?

47-17   Where was the 100th British Open Championship contested and who won?

47-18   Which world famous golf architect developed his "Defensive Camouflage," used in golf course design, from serving in the Boer War and World War I?

47-19   **T or F** Tiger Woods is the oldest of the youngest to win the four major championships.

47-20   What was the first complete book on golf written by a major championship winner?

ANSWERS

GROUP
47

47-1   The Crow's Nest in the world famous clubhouse

47-2   New Course (1895), Jubilee (1897), Eden (1914) and Strathtyrum (1993)

47-3   St. Andrews, Scotland

47-4   Orville Moody in the U.S. Open, 1969; Ben Curtis in the British Open, 2003; and the PGA Championship won by John Daly, 1991

47-5   1978 Masters Tournament, his 9th major championship victory

47-6   113 under par, 67.92 strokes per round average

47-7   1954 at Baltusrol Golf Club (Lower Course), Springfield, NJ

47-8   Craig Wood

47-9   #12 and #13, Byron Nelson makes birdie (2), eagle (3) while Ralph Guldahl shoots a bogey 5 and 6, a six short swing!

47-10   The Ohio State University, in the shadow of the "Horseshoe," 2355 Olentangy River Road, Columbus, OH, 614-247-5959, www.nicklausmuseum.org. A nice place to visit before a "Buckeye" football game!

47-11   The Masters Tournament since 1986

47-12   Ben Crenshaw, University of Texas (1971, 1972, 1973); Phil Mickelson, Arizona State University (1989, 1990 and 1992)

47-13   Sam Snead, 1950

47-14   Nick Price also won a PGA Championship in 1992

47-15   Byron Nelson at Philadelphia Country Club beating Craig Wood and Denny Shute in the play-off

47-16   Curtis Strange in 1988

47-17   1971 at Royal Birkdale Golf Club, Southport, England, won by Lee Trevino

47-18   Dr. Alister MacKenzie

47-19   True; Tiger Woods, 1997 Masters, 21 years, 3 months; "Young" Tom Morris, 1868 British Open, 17 years, 5 months; John McDermott, 1911 U.S. Open, 19 years, 10 months; Gene Sarazen, 1922 PGA Championship, 20 years, 5 months

47-20   *The Game of Golf* by Willie Park, Jr., 1896

GROUP

QUESTIONS

48-1   Oakmont has hosted eight U.S. Open Championships. Which course is second, hosting seven U.S. Open Championships?

48-2   Who did Doug Ford beat four and three in match-play to win the 1955 PGA Championship at Meadowbrook Country Club?

48-3   What is the smallest field of the four major championships?

48-4   Course logo: "Lone Cypress" on contemporary rocks?

48-5   Who took up the game of golf after returning from the Vietnam War and went on to win three major championships?

48-6   Who has completed the most 72-hole tournaments in the U.S. Open Championships?

48-7   Who was the low amateur by three strokes in the 1966 U.S. Open at the Olympic Club?

48-8   Which Masters winner in the 1970s missed the cut the year before and the year after his win?

48-9   Which two major winners won both the U.S. Open Championship and the U.S. Junior Amateur?

48-10   **T or F** Gary Player's winning streak of at least one sanctioned international pro tournament victory for 27 years straight is 10 years longer than anyone else.

48-11   Since WWII, who is the only major winner to have also won the British Amateur Championship?

48-12   Who was the "Dean of American Sports Writers?" Career span from Bobby Jones to Ben Hogan.

48-13   Who was the first winner of the "PGA Player of the Year Award" for four consecutive years?

48-14   In which British Open Championship did the now famous "Bottle Shot" occur? It probably cost Harry Bradshaw the Open Championship.

48-15   Traditionally, what are the colors of the flags for the "outward" and "inward" nines?

48-16   Which of the brothers that played in the 1932 U.S. Open Championship won in 1934?

48-17   Name the six players who have won both the U.S. Open and British Open in the same year?

48-18   Who made the most famous collapse on the 18th hole in the final round to lose a U.S. Open?

48-19   What type of feathers were used in the early golf balls called "featherie?"

48-20   **T or F** Ben Hogan shot a lower score in each of his previous rounds during the British Open Championship at Carnoustie in 1953.

ANSWERS

GROUP

48

48-1   Baltusrol Golf Club, Springfield, NJ

48-2   Dr. Cary Middlecoff

48-3   The Masters Tournament

48-4   Pebble Beach Links Club, Pebble Beach, CA

48-5   Larry Nelson, won the U.S. Open Championship 1983; PGA Championship 1981 and 1987

48-6   Jack Nicklaus, 35 times

48-7   Johnny Miller, his home course

48-8   Tommy Aaron, won in 1973, missed cut in 1972 and 1974

48-9   Johnny Miller and Tiger Woods

48-10   True! WOW!

48-11   Jose Maria Olazabal won the Masters Tournament twice, once in 1994 and 1999

48-12   Mr. Grantland Rice

48-13   Tom Watson (1977, 1978, 1979 and 1980); Tiger Woods has won five years in a row as of 2007

48-14   1949, Royal St. George's Golf Club; ball was lying in a broken beer bottle; player was entitled to a free lift and drop! You've got to know the rules!

48-15   Outward nine, white flags and inward nine, red flags

48-16   Olin Dutra at Merion Golf Club, East Course, Ardmore, PA

48-17   Bobby Jones, 1926 and 1930, Gene Sarazen 1932, Ben Hogan 1953, Lee Trevino 1971, Tom Watson 1982 and Tiger Woods 2000

48-18   Sam Snead, 1939. Sam made an eight, but only needed a par five to win. He finished fifth behind winner Byron Nelson who won in a play-off.

48-19   Boiled goose feathers

48-20   True; 73, 71, 70 and 68

QUESTIONS

Who was the Golf Architect?

49-1   Bethpage State Park, Black, Farmingdale, NY

49-2   Columbus Country Club, Columbus, OH

49-3   Oakland Hills Country Club (South), Bloomfield Hills, MI

49-4   Merion Golf Club, Ardmore, PA

49-5   Inverness Club, Toledo, OH

49-6   Scioto Country Club, Upper Arlington (Columbus), OH

49-7   Congressional Country Club (redesign), Bethesda, MD

49-8   Carnoustie Golf Links (remodeling), Carnoustie, Scotland

49-9   Turnberry (Ailsa Course), Turnberry, Scotland

49-10   Baltusrol Golf Club (Lower), Springfield, NJ

49-11   The Olympic Club (Lakes Course), Daly City, CA

49-12   Valhalla Golf Club, Louisville, KY

49-13   Oakmont Country Club, Oakmont, PA

49-14   Hazeltine National Golf Club, Chaska, MN

49-15   Pinehurst #2, Pinehurst, NC

49-16   Pebble Beach Golf Links, Pebble Beach, CA

49-17   Medinah Country Club, Medinah, IL

49-18   Whistling Straits, Kohler, WI

49-19   Augusta National Golf Club, Augusta, GA

49-20   Winged Foot Golf Club (Western), Mamaroneck, NY

ANSWERS

GROUP

49

Who was the Golf Architect?

49-1   A.W. Tillinghast

49-2   Donald Ross

49-3   Donald Ross, redesigned by Robert Trent Jones, and later by Rees Jones

49-4   Hugh Wilson

49-5   Donald Ross

49-6   Donald Ross, updated in 2008 by Jack Nicklaus

49-7   Robert Trent Jones

49-8   "Old" Tom Morris was first architect, remodeled by James Braid

49-9   Mackenzie Ross

49-10   A.W. Tillinghast

49-11   Wilfrid Reid, remodeled by Sam Whiting and Willie Watson

49-12   Jack Nicklaus

49-13   Henry Clay Fownes (only course he designed), improved by his son
        William Clarke Fownes, Jr.

49-14   Robert Trent Jones

49-15   Donald Ross

49-16   Jack Neville and Douglas Grant

49-17   Tom Bendelon

49-18   Pete Dye

49-19   Dr. Alister MacKenzie and Bobby Jones

49-20   A.W. Tillinghast

GROUP

50 QUESTIONS

50-1   Who set the Masters Tournament scoring record and won by 12 strokes?

50-2   What type of grass grows on Oakmont Country Club's world famous "fast" greens?

50-3   Who won five British Opens, twice the runner-up at the British Open and a member of the "Great Triumvirate?"

50-4   **T or F** "The Big Three" consisting of Jack Nicklaus, Arnold Palmer and Gary Player, all won their last major championship at the Masters Tournament.

50-5   What is the major championship tournament record for the lowest aggregate score?

50-6   Who was the first winner of the U.S. Open Championship to shoot four rounds under par?

50-7   How old was major winner Seve Ballesteros when he started to play as a professional golfer?

50-8   Who was the first foreign player to win the Masters Tournament?

50-9   In which U.S. Open Championship play-off did Lee Trevino toss a rubber snake toward his opponent to unnerve him on the first tee?

50-10   Who conceived the idea of the "Champions Dinner" at the Masters Tournament the Tuesday evening before the start of the tournament?

50-11   Who was the first back-to-back winner of the Masters Tournament?

50-12   Who has the most Top 5 finishes in the Masters Tournament?

50-13   Which major winner is also the youngest winner of the U.S. Amateur Championship?

50-14   Who won the U.S. Open Championship by a record of 11 shots, and held the record until broken by Tiger Woods in 2000, by 15 shots?

50-15   How many of Ben Hogan's nine major championships were won in a play-off?

50-16   How many times was Jack Nicklaus a runner-up to Tom Watson in a major championship?

50-17   In which British Open Championship did Arnold Palmer win, setting the stage for American pros to return and play in the British Open Championship?

50-18   Through 2008, how many times has the Old Course St. Andrews hosted the British Open Championship?

50-19   Which player has had the most 54-hole leads in the U.S. Open Championship?

50-20   **T or F** There is no ball washer on the first tee at the Augusta National Golf Club.

ANSWERS

50-1   Tiger Woods, 1997 shoots 270, 18 under par

50-2   Pittsburgh Poa Annua

50-3   James Braid, won 1901, 1905, 1906, 1908, 1910; runner up 1897 and 1909

50-4   True, Jack Nicklaus (18), Gary Player (9) Arnold Palmer (7), a total of 34 major championships.

50-5   267 by Greg Norman, 1993 at British Open Championship at Royal St. George's Golf Club

50-6   Lee Trevino in 1968 at Oak Hill Country Club, Rochester, NY; 69-68-69-69 = 275

50-7   17 years old

50-8   Gary Player, 1961 Masters Tournament, 8 under par, 280

50-9   1971 at Merion Golf Club (East Course), beating Jack Nicklaus 68 to 71... good gamesmanship!

50-10   Ben Hogan in 1951, started in 1952 when the previous year's champion (Hogan) hosts the dinner

50-11   Jack Nicklaus, 1965 and 1966

50-12   Jack Nicklaus with 15; the most Top 10 finishes with 22

50-13   Tiger Woods, 18 years old, winning three in a row 1994–1995 and 1996; also won three U.S. Junior Amateurs 1991, 1992 and 1993

50-14   Willie Smith, 1899, U.S. Open Championship held at Baltimore (Roland Course) Country Club

50-15   One, the 1950 U.S. Open Championship. All others he won by two strokes or more

50-16   Four times, 1977 and 1981 Masters, 1977 British Open and 1982 U.S. Open Championship

50-17   1961 at Royal Birkdale Golf Club, Southport, England

50-18   27 times, Prestwick is second with 24

50-19   Six times by Bobby Jones, winning four championships

50-20   True! Why would you need one? Wouldn't you be playing with a new sleeve of balls?

GROUP

51 QUESTIONS

51-1   Who is the only player to beat Jack Nicklaus in a major championship play-off?

51-2   Where is the Arnold Palmer plaque located at Augusta National Golf Club?

51-3   Did the 2007 U.S. Open Championship winner at Oakmont make the cut in 2008 at Torrey Pines?

51-4   In eleven starts in the U.S. Open, how many times did Bobby Jones finish either first or second?

51-5   Between McDermott's 1911 win and Jim Furyk's 2003 win in the U.S. Open Championships, how many Americans and how many international players have won?

51-6   Which three major championship winners won the inaugural Payne Stewart Award in 2000?

51-7   Name the three major winners designing golf courses at the Cliffs Communities in the Carolinas.

51-8   **T or F** Torrey Pines (2008 U.S. Open) was ranked in the Top 100 Greatest American Golf Courses by *Golf Digest* magazine for 2008.

51-9   Which major championship player was the first foreign-born player to win the American Professional Golfers' Association Tour money title?

51-10   Who did Paul Azinger beat in a play-off for the 1993 PGA Championship at the Inverness Club?

51-11   Which major championship winner led in the final round in 1995, 1996 and 1997 U.S. Open Championship, but never won?

51-12   **T or F** Padraig Harrington played the last 54 holes at Royal Birkdale in 2008 one under par.

51-13   **T or F** Ben Hogan was not exempt from qualifying for the 1962 U.S. Open Championship at Oakmont Country Club, where he had won before.

51-14   Which player took an eight on "The Cardinal" hole, but still won the British Open by eight shots?

51-15   When was the first U.S. Open Championship extended to 72 holes of stroke play?

51-16   What did Tiger Woods shoot in his second round of the 2007, 89th PGA at Southern Hills?

51-17   What is the lowest score, under par, for 72 holes in the U.S. Open Championship?

51-18   Where and in what year was the "Blast Furnace Open" (U.S. Open Championship) played ?

51-19   Who refereed the play-off between Boros, Culpit and Palmer to decide the 1963 U.S. Open Championship at The Country Club in Brookline, MA?

51-20   Which amateur went from caddy to player by qualifying for the 1966 U.S. Open Championship at the Olympic Club?

ANSWERS

51-1   Lee Trevino, U.S. Open Championship at Merion Golf Club, East Course, 1971

51-2   Behind the 16th tee, dedicated April 4, 1995

51-3   No, he was cut at 13 over par

51-4   Eight times; four wins, four seconds, retired at age 28 in 1930

51-5   9 international players and 76 U.S. players. However, the international players have won the last four going into the into the 2008 U.S. Open Championship. Tiger Woods won in 2008 to stop their streak.

51-6   Byron Nelson, Jack Nicklaus and Arnold Palmer

51-7   Jack Nicklaus (2), Gary Player and Tiger Woods

51-8   False. Not ranked in the Top 100 yet

51-9   Gary Player, 1961

51-10   Greg Norman, second extra hole

51-11   Tom Lehman

51-12   True, winning the British Open Championship at plus three over par

51-13   True, first time since 1941 he did not try to qualify for the championship

51-14   James Braid, 1908 (291) at Prestwick

51-15   1898 at Myopia Hunt Club, South Hamilton, MA

51-16   63; tying the record for the lowest round in a major championship. Winning his fourth PGA Championship, 13th major championship over-all

51-17   −12 (272) Tiger Woods, Pebble Beach Golf Links 2000. 15-shot winning margin; the record for all major championships

51-18   1958 U.S. Open Championship at Southern Hills Country Club, Tulsa, OK, 100-plus degree temperatures all week long. Won by Tommy Bolt.

51-19   1913 winner Francis Ouimet; 50th Anniversary of his great win over Harry Vardon and Ted Ray

51-20   Johnny Miller finishing tied for 8th place; best amateur finish in the field

QUESTIONS

GROUP 52

52-1   In the first two rounds of the 2008 U.S. Open at Torrey Pines, how many rounds were in the 80s?

52-2   Who holds the record for the most Top 10 finishes (18) in the U.S. Open Championship?

52-3   What was the span in years between Jack Nicklaus' first and last U.S. Open wins?

52-4   Which major winner, considered by many as the greatest putter ever, never three-putted in the 1948 season in tournament play?

52-5   How many play-offs have there been in the first 108 U.S. Open Championships?

52-6   What famous landmark hotel is located on a British Open Championship course? It was a military hospital in World War II.

52-7   Who was the youngest winner of the British Open since Seve Ballesteros in 1979?

52-8   Who one-putted each of the last three greens to beat Phil Mickelson in the 1999 U.S. Open Championship at Pinehurst #2?

52-9   Which major winner succeeded Spaniard Seve Ballesteros as the leading player from Spain?

52-10   Who was the first two-time winner of the Masters Tournament?

52-11   Which player has had the most birdies in a Masters Tournament?

52-12   **T or F** Hal Sutton lead wire-to-wire in the 1983 PGA Championship at Riviera Country Club beating Jack Nicklaus.

52-13   Who is the only player to have won the U.S. Open Championship with both the Gutta-Percha and Rubber-Cored golf ball?

52-14   How many consecutive Masters Tournaments did Arnold Palmer play in during his career?

52-15   Phil Mickelson's famous last hole double-bogey collapse occurred in which major championship?

52-16   Who said, "The reason the Road Hole is the greatest par four in the world, is because it's a par five."

52-17   Who is the only U.S. Open Champion to birdie the last hole (#18) in each and every round?

52-18   **T or F** Ben Hogan went wire-to-wire to win the 1953 U.S. Open Championship at Oakmont Country Club; beating Sam Snead by six strokes.

52-19   How old was "Old" Tom Morris, Sr. when he competed in his last British Open Championship?

52-20   Who was the only professional to win the U.S. Open Championship from 1914 to 1919?

ANSWERS

GROUP
52

52-1   40 rounds, 20 rounds each on day one and day two

52-2   Jack Nicklaus, he won four times (1962, 1967, 1972 and 1980)

52-3   18 years, 1962 Oakmont Country Club; 1980 Baltusrol (Lower)

52-4   Bobby Locke

52-5   Thru 2008, 33 with Tiger Woods vs. Rocco Mediate at Torrey Pines Golf Course

52-6   The Turnberry Hotel, original name: Station Hotel known by White Facade and Russet Red Roof

52-7   Justin Leonard, age 25

52-8   Payne Stewart, winning his second U.S. Open Championship

52-9   Jose Maria Olazabal, two-time winner of the Masters Tournament in 1994 and 1999

52-10   Horton Smith, 1934 and 1936

52-11   Phil Mickelson with 25 birdies in 2001

52-12   True

52-13   Willie Anderson, 1901–1903 (also won 1904 and 1905)

52-14   50, last one in 2004 (1954 thru 2004) Hell of a run! Gary Player has 51 tournaments

52-15   2006 U.S. Open Championship at Winged Foot Golf Club, ranks second behind Sam Snead's triple bogey in the 1939 U.S. Open

52-16   Ben Crenshaw

52-17   Walter Hagen, 1914 at Midlothian Country Club, Blue Island, IL

52-18   True, Ben Hogan's fourth U.S. Open Championship

52-19   75 years old, 1896 at Muirfield, Gullane, Scotland

52-20   Walter Hagen, 1914 and 1919; Amateurs Jerome Travers (1915), Chick Evans, Jr. (1916); No U.S. Open Championship in 1917 and 1918 because of World War I.

QUESTIONS

GROUP 53

53-1   In what year was the first U.S. Open televised in prime time in the Eastern United States?

53-2   Which NFL quarterback tried to qualify for the 2008 U.S. Open Championship at Torrey Pines?

53-3   Who shares the record with Jack Nicklaus for 11 Top Fives in the U.S. Open Championship?

53-4   Who are the only players to win the British Open Championship in three different decades?

53-5   Before grass-cutting machines and mowers, what did greenskeepers rely on to keep grass closely cropped?

53-6   On which hole did Nick Faldo win two play-offs to win the Masters Tournament in 1989 and 1990?

53-7   How many major championships did Mark O'Meara compete in before winning his first?

53-8   Which major championship did Tiger Woods consider his best victory so far through 2008?

53-9   Which four players have led (including ties) every round of a British Open Championship?

53-10   Who is the best of the current major winners to never have won a U.S. Open Championship?

53-11   What is the best 4th round shot by the winner in the British Open Championship?

53-12   By how many strokes did Francis Ouimet beat Harry Vardon and Ted Ray in the 1913 U.S. Open play-off at The Country Club?

53-13   What was the first U.S. Open Championship contested without a defending champion?

53-14   Who won the first stroke-play PGA Championship?

53-15   Which U.S. Open winner also won the U.S. and British Amateurs two years back-to-back?

53-16   **T or F** Francis Ouimet led his play-off with Harry Vardon and Ted Ray in the 1913 U.S. Open Championship from the start.

53-17   What story captivated the press during the 137th British Open at Royal Birkdale in 2008?

53-18   What was the average square footage of the greens at Oakmont Country Club in 2007 during the U.S. Open Championship?

53-19   How many Top 10 finishes in the major championships did Jack Nicklaus have in his career?

53-20   On which major championship golf course did the golf architect shape Native American burial mounds into bunkers?

ANSWERS

GROUP

53

53-1   2008 at Torrey Pines Golf Course, South Course, La Jolla, San Diego, CA

53-2   Dallas Cowboys quarterback Tony Romo, shot 75 and did not qualify

53-3   Willie Anderson, he won four times 1901, 1903, 1904 and 1905

53-4   Gary Player, 1959, 1968 and 1974; Harry Vardon 1896, 1898, 1899, 1903, 1911 and 1914; J.H. Taylor 1894, 1895, 1900, 1909 and 1913

53-5   Sheep and rabbits

53-6   #11, Par 4, 455 yards, "White Dogwood"

53-7   57: 14 Masters, 15 U.S. Opens, 13 British Opens and 15 PGAs…won two in 1998 (the Masters and the British Open at the Royal Birkdale Golf Club, Southport, England)

53-8   2008 U.S. Open Championship play-off win over Rocco Mediate at Torrey Pines Golf Course

53-9   Harry Vardon (1899 and 1903), J.H. Taylor (1900), Lee Trevino (1971) and Gary Player (1974)

53-10 Phil Mickelson (2008 World Ranking #2) has been second, three times through 2008

53-11 Greg Norman, a 64 in 1993 at Royal St. George's Golf Club, Sandwich, England

53-12 Harry Vardon by five shots, Ted Ray by six shots

53-13 1901 at Myopia Hunt Club, South Hamilton MA, previous winner was Harry Vardon

53-14 Dow Finsterwald, 1958 at Lianerch Country Club, Havertown, PA

53-15 Larry Little, 1940 U.S. Open Champion; 1934 and 1935 Amateur Championships

53-16 False; all three were tied at 38 after the front nine, then Francis Ouimet shot 34, Harry Vardon 39, and Ted Ray 40, on the back nine.

53-17 Greg Norman, leading going into the 4th round at Royal Birkdale Golf Club, Southport, England

53-18 6,800 square feet, large, fast and undulating

53-19 73: 56 Top Five, 48 Top Three, 19 Runner-up finishes

53-20 Shinnecock Hills Golf Club, Shinnecock, NY, by Willie Dunn, course designer

GROUP
54 QUESTIONS

54-1 Where is the Jack Nicklaus plaque located at the Augusta National Golf Club?

54-2 **T or F** From 1940 to 1960 Ben Hogan never finished outside the Top 10 in the U.S. Open.

54-3 What is the average distance (speed) measured by the Stimpmeter for the U.S. Open greens?

54-4 Who was the first international player to win the Professional Grand Slam?

54-5 Where is the Arnold Palmer Center for Golf History located?

54-6 Who won the first U.S. Open Championship played at a "public" golf course?

54-7 What was the main topic discussed during the 2008 U.S. Open Championship at Torrey Pines?

54-8 What club has hosted seven U.S. Open Championships on three different courses?

54-9 Who was the last player through 2008 to have a double-digit winning season in the United States?

54-10 Which major championship winner has won the most British Amateur Championships (considered a major) at the time?

54-11 **T or F** There were no amateurs in the very first U.S. Open Championship in 1895.

54-12 What was the most one-sided victory match in the PGA Championship?

54-13 Where did the term "Grand Slam" come from?

54-14 Which players had the following stats for PGA match winning percentage, .822% (37/45) and second place .8148% (22/27)?

54-15 What is the nickname of the Olympic Club?

54-16 Who redesigned "The Monster" at Oakland Hills for the 2008 PGA Championship?

54-17 What was the leading golf magazine in the 1920s and 1930s with major championship winners contributing golf columns?

54-18 What day did Tiger Woods turn professional golfer?

54-19 What was the injury to Tiger Woods left leg during the 2008 U.S. Open at Torrey Pines?

54-20 The biographical movie "The Greatest Game Ever Played" is about which major championship?

ANSWERS

54-1   On the drinking fountain between #16 and #17, dedicated April 4, 1998

54-2   True, no wonder he is considered one of the all-time great golfers.

54-3   13 foot roll out! FAST GREENS!

54-4   Gary Player, 1965, and he is still the only international player to win the Grand Slam

54-5   USGA Headquarters, Far Hills, NJ 07931
        Phone: 908-234-2300, website: www.usga.org

54-6   Jack Nicklaus, 1972 at Pebble Beach Golf Links, Pebble Beach, CA

54-7   Tiger Wood's knee. What about Hogan's legs, Trevino's lightning strike, Nicklaus' hip,
        Crenshaw's back, Ballesteros' back? Injuries are part of the game.

54-8   Baltusrol; the original course (1903), Lower (1954, 1967, 1980 and 1993)
        and Upper Course (1936)

54-9   Sam Snead, 1950 with 11 wins

54-10   John Ball, eight times: 1888, 1890, 1892, 1894, 1899, 1907, 1910 and 1912

54-11   False; there waas one—A.W. Smith out of 11 players. Finished three shots behind winner
        Horace Rawlins

54-12   1938, 8 and 7, Paul Runyan over Sam Snead at Shawnee Inn, Smithfield Twp., PA

54-13   A term used in the card game, Contract Bridge

54-14   Byron Nelson (.822 record); Ben Hogan (.8148 second)

54-15   "Giant Killer" Ben Hogan, Arnold Palmer, Tom Watson and Payne Stewart

54-16   Rees Jones, his father Robert Trent Jones, Sr. renovated in 1950 for the U.S. Open
        Championship, original design by Donald Ross

54-17   *The American Golfer*

54-18   August 27, 1996

54-19   Torn ACL and stress fracture to the tibia

54-20   1913 U.S. Open Championship won by amateur Francis Ouimet over Harry Vardon and
        Ted Ray

55-1 Ben Hogan set the 72-hole scoring record of 276 in the 1948 U.S. Open. How long did the record stand?

55-2 Who had 13 out of 15 tries as a Top 10 finisher in the Masters Tournament, winning three times?

55-3 Jockie's Burn, a fast running stream comes into play on four of the first six holes at which British Open Championship course?

55-4 Who was the first player outside of Scotland to win the British Open Championship?

55-5 Willie Park, Sr. and Willie Park, Jr. won how many British Open Championships?

55-6 What was the first major championship Tiger Woods missed in his pro career?

55-7 Which one was the only U.S. Open Championship that Bobby Jones finished out of the Top 10?

55-8 **T or F** Byron Nelson, during the match-play era of the PGA Championship, was in the final match five out of six times from 1939 to 1945.

55-9 Who was the first winner of the U.S. Open Championship to shoot four rounds under 80?

55-10 Between 1934 and 1960, how many Americans won the British Open Championship?

55-11 In the PGA Championship, who qualified for 28 match-plays, had 57 victories and 25 defeats in 82 matches?

55-12 What was the first year the USGA charged an admission fee to attend the U.S. Open Championship?

55-13 Which four players through 2008 have not defended their PGA Championship title?

55-14 Which tournament was Lee Trevino's first win?

55-15 Who was golf's "Greatest Showman and Bon Vivant," establishing the standard or status for professional golfers?

55-16 How many sub-par rounds were shot during the whole of the 1951 U.S. Open at Oakland Hills?

55-17 Through 2008, how many different players have been play-off losers in the U.S. Open?

55-18 In what year and on which course did the USGA celebrate the 100th U.S. Open Championship?

55-19 Who beat Ben Crenshaw with phenomenal putts to win the 1979 PGA Championship at Oakland Hills in a play-off?

55-20 Who was the first player to win five British Open Championships?

ANSWERS

55-1   19 years, broken by Jack Nicklaus, 1967 (275) at Baltusrol Golf Club, Lower Course

55-2   Gary Player won in 1961, 1974 and 1978; second in 1962 and 1965

55-3   Carnoustie Golf Links, Carnoustie, Scotland

55-4   John Ball, 1890. He also was the first player to win the British Amateur in the same year.

55-5   Six times: Sr., 1861, 1862, 1864 and 1867; Jr., 1887 and 1889

55-6   2008 British Open at Royal Birkdale Golf Club and then the PGA Championship at Oakland Hills

55-7   1927, at Oakmont Country Club; he finished tied for 11th, eight shots back

55-8   True, 1939 to 1945 (1943 no PGA...WWII), winning 1940 and 1945

55-9   Laurie Auchterlonie (78-78-64-77), 1902 at Garden City Golf Club, Garden City, NY

55-10   Two; Sam Snead 1946 at the Old Course St. Andrews and Ben Hogan 1953 at Carnoustie

55-11   Gene "Squire" Sarazen

55-12   1922, $1.00 a round or $5.00 for the week

55-13   Walter Hagen (1922) exhibition, Sam Snead (1943 World War II) injury, Ben Hogan (1949) auto accident, Tiger Woods (2008) knee surgery

55-14   A major championship, 1968 U.S. Open at Oak Hill Country Club (East), shooting 69-68-69-68

55-15   Walter Hagen in the "Roaring 20s"

55-16   Two! Ben Hogan shot a 67 to win

55-17   38 times, Arnold Palmer three times, Bobby Jones twice

55-18   2000 at Pebble Beach Golf Links, winner was Tiger Woods 272 (−12)

55-19   David Graham, three-hole play-off, par-par-birdie

55-20   James Braid, 1901, 1905, 1906, 1908 and 1910

"Who Said?"

56-1 "Son, you are going to be a great player."

56-2 "The older you get, the more thrilling it gets because the harder it gets."

56-3 "The older I get, the better I used to be."

56-4 "Golf is 90% inspiration and 10% perspiration."

56-5 "Forget your opponents; always play against par."

56-6 "The harder you work, the luckier you get."

56-7 "If you want to increase your success rate. Double your failure rate."

56-8 "Golf and sex are the only things you can enjoy without being good at them."

56-9 "At my best, I never came close to the golf Byron Nelson shoots."

56-10 "Don't play too much golf. Two rounds a day are plenty."

56-11 "I'm glad I brought this course—'The Monster'—to its knees."

56-12 "The mark of a great player is his ability to come back. The great champions have all come back from defeat."

56-13 "The man who can putt is a match for anyone."

56-14 "I got a W."

56-15 "I like trying to win. That's what golf is all about."

56-16 "You're only here for a short visit. Don't hurry, don't worry and be sure to smell the flowers along the way."

56-17 "The toughest thing for most people to learn in golf is to accept bad holes—and then forget about them."

56-18 "He is so hard to beat, he's unreal."

56-19 "A kid grows up a lot faster on the golf course. Golf teaches you how to behave."

56-20 "Golf is like solitaire. When you cheat, you only cheat yourself."

ANSWERS

GROUP 56

"Who Said?"

56-1   Ben Hogan to Gary Player in 1958

56-2   Jack Nicklaus, after winning the U.S. Open Championship at Baltusrol in 1980

56-3   Lee Trevino

56-4   Johnny Miller

56-5   Sam Snead

56-6   Gary Player

56-7   Tom Watson

56-8   Jimmy Demaret

56-9   Bobby Jones

56-10   Harry Vardon

56-11   Ben Hogan, upon winning the 1951 U.S. Open Championship at Oakland Hills Country Club

56-12   Sam Snead

56-13   Willie Park, Jr.

56-14   Tiger Woods after winning his 14th major championship, the U.S. Open at Torrey Pines

56-15   Jack Nicklaus

56-16   Walter Hagen

56-17   Gary Player

56-18   Rocco Mediate after losing the 2008 U.S. Open Championship play-off to Tiger Woods

56-19   Jack Nicklaus

56-20   Tony Lema

GROUP 57 QUESTIONS

57-1   Which organization runs the U.S. Open Championship tournament?

57-2   The home course for Ben Hogan, Colonial in Ft. Worth, Texas, hosted the U.S. Open Championship one time in what year?

57-3   How many holes did it take for Tiger Woods to win his 14th major championship title?

57-4   Who was the first amateur (major championship winner of two British Opens) to win both the U.S. and British Amateur Championships in the same year?

57-5   Who was known as the "Golfing Robot?"

57-6   Who did Ian Woosnam beat on the 72nd hole of the 1991 Masters after being tied at 11 under?

57-7   Based on official world golf rankings, which major championship has the strongest field?

57-8   **T or F** Famous golf architect Donald Ross played in the U.S. Open Championship.

57-9   What was the first U.S. Open Championship where the winner won a million dollars?

57-10   What major win did Sam Snead call, "His biggest thrill in golf?"

57-11   **T or F** Charles "Chick" Evans, Jr. never placed ahead of Bobby Jones in the eight U.S. Opens they competed in against each other.

57-12   Who was the first player to finish all four rounds at double-digits under par in the U.S. Open?

57-13   Before Tiger Woods sat out the last two majors in 2008 (British Open and PGA), what was his major championship record to that point?

57-14   When Gary Player won the 1965 U.S. Open at Bellerive, what feat did he accomplish?

57-15   Which major winner was born on St. Patrick's Day?

57-16   How many shots did John Mahaffey come from behind to win the 1978 PGA Championship at Oakmont Country Club?

57-17   Who holds the record for the most wins before winning his first major championship?

57-18   Who came back from 18th place after two rounds, eight shots back to beat Gene Sarazen by one to win the 1934 U.S. Open Championship?

57-19   Who was the last European to win the PGA Championship in the match-play format?

57-20   Which player shot a 32 each time on the back nine in two of the final rounds to win two majors in the same year?

ANSWERS

57-1   USGA, the United States Golf Association, www.usga.org

57-2   1941, won by Craig Wood, 284 (+4)

57-3   91 holes, sudden-death play-off over Rocco Mediate at the 2008 U.S. Open Championship, Torrey Pines, La Jolla, CA

57-4   Harold Hilton, 1911

57-5   Bobby Locke

57-6   Tom Watson and Jose Maria Olazabal

57-7   The PGA Championship

57-8   True, eight times, finishing in the Top 10, four times

57-9   2002, Tiger Woods at Bethpage State Park, Black Course, Farmingdale, NY

57-10   1942 PGA Championship, beating Jim Turnesa 2 and 1(match-play) at Seaview Country Club, NJ

57-11   False, 1920 and 1921, Chick Evans. Both times he was one shot ahead.

57-12   Tiger Woods, 2000, 272 (−12) at Pebble Beach Golf Links, 15-stroke victory margin

57-13   14 wins in 46 major championships

57-14   He became the third player to win the four majors with Gene Sarazen and Ben Hogan. Jack Nicklaus and Tiger Woods followed later.

57-15   Bobby Jones, March 17, 1902

57-16   Seven shots!

57-17   Ben Hogan won 30 times before winning the 1946 PGA Championship at Portland Golf Club

57-18   Olin Dutra, he also won the 1932 PGA Championship in match-play 4 and 3 over Frank Walsh

57-19   Tommy Armour (Scottish) 1930 at Fresh Meadow Country Club, Great Neck, NY winning one up over Gene Sarazen

57-20   Padraig Harrington, 2008 British Open (Royal Birkdale) and PGA Championship (Oakland Hills)

GROUP 58   QUESTIONS

58-1   Who one-putted the last six holes to win the 2004 U.S. Open Championship at Shinnecock Hills?

58-2   Name the three winners of the U.S. Open Championship at The Country Club in Brookline, MA?

58-3   Who won the 1956 Masters Tournament and the PGA Championship?

58-4   Which major championship winners have won the Fred Haskins Award three times in a row as the Outstanding College Player?

58-5   Who was the player that won the Masters Tournament for his sixth consecutive tournament win?

58-6   What famous hole most likely cost Tom Watson a record-tying 6th victory in the 1984 British Open Championship?

58-7   **T or F** Tiger Woods, through 2008, has won all three of his first U.S. Open Championships on public golf courses, not country clubs.

58-8   Which major championship winner was one of the original founders of the PGA Championship?

58-9   Who shot an eight on #9, Par 3, 182 yards at Baltusrol Golf Club in the 4th round and still won the U.S. Open Championship?

58-10   Who hit a 249-yard 5 wood to eagle #17 in the final round to win a British Open Championship?

58-11   What is the last major to earn qualifying points to make the U.S. Ryder Cup Team?

58-12   **T or F** There has been a hole played in the U.S. Open Championship as a Par 6.

58-13   How many pot bunkers were there at Royal Birkdale Golf Club during the British Open in 2008?

58-14   What was the first U.S. Open Championship to cut the field after two rounds?

58-15   Which U.S. Open winner was previously an Honor Guard for President Kennedy?

58-16   Who was the last player to win the U.S. Open Championship while wearing a tie?

58-17   Which major championship winner, when an amateur, shot 66-69-75 (bad weather) and still had a four-shot lead in the Masters Tournament to then shoot an 80 and lose by one?

58-18   Name the four major championship winners from South Africa.

58-19   Who won by the largest margin in a Masters Tournament play-off?

58-20   What two New Zealanders have won a major championship tournament?

ANSWERS

58-1   Retief Goosen, his second U.S. Open Championship title

58-2   1913, Francis Ouimet; 1963, Julius Boros; and 1989, Curtis Strange

58-3   Jack Burke, Jr.

58-4   Ben Crenshaw (University of Texas) 1971, 1972, 1973; Phil Mickelson (Arizona State University) 1990, 1991, 1992

58-5   Jimmy Demaret, 1940

58-6   17th hole, "The Road Hole," his second shot ended up against the wall over the green and road

58-7   True! Pebble Beach Golf Links 2000, Bethpage State Park (Black) 2002, Torrey Pines 2008

58-8   Walter Hagen, winning five PGA Championships 1921, 1924, 1925, 1926 and 1927

58-9   1903, Willie Anderson (307)

58-10   Padraig Harrington, 2008 at Royal Birkdale Golf Club, Southport, England

58-11   The PGA Championship

58-12   True; 1912, #10 at the Country Club of Buffalo, 606 yards

58-13   123...Pot Bunkers!

58-14   1904 at Glen View Club, Golf, IL, won by Willie Anderson

58-15   Lou Graham

58-16   Ralph Guldahl, won 1937 and 1938 U.S. Open Championships. He also won the 1939 Masters Tournament

58-17   Ken Venturi, 1956

58-18   Gary Player, Ernie Els, Retief Goosen and Trevor Immelman

58-19   Billy Casper, five shots, 1970 beating Gene Littler 69 to 74

58-20   Bob Charles, 1963 British Open; Michael Campbell, 2005 U.S. Open Championship

GROUP 59 QUESTIONS

59-1 What year did the USGA add International Sectional Qualifying locations in Europe and Japan for the U.S. Open Championship?

59-2 Which hole knocked Phil Mickelson out of the 2008 U.S. Open Championship at Torrey Pines?

59-3 When was the first U.S. Open Championship telecast on color TV?

59-4 Which major championship winner has the record for the lowest scoring average for a season?

59-5 Who was the first player to go 91 holes to win the U.S. Open Championship?

59-6 Sir Henry Cotton won how many British Open Championships?

59-7 How many rounds in the 2007 U.S. Open Championship at Oakmont were shot at par or better?

59-8 Who is the oldest participant in the PGA Championship on record?

59-9 Who is the last Scotsman to win the U.S. Open Championship?

59-10 Who was the highest-ranked player in the 137th British Open Championship at Royal Birkdale?

59-11 What is the world's most exclusive golf tournament?

59-12 Who was the first player to break the 300-shot barrier and win his first of two U.S. Open Championships after three runner-up finishes?

59-13 In which U.S. Open Championship did Jack Nicklaus shoot 81, Arnold Palmer, 79, and Gary Player, 80, in the opening round?

59-14 Which major championship golf course was designed by A.W. Tillinghast; restored by Rees Jones and called "Man Killer?"

59-15 **T or F** Jack Fleck beat Ben Hogan in the 1955 U.S. Open with his new set of Hogan irons.

59-16 Which future major championship winner was Ken Venturi's playing partner in the fourth round when he won the 1964 U.S. Open Championship at Congressional Country Club?

59-17 Which major championship winner had three runner-up finishes in the Masters, U.S. Open and British Open Championships in the same year?

59-18 What kind of grass is called "sponge grass?"

59-19 **T or F** Johnny Miller hit all the greens in regulation during the fourth round in the 1973 U.S. Open Championship at Oakmont Country Club...shooting 63.

59-20 Which golf courses were said to be formed by the hand of the Almighty?

ANSWERS

59-1   2005, helps build a worldwide international field

59-2   #13, Par 5, Mickelson makes a quad (9); Tiger Woods eagles the hole (3) for a six-shot swing

59-3   1965 at Bellerive Country Club, St. Louis, MO, won by Gary Player

59-4   Tiger Woods 2006 (68.17); beating Byron Nelson's record of 1945 (68.33)

59-5   Hale Irwin (age 45, oldest at the time), 1990 at Medinah #3, winning play-off over
        Mike Donald

59-6   Three championship wins; 1934 (Royal St. George's), 1937 (Carnoustie) and 1948
        (Muirfield)

59-7   Eight rounds; Oakmont is still one of the toughest championship golf courses in all
        of America

59-8   Gene Sarazen, age 70 in 1972 at Oakland Hills Country Club; youngest champion at the age
        of 20 in 1922 at Oakmont Country Club

59-9   Tommy Armour, play-off win over Harry Cooper 76 to 79, 1927 at Oakmont Country Club

59-10   Phil Mickelson #2, Sergio Garcia—the British bookies' favorite at 8 to 1

59-11   The PGA Grand Slam of Golf; features the four winners of each major championship that
        season (began in1979)

59-12   Alex Smith, 1906 at Onwentsia Club, Lake Forest, IL

59-13   June 18, 1970, at Hazeltine National Golf Club, one round under par all day from
        the competition

59-14   Bethpage State Park, Black Course, NY

59-15   True! Ben Hogan also made good golf clubs!

59-16   Raymond Floyd

59-17   Ernie Els, 2000

59-18   Kikuya ("Ki-Screw-Ya"), famous at Torrey Pines Golf Course during the 2008 U.S. Open

59-19   True! He also only had 29 putts

59-20   "Old" Tom Morris, Sr. speaking of the treeless, wind swept Scottish golf courses

60 QUESTIONS

60-1   From green cut to second cut primary rough, how many cuts were there in the 2008 U.S. Open?

60-2   What major championship golf course was one of the first glider ports developed by the famous aviator Charles Lindbergh during the Great Depression?

60-3   What course do many players label "most difficult" among the majors in the United States?

60-4   Which major winner holds the record for the most appearances on the European Ryder Cup Team?

60-5   Who was in fourth place when Francis Ouimet won the 1913 U.S. Open Championship beating Harry Vardon and Ted Ray in the play-off at Brookline?

60-6   Who needed only 11 putts on the last nine holes to win his second U.S. Open Championship by two shots over Phil Mickelson?

60-7   **T or F** Bobby Jones and Jack Nicklaus each held the U.S. Amateur and U.S. Open Championship titles at one time, but in different years during their careers.

60-8   **T or F** Ben Hogan has been tied for the record of "worst start" by a champion in winning a U.S. Open Championship.

60-9   Who was the first player to win both the U.S. Open and PGA Championship in the same year since Gene Sarazen in 1922?

60-10 Who was the oldest winner of the U.S. Open Championship before Julius Boros won in 1963?

60-11 What golf course designed by MacKenzie is considered the "Best Collegiate Golf Course?"

60-12 How many U.S. Amateur Championships did 1916 U.S. Open Champion "Chick" Evans play in?

60-13 Who shot a back-nine 30, birdied seven of the last ten holes, shooting a 64 to come from seven shots behind to win a green jacket at the Masters Tournament?

60-14 Which amateur lead the 1976 U.S. Open at the Atlanta Athletic Club after the first round?

60-15 Name the five current (2008) professional players with three major championship wins or more.

60-16 Which opening hole is considered the toughest in all of the major championships?

60-17 What did Jack Nicklaus shoot in his first U.S. Open Championship at Inverness in 1957 at age 17?

60-18 How many Top 10s did Trevor Immelman have in 2008 before his Masters Tournament win?

60-19 From what two universities has Jack W. Nicklaus received Honorary Doctorates?

60-20 Which two Australians have won the U.S. Open Championship?

ANSWERS

GROUP 60

60-1   Five cuts: green (shortest), fairway, intermediate, first cut rough, second cut primary rough

60-2   Torrey Pines Golf Course, host of the 2008 U.S. Open Championship

60-3   Medinah Country Club #3 and Oakmont Country Club are both considered #1... a good argument!

60-4   Nick Faldo, 11 times from 1977 thru 1997

60-5   Walter Hagen

60-6   Retief Goosen, 2004 at Shinnecock Hills Golf Club, Shinnecock Hills, NY

60-7   True, Bobby Jones 1930, Jack Nicklaus 1961–1962

60-8   True! 76 in 1951 at Oakland Hills, tied by Jack Fleck 1955 Olympic Club

60-9   Ben Hogan in 1948

60-10 43 years earlier, Ted Ray a month younger in 1920 at Inverness Club, Toledo, OH

60-11 The Scarlet Course at The Ohio State University, Upper Arlington (Columbus), OH

60-12 49 times, he established Evans Caddie Scholarship Foundation

60-13 Gary Player, 1978, 277 (–11)

60-14 Amateur, Mike Reid shoots a 67 being the only player to break par in the first round

60-15 Ernie Els, Padraig Harrington, Phil Mickelson, Vijay Singh and Tiger Woods

60-16 #1, 455 yards, Par 4 at Augusta National Golf Club in the Masters Tournament

60-17 Birdied first hole, shot 80-80, missed cut

60-18 None, he had made only four cuts out of eight tournaments earlier in the year/season.

60-19 The Ohio State University, Columbus, OH 1972; St. Andrews University, St. Andrews, Scotland 1984

60-20 David Graham (1981), Geoff Ogilvy (2006)

QUESTIONS

61-1 Who shot four separate rounds of 73 in the British Open Championship, then won in a play-off?

61-2 Who was the first player to shoot four rounds in the 60s, in a 1960s major tournament?

61-3 **T or F** The PGA Championship was the first major win for both Sam Snead and Ben Hogan.

61-4 What is a "Shampoo Shot?"

61-5 Who shot a total of 136 in the final 36 holes at Oakmont Country Club, that was a record for 50 years, in the U.S. Open Championship?

61-6 Who combed his hair to look good for the photographers before holing out on the 72nd hole to win the U.S. Open Championship?

61-7 What year did the most amateurs compete in the Masters Tournament?

61-8 Name the four players who have won both the British Open Championship and PGA Championship in the same year.

61-9 As of 2008, name the five players who have led the Masters Tournaments three times or more after the first round.

61-10 How many former amateurs who played in the Masters Tournament later won as professional golfers?

61-11 Who birdied #18 twice, which was the hardest hole during the 1978 U.S. Open Championship, to win at Cherry Hills?

61-12 "Nae wind, Nae rain, Nae golf" is a famous golf phrase from what golfing country?

61-13 After which U.S. Open Championship did the USGA go back to an 18-hole play-off?

61-14 Who was the first wire-to-wire winner of the PGA Championship in medal-play?

61-15 When the present day Oakmont Country Club opened in 1904, what was par?

61-16 After the 2008 PGA Championship, who had more Top 10s in the major championships, Phil Mickelson or Ernie Els?

61-17 Which U.S. Open Championship was the first to exceed $1 million in purse money?

61-18 What world ranking did Padraig Harrington attain after winning the 2008 British Open?

61-19 What was the overall average score during the 2008 U.S. Open Championship?

61-20 Who was the first round leader in the 1973 and 1974 U.S. Open Championships?

ANSWERS

GROUP
61

61-1   Denny Shute, 1933 at the Old Course St. Andrews, Scotland

61-2   Arnold Palmer 68-68-69-69, 1964, runner-up in PGA Championship at
         Columbus Country Club

61-3   True, Sam Snead 1942 and Ben Hogan 1946

61-4   Term from the British Open, hitting a sand shot into the famous winds of the British Isles

61-5   Gene Sarazen 1932, broken by Larry Nelson 1983, with 132 shots

61-6   Ralph Guldahl 1937 at Oakland Hills Country Club, South Course, Bloomfield Hills, MI

61-7   1966, 26 amateurs

61-8   Walter Hagen (1924), Nick Price (1994), Tiger Woods (2000 and 2006) and Padraig
         Harrington (2008)

61-9   Four times: Lloyd Mangrum, Arnold Palmer, Gary Player and Justin Rose; three times:
         Jack Nicklaus

61-10   12 players, last one was 2008 winner, Trevor Immelman

61-11   Andy North, he had two of the only 11 birdies all week on #18

61-12   "The Scots"—Scotland, if there is no inclement weather on the 1st tee, then golf isn't
         really golf

61-13   1931, it was a 36 hole play-off at that time

61-14   Bobby Nichols, 1964 at Columbus Country Club, Columbus, OH, 271 (–9)

61-15   Par 80, eight Par 5s, one Par 6..."Hardest Course in the World"

61-16   Phil Mickelson 20, Ernie Els 19, both have won three major championships

61-17   1988, 75th Anniversary of Francis Ouimet's win, held at the Country Club. Curtis Strange
         won $180,000; purse $1,006,763.93

61-18   Third, behind Tiger Woods #1 and Phil Mickelson #2

61-19   First round 75.58, second 74.96 (75.27), third 74.36 (75.08) and fourth round 72.87
         (74.71)...3 plus shots over par 71, 7,643 yards at Torrey Pines

61-20   Gary Player, (67) at Oakmont Country Club 1973, (70) at Winged Foot Golf Club
         West 1974

62 QUESTIONS

62-1   Where was the first U.S. Open Championship played west of the Mississippi River?

62-2   What other famous sporting event scheduling caused a delay in the first U.S. Open Championship until October 4, 1895?

62-3   Who has the best record in stroke-play PGA Championships?

62-4   **T or F** Tommy Bolt was a leader in each round of the 1958 U.S. Open when he won at Southern Hills.

62-5   After which U.S. Open Championship did the USGA take over control from the host club in regards to course layout and preparation?

62-6   Where and when did Tiger Woods shoot his worst score in a major championship?

62-7   Who was the first player to defend his U.S. Open Championship after Ben Hogan in 1950–1951?

62-8   In which two major championships do the players start on #10 and #1 during the first two rounds?

62-9   Who are the only three players to have won the Masters on both Bermuda and bent grass greens?

62-10 Who shot the lowest score ever in a U.S. Open Championship play-off?

62-11 Who had a bad wrist, and who had a bad knee, but both won major championships in the same year?

62-12 **T or F** The first British Open Championship played outside of Scotland was also won by an Englishman for the first time.

62-13 Name the three players who finished under par in the 2008 PGA Championship at Oakland Hills.

62-14 The last three holes at Oakhill Country Club, during the 1956 U.S. Open—how did the top six finishers play them against par?

62-15 Which great putter only took 114 putts (28-31-27-28) in four rounds, including 31 one-putts, and one three-putt, winning a major championship?

62-16 In 1929 Bobby Jones won his U.S. Open Championship play-off against Al Espinosa by how many shots?

62-17 **T or F** Sam Snead never won the PGA Championship in the stroke-play era.

62-18 Who was the last player to win the Masters Tournament on his first attempt?

62-19 What is the number one opponent on the back nine on a Sunday afternoon in a major championship?

62-20 On what course did Ben Hogan play his first and last U.S. Open Championship?

ANSWERS

GROUP 62

62-1   1938, Cherry Hills Country Club, Denver, CO

62-2   The America's Cup Yacht Races

62-3   Jack Nicklaus, 14 times out of 37 in Top 5, five victories—1963, 1971, 1973, 1975 and 1980

62-4   True, 71-71-69-72 = 283

62-5   1951 at Oakland Hills Country Club, in Bloomfield Hills, MI

62-6   British Open at Muirfield in 2002, a score of 81

62-7   Curtis Strange, 1988–1989

62-8   U.S. Open Championship and PGA Championship; (author wishes they all started on #1)

62-9   Seve Ballesteros, Jack Nicklaus and Tom Watson

62-10   Fuzzy Zoeller, 67 beating Greg Norman, 75

62-11   2008 Tiger Woods (knee) U.S. Open Championship, Padraig Harrington (wrist) British Open Championship

62-12   True, Royal St. George's, Sandwich, England. Won by John Henry "JH" Taylor, 1894

62-13   Padraig Harrington –3, Ben Curtis and Sergio Garcia –1; no other player was at even par

62-14   Middlecoff (winner +8); Boros (tied for second +1); Hogan (tied for second +4); Furgol (tied for fourth +4); Kroll (tied for fourth +6); Thomson (tied for fourth +6); tough stretch of three holes

62-15   Billy Casper winning the 1959 U.S. Open Championship at Winged Foot Golf Club

62-16   36-hole play-off, 23 shots—141 vs. 164

62-17   True, but he finished third, three times in 21 attempts

62-18   Fuzzy Zoeller, 1979

62-19   "Old Man Par." Think about how many great players and Hall of Fame members have lost by not beating par!

62-20   Baltusrol Golf Club, Springfield, NJ

GROUP

63 QUESTIONS

Where was I born?

	Player's Name	Legal Name	Nickname
63-1	Jack Nicklaus	(Jack William Nicklaus)	"The Golden Bear"
63-2	Retief Goosen	(Retief Goosen)	"The Little Easy"
63-3	Lee Trevino	(Lee Buck Trevino)	"The Merry Mex"
63-4	Bobby Jones	(Robert Tyre "Bobby" Jones)	"Bobby"
63-5	Tommy Armour	(Thomas Dickson Armour)	"The Silver Scot"
63-6	Gene Sarazen	(Eugenio Saraceni)	"The Squire"
63-7	Tiger Woods	(Eldrick Tont "Tiger" Woods)	"Tiger"
63-8	Tom Watson	(Thomas Sturges "Tom" Watson)	"Huckleberry Dillinger"
63-9	Ernie Els	(Theodore Ernest "Ernie" Els)	"The Big Easy"
63-10	Geoff Ogilvy	(Geoff Charles Ogilvy)	"Full Monty"
63-11	Billy Casper	(William Earl "Billy" Casper)	"Buffalo Bill"
63-12	Lee Janzen	(Lee McLeod Janzen)	"The Terminator"
63-13	Ben Hogan	(William Ben Hogan)	"The Hawk"
63-14	Curtis Strange	(Curtis Northrop Strange)	"Brutus"
63-15	Gary Player	(Gary Player)	"The Black Knight"
63-16	Walter Hagen	(Walter Charles Hagen)	"The Haig"
63-17	Hale Irwin	(Hale S. Irwin)	"Stitch"
63-18	Byron Nelson	(John Byron Nelson)	"Lord Byron"
63-19	Julius Boros	(Julius Nicholas Boros)	"Moose"
63-20	Arnold Palmer	(Arnold Daniel Palmer)	"The King"

ANSWERS

GROUP
63

Where was I born?

	Player's Name	Location	Date of Birth
63-1	Jack Nicklaus	Columbus, Ohio	01-21-1940
63-2	Retief Goosen	Pietersburg (now Polokwane) South Africa	02-03-1969
63-3	Lee Trevino	Dallas, Texas	12-01-1939
63-4	Bobby Jones	Atlanta, Georgia	03-17-1902
63-5	Tommy Armour	Edinburgh, Scotland	09-24-1894
63-6	Gene Sarazen	Harrison, New York	02-27-1902
63-7	Tiger Woods	Cypress, California	12-30-1975
63-8	Tom Watson	Kansas City, Missouri	09-04-1949
63-9	Ernie Els	Johannesburg, South Africa	10-17-1969
63-10	Geoff Ogilvy	Adelaide, Australia	06-11-1977
63-11	Billy Casper	San Diego, California	06-24-1931
63-12	Lee Janzen	Austin, Minnesota	08-28-1964
63-13	Ben Hogan	Stephenville, Texas	08-13-1912
63-14	Curtis Strange	Norfolk, Virginia	01-30-1955
63-15	Gary Player	Johannesburg, South Africa	11-01-1935
63-16	Walter Hagen	Rochester, New York	12-21-1892
63-17	Hale Irwin	Joplin, Missouri	06-03-1945
63-18	Byron Nelson	Waxahachie, Texas	02-04-1912
63-19	Julius Boros	Bridgeport, Connecticut	03-03-1920
63-20	Arnold Palmer	Latrobe, Pennsylvania	09-10-1929

64 QUESTIONS

64-1   How many bunkers did Oakmont Country Club have during the 2007 U.S. Open Championship?

64-2   When and where was the PGA Championship Tournament organized?

64-3   Who hit a 2 iron out of the rough, 200 yards over water to six feet on #18 to win a U.S. Open?

64-4   Who is the oldest Masters Champion to shoot even par 72?

64-5   Name the three British Open Champions to shoot four rounds under 70.

64-6   Who was the "odds on favorite" to win the 2008 PGA Championship at Oakland Hills?

64-7   **T or F** The most penal U.S. major championship golf course is Oakmont Country Club, known for its wondering streams throughout the course like Carnoustie in Scotland.

64-8   The Royal Bank of Scotland printed which major winner on a "special" issue of two million five pound notes?

64-9   How many players were under par after 36 holes in each of the four major championships in 2008?

64-10   Which two players have shot the highest winning final round of 75, still winning the Masters?

64-11   Who received a special exemption to play in the 1990 U.S. Open Championship and won it?

64-12   Which major winner was the first "lefty" inducted into the World Golf Hall of Fame?

64-13   Which player never finished worse than second in the British Open between 1952 and 1958?

64-14   Tiger Woods has the record for the most weeks ranked #1, who is ranked #2?

64-15   Who was the first winner of the U.S. Open Championship to win $1,000?

64-16   How many consecutive Top 5 finishes did Bobby Jones have in the U.S. Open Championship?

64-17   **T or F** The average score for the first round in the 2008 British Open Championship was 76, with 19 rounds in the 80s.

64-18   Who was the last player to *not* defend his PGA Championship before 2008?

64-19   At what major championship was Tiger Woods' "Tiger Slam" stopped?

64-20   **T or F** Royal Birkdale was redesigned. 155 yards longer on six holes, 6 total net new bunkers (20 new) and one new green at #17 for the 2008 British Open Championship.

ANSWERS

64-1   210, counting the "Church Pews" as one

64-2   Taplow Club at the Hotel Martinique in New York City, January 17, 1916

64-3   Bobby Jones, 1923 at Inwood Country Club, Inwood, NY

64-4   Gay Brewer, 1998

64-5   Greg Norman (1993), Nick Price (1994) and Tiger Woods (2000)

64-6   Phil Mickelson 10-1, British Open winner Padraig Harrington 15-1

64-7   False. There are no streams, ponds or lakes on the course, but plenty of sand traps.

64-8   Jack Nicklaus

64-9   Masters 19, U.S Open Championship 8, British Open Championship one, PGA
        Championship one

64-10   Arnold Palmer 1962, Trevor Immelman 2008

64-11   Hale Irwin, his third U.S. Open Championship victory played at Medinah #3, Medinah, IL

64-12   Bob Charles from New Zealand, winner of the 1963 British Open Championship

64-13   Peter Thomson, winning in 1954, 1955, 1956, 1958 and 1965

64-14   Greg Norman

64-15   Billy Burke 1931

64-16   Six, 1921–1926, winning in 1923 and 1926

64-17   True! Tough winds (30-plus mph) and rain

64-18   Ben Hogan, 1949, recovering from a car accident

64-19   2001 U.S. Open Championship at Southern Hills, won by Retief Goosen

64-20   True. Most major championship courses are always redesigned before the tournament.

GROUP

65 QUESTIONS

65-1   Who was the first Irishman to win back-to-back British Open Championships?

65-2   Course logo: National Capital Dome?

65-3   **T or F** Julius Boros had a total of 40 putts on his last 27 holes at the Northwood Club to stop Ben Hogan winning his third consecutive U.S. Open Championship.

65-4   How many times did Nick Price play in the British Open Championship before he won one?

65-5   Who is the only player in the U.S. Open Championship history to receive the winner's trophy from the President of the United States?

65-6   Who has had the largest lead after 36 holes and 54 holes in the British Open Championship?

65-7   **T or F** Arnold Palmer beat Jack Nicklaus statistically in the 1967 U.S. Open Championship in one-putts, driving and fairways hits.

65-8   Which U.S. Open Championship winner won eight events in a row to set the record until broken by Byron Nelson's eleven straight in 1945?

65-9   Who, to win his first Masters Tournament, hit more fairways than anybody (straight driver), was 2nd in G.I.R., 4th in putting and 4th in driving?

65-10   The quote, "To try for the green or not," is most famous at what hole in which major?

65-11   **T or F** In 1970, Billy Casper, winning the Masters Tournament, only three-putted three times.

65-12   Which major championship player is credited with the golfing term "Yips?"

65-13   What championship course has now hosted six U.S. Opens, three PGAs, and one Ryder Cup?

65-14   **T or F** Walter Hagen's first tournament win was the 1914 U.S. Open Championship.

65-15   On what golf course did the 1996 U.S. Open Champion Steve Jones qualify?

65-16   Which player, through the 2008 season, has 14 Top 10s in the majors but is 0-for-41?

65-17   How many holes-in-one have occurred on #16, 169-yard, Par 3 at the Augusta National Golf Club, during the Masters Tournament, through 2008?

65-18   How many different players were tied for the lead at one time during the fourth round in the 1986 U.S. Open Championship at Shinnecock Hills?

65-19   What state has the most native sons who have won the U.S. Open Championship?

65-20   What is the biggest difference in scores between rounds by the winner of the British Open?

ANSWERS

GROUP
65

65-1 Padraig Harrington, 2007 Carnoustie and 2008 Royal Birkdale Golf Club

65-2 Congressional Country Club (Blue), Bethesda, MD. Hosting 2011 U.S. Open Championship

65-3 True; a hot putter, 1952 winner at Northwood Club, Dallas, TX

65-4 16 times, finally winning in 1994 at Turnberry Ailsa Course, Turnberry, Scotland

65-5 James Barnes, 1921, from President Harding at Columbia Country Club, Chevy Chase, MD

65-6 Henry Cotton, 1934, 36 holes (9 strokes), 54 holes (10 strokes) at Royal St. George's Golf Club

65-7 True, but Jack Nicklaus was #1 in greens in regulation...winning!

65-8 Johnny Farrell 1927; 1928 U.S. Open Champion

65-9 Trevor Immelman in 2008

65-10 #13, Par 5, 510 yards at the Masters Tournament

65-11 False; Billy Casper never three-putted, one of the reasons he is considered one of the all-time great putters

65-12 Tommy Armour "putting with twitchy nerves"

65-13 Oakland Hills Country Club (South Course), Bloomfield Hills, MI

65-14 True! Midlothian Country Club, Midlothian, IL (+2) 290

65-15 Brookside Golf and Country Club, Columbus, OH. Same course Rocco Mediate had to qualify on in 2008 for the U.S. Open Championship at Torrey Pines. Denny Shute, major winner, was a pro here!

65-16 Sergio Garcia

65-17 11 at #16, 19 total overall on the course

65-18 Nine: Beck, Crenshaw, McCumber, Norman, Stewart, Sutton, Trevino, Tway and Wadkins... but Raymond Floyd won shooting a 66 = 279

65-19 California

65-20 In 1934, by Henry Cotton at Royal St. George's, 2nd round 65, and fourth round 79 (14 shot difference)

GROUP

66 QUESTIONS

66-1 **T or F** Ben Hogan never played in the match-play format of the PGA Championship after his 1949 automobile accident.

66-2 Who was the only PGA Champion in the 1950s to win other major championships?

66-3 How many times did Arnold Palmer finish runner-up in the PGA Championship?

66-4 When was the last U.S. Open Championship in which all champions were exempt from qualifying?

66-5 Which major in 2008 had an asterisk (*) placed beside the winners' name because Tiger Woods was not competing?

66-6 Which trophy did the Honourable Company of Edinburgh Golfers play for in the year 1744 (date approximate)?

66-7 How many times did Tiger Woods and Rocco Mediate trade the lead in their 2008 U.S. Open Championship play-off?

66-8 **T or F** In 1972, Jack Nicklaus either led or shared the lead in both the Masters Tournament and U.S. Open Championship at Pebble Beach in every round.

66-9 How many holes did Mark O'Meara, 1998 Masters Champion, lead outright during the tournament?

66-10 What did Larry Nelson shoot in the last two rounds at Oakmont in 1983 to win the U.S. Open?

66-11 Which two major winners created what we recognize as "Signature Golf Course Design?"

66-12 Who missed a two-foot putt on the 72nd hole to fall back into a tie with Mark Brooks in the U.S. Open Championship?

66-13 Which one of the four majors was the first to implement a sudden-death play-off?

66-14 Through 2004, how many Masters Tournament records did Jack Nicklaus own or tie?

66-15 Which major championship winner has been the American Ryder Cup Team Captain the most times?

66-16 Which four major winners also won an NCAA Individual and U.S. Amateur Championship?

66-17 Who is credited with adding the word "birdie" to golf lexicon?

66-18 Name the six players who have won both the U.S. Open and British Open in the same year?

66-19 Who holds the record of seven consecutive scores of three, from holes 10 to 16 in the U.S. Open?

66-20 **T or F** Tiger Woods won each major championship the same year that Jack Nicklaus played in his last as a competitor.

ANSWERS

GROUP
66

66-1   True, Ben Hogan played stroke-play starting back in 1958

66-2   Sam Snead, won 1951 PGA Championship and 1952 and 1954 Masters Tournament

66-3   Three times, 1964, 1968 and 1970; never won a PGA Championship

66-4   1954, in 1955 the exemption went to only the last five years' champions

66-5   2008 British Open Championship—really just a fabrication of the sportswriters

66-6   Silver Club, a famous watercolor painting by David Allan, 1787, depicts the "Prize of the Silver Golf"

66-7   Three times on the front nine, 2 times on the back nine, with Tiger Woods' birdie on the eighteenth hole to tie. Tiger Woods won in sudden-death.

66-8   True, winning both

66-9   One! 72nd and final hole

66-10   65-67, setting the U.S. Open Championship record for the last 36 holes

66-11   Jack Nicklaus and Arnold Palmer

66-12   Retief Goosen 2001 U.S. Open Championship; then won the play-off 70-72

66-13   PGA Championship in 1977 for the first time

66-14   54 tournament records

66-15   Walter Hagen, six times, Ben Hogan and Sam Snead three times each

66-16   Justin Leonard, Phil Mickelson, Jack Nicklaus and Tiger Woods

66-17   A.W. Tillinghast, famous golf architect

66-18   Ben Hogan in 1953; Bobby Jones in 1926 and 1930, Gene Sarazen in 1932, Lee Trevino in 1971, Tom Watson in 1982 and Tiger Woods in 2000

66-19   Hubert Green, 1977, at Southern Hills Country Club, Tulsa, OK

66-20   True. 2000 U.S. Open and PGA Championships; 2005 Masters and British Open Championship

GROUP

67 QUESTIONS

67-1 What year did Ben Hogan set the Masters Tournament scoring record at 14 under par (274)?

67-2 From 1973 to 1983 Tom Watson and Jack Nicklaus won how many major championships?

67-3 What was the first U.S. Open Championship to use telephones to aid in scoring?

67-4 What hole at Oakmont Country Club arguably has determined the U.S. Open Championship winner more than any other hole?

67-5 Starting with Arnold Palmer (1961–1962) name the other four players who have won back-to-back British Open Championships.

67-6 Who played the last four holes in the 1977 U.S. Open at Southern Hills under a threat on his life?

67-7 Through 2008, what is Tiger Woods record when leading, or sharing the lead, going into the final round of a major championship?

67-8 How many major championships did Walter Hagen win when Bobby Jones was also in the field?

67-9 Fred Couples' consecutive cut streak at the Masters ended which year and at how many cuts?

67-10 Who is the only other player next to Lee Trevino to shoot four sub-70 rounds in the U.S. Open?

67-11 **T or F** After shooting a 63 in the opening round of the 1980 U.S. Open, Tom Weiskopf never shot a round in the 60s again in a U.S. Open Championship.

67-12 Who one-putted eight of the last 11 holes to once again beat Sergio Garcia in a major championship?

67-13 **T or F** No Asian-born player has won a major championship in his first appearance.

67-14 How many times did Jack Nicklaus win the Vardon Trophy for lowest scoring average?

67-15 Which British Open Championship winner received a replica of the Red Morocco Belt with silver cups to celebrate the 125th Anniversary of the Open Championship?

67-16 What shot did Ben Hogan consider his biggest disappointment in a major championship?

67-17 **T or F** Major Championship winners Bobby Jones and Ben Hogan both had seven consecutive Top Ten finishes in the U.S. Open Championship.

67-18 What is considered by many as the majors "ultimate surprise victory?"

67-19 Who has the lowest winning score at 11 under par at Winged Foot Golf Club (West Course)?

67-20 Which years did Jack Nicklaus establish his first, second and third "Career Grand Slams"?

67-1   1953, broke record by five shots. Record stood until Jack Nicklaus broke it in 1965 with 17 under

67-2   Tom Watson, eight majors, total 28 wins; Jack Nicklaus, six major wins, total 18 wins

67-3   1926 at Scioto Country Club, Columbus, OH, Bobby Jones, winner 293 (+5)

67-4   #17, uphill Par 4, 322 yards with famous "Big Mouth" bunker

67-5   Lee Trevino (1971–1972), Tom Watson (1982–1983), Tiger Woods (2005–2006) and Padraig Harrington (2007–2008)

67-6   Hubert Green, winning by one shot over Lou Graham

67-7   Perfect 14-0!

67-8   None, won 11 when Bobby Jones was not in the field

67-9   2008, 23 cuts in a row

67-10 Lee Janzen, 1993 at Baltusrol Golf Club shooting 67-67-69-69

67-11 True

67-12 Padraig Harrington, winning the 2008 PGA Championship and winning three of the last six majors

67-13 True—but it will happen some day

67-14 Jack Nicklaus never won the Vardon Trophy

67-15 Sandy Lyle at Royal St. George's Golf Club in 1985

67-16 Third shot at #17, Par 5, 518 yards at Cherry Hills. Shot hitting bank by green and backing up and going into the greenside pond

67-17 True, Bobby Jones (1920–1926); Ben Hogan (1950–1956)

67-18 Rookie John Daly's 1991 PGA Championship victory at Crooked Stick, 9th alternate taken to play

67-19 Davis Love III, winning the 1997 PGA Championship

67-20 First 1966, second 1971 and third 1978

68 QUESTIONS

68-1   Which famous caddy at Oakmont Country Club, caddied for Bobby Jones, Sam Snead, Jack Nicklaus, Arnold Palmer, Gary Player and many other famous golfers?

68-2   After Sam Snead in 1951, who was the next two-time winner of the PGA Championship?

68-3   Who are the only American brothers to win the same major championship?

68-4   Who was the Scioto club pro during the 1926 U.S. Open Championship won by Bobby Jones?

68-5   What major championship golf course was called "The Green?"

68-6   In which major championship, which probably cost him a win, did T.C. Chen have a double-hit chip?

68-7   What year was the Stimpmeter invented?

68-8   When was the first time a penalty for slow play was called in the U.S. Open Championship?

68-9   Who beat Bobby Jones by three strokes to win a U.S. Open Championship and never won again?

68-10 **T or F** The 2008 Masters Tournament did not have an amateur make the 36-hole cut.

68-11 Through 2008, Greg Norman has lead in eight majors after 54 holes. How many did he win?

68-12 Who finished second to Tom Watson in four of his eight major championship wins?

68-13 How many players made the cut in all four of the 2008 major championships?

68-14 Who did Lou Graham beat in a play-off to win the 1975 U.S. Open Championship at Medinah #3?

68-15 When was the first time the U.S. Open Championship went to a sudden-death format after an 18-hole play-off was tied after 90 holes?

68-16 Which five players have won the Masters and the U.S. Open Championship in the same year?

68-17 Which major champion was said to have "owned his swing?"

68-18 When was the last year that all four major championships were won by first-time winners?

68-19 Which major championship marked the "Changing of the Guard" from Palmer to Nicklaus?

68-20 Name the course after which Gary Player named his timber farm. He won a major championship there.

ANSWERS

68-1   James "JP" Pernice, member of Professional Caddies Hall of Fame Association. *See The James F Pernice Oakmont Caddy Scholarship Fund Foundation for further details.*

68-2   Jack Nicklaus, 1963 and 1971, also won in 1973, 1975 and 1980

68-3   Lionel (1957) and Jay (1960) Herbert, PGA Championships

68-4   1909 U.S. Open Championship winner George Sargent at Englewood Golf Club, Englewood, NJ

68-5   The Old Course St. Andrews...the entire course! "Putting ground" was one club length around the hole.

68-6   1985 U.S. Open Championship at Oakland Hills—now a popular saying by T.C. Chen

68-7   1936, used to measure "the speed," distance of putts

68-8   1978 at Cherry Hills Country Club, Denver, CO

68-9   Cyril Walker, 1924 U.S. Open Championship at Oakland Hills, Bloomfield, MI

68-10   True! No winner for the last three years of the Silver Cup

68-11   One, 1986 British Open Championship at Turnberry (Ailsa Course), Turnberry, Scotland

68-12   Jack Nicklaus, 1977 and 1981 Masters, 1977 British Open and 1982 U.S. Open Championship

68-13   Eleven players, led by Padraig Harrington

68-14   John Mahaffey 71 to 73

68-15   1990 at Medinah #3, Hale Irwin beating Mike Donald on the first hole with a birdie three

68-16   Craig Wood (1941), Ben Hogan (1953), Arnold Palmer (1960), Jack Nicklaus (1972) and Tiger Woods (2002)

68-17   Ben Hogan, absolutely one of the all-time great ball strikers!

68-18   2003, Masters Tournament Mike Weir, U.S. Open Championship Jim Furyk, British Open Ben Curtis, PGA Championship Shaun Micheel

68-19   1967, U.S. Open Championship at Baltusrol. After this tournament Arnold Palmer never won another major championship, Jack Nicklaus won 12 more for a total of 18.

68-20   Bellerive, his 1965 U.S. Open Championship win in St. Louis, MO

69-1   How many "links" golf courses are in the British Open Championship rotation?

69-2   Who is the oldest winner of the British Open Championship?

69-3   What is the "oldest" top-ranked championship golf course in the United States?

69-4   What year did scheduling conflicts overlap that made it difficult for Ben Hogan to win all four major championships in a single season?

69-5   Who birdied five of the last six holes to shoot a 66 and win the 1959 Masters Tournament?

69-6   Which two current major championship winners are right-handed, but play golf left-handed?

69-7   Who has the most appearances in the Masters Tournament?

69-8   **T or F** Trevor Immelman won wire-to-wire in the 72nd, 2008 Masters Tournament.

69-9   What major championship win started the famous "Tiger Slam?"

69-10   Who came from behind to win the 1957 Masters Tournament over Sam Snead by three strokes?

69-11   What is the proper name of Muirfield in Scotland?

69-12   How many under par was Raymond Floyd on the par 5s during the 1976 Masters Tournament?

69-13   How many tournaments did Ben Hogan win before WWII, 1940–1942 and then after 1946–1949 before his automobile accident?

69-14   How many and in which majors was Jack Nicklaus second (or tied for second) in 1964?

69-15   **T or F** Winning the PGA Championship qualifies you to play in the other three majors for five years and earn a life time qualification in the PGA Championship.

69-16   Who won one PGA Championship, had two seconds in the Masters, one tie for second in the U.S. Open and a tie for fourth in the British Open Championship?

69-17   Who was the first player to win the "Career Grand Slam" (victories in all four majors)?

69-18   What is the diameter of the standard (Big Ball) golf ball, and what was the diameter of the smaller ball used until 1974?

69-19   Who hit an "explosion" shot with his ball totally submerged in water at #15 in the Masters Tournament to then sink the birdie putt and win the 1947 Masters Tournament?

69-20   **T or F** Ben Hogan only entered six tournaments in 1953, but won five of them including the Masters Tournament, the U.S. Open and the British Open Championships.

ANSWERS

GROUP
69

69-1   Nine; all of them are "links" courses

69-2   "Old" Tom Morris, Sr., 1867, 46 years old

69-3   Oakmont Country Club, Oakmont, PA, built in 1903

69-4   1953, The PGA Championship and the British Open Championship overlapped

69-5   Art Wall, Jr.

69-6   Phil Mickelson and Mike Weir

69-7   Record set at 51 appearances in 2008 by Gary Player

69-8   True, shooting 68-68-69-75

69-9   2000 U.S. Open Championship at Pebble Beach Golf Links

69-10   Doug Ford, he holed-out from a bunker on the 72nd hole

69-11   "The Honourable Company of Edinburgh Golfers"

69-12   16 under for four rounds, score of 271, winning by eight strokes

69-13   15, 1940–1942 and 32, 1946–1949

69-14   Three times: Masters (tied for second), British Open Championship (2nd), the PGA Championship (tied for second)

69-15   True, plus The Players Championship for five years

69-16   Davis Love III

69-17   Gene Sarazen, U.S. Open 1922 and 1932, PGA 1922, 1923 and 1933, British Open Championship 1932 and the Masters 1935

69-18   1.68 inches minimum "Big" ball; 1.66 inches "Small" ball

69-19   Jimmy Demaret

69-20   True! One of golf's truly all-time great years

70 QUESTIONS

Where was I born?

	Player's Name	Legal Name	Nickname
70-1	Harry Vardon	(Harry Vardon)	"Mr. Golf"
70-2	Sam Snead	(Samuel Jackson "Sam" Snead)	"Slammin' Sammy"
70-3	James Braid	(James Braid)	"Inventor"
70-4	Henry Cotton	(Sir Henry Thomas Cotton)	"Maestro"
70-5	Tony Jacklin	(Tony Jacklin)	"Tony"
70-6	John Daly	(John Patrick Daly)	"Long John"
70-7	Tom Morris, Sr.	(Thomas Mitchell "Tom" Morris, Sr.)	"Old Tom"
70-8	Mark O'Meara	(Mark Francis O'Meara)	"Mark"
70-9	Sandy Lyle	(Alexander Walter Barr "Sandy" Lyle)	"Sandy"
70-10	Ted Ray	(Edward R.G. "Ted" Ray)	"Ted"
70-11	Greg Norman	(Gregory John Norman)	"The Shark"
70-12	Bobby Locke	(Arthur D'Arcy "Bobby" Locke)	"Bobby"
70-13	Denny Shute	(Herman Densmore "Denny" Shute)	"Denny"
70-14	Seve Ballesteros	(Severiano "Seve" Ballesteros)	"Seve"
70-15	Nick Faldo	(Nicholas "Nick" Alexander Faldo)	"Nick"
70-16	J.H. Taylor	(John Henry "J.H." Taylor)	"J.H."
70-17	Nick Price	(Nicholas Raymond Leige Price)	"Nicky"
70-18	Peter Thomson	(Peter William Thomson)	"Melbourne Tiger"
70-19	Paul Runyan	(Paul Scott Runyan)	"Little Poison"
70-20	Jimmy Demaret	(James Newton Demaret)	"Singing Texan"

ANSWERS

GROUP
70

Where was I born?

	Player's Name	Location	Date of Birth
70-1	Harry Vardon	Grouville, Jersey, Channel Islands	05-09-1870
70-2	Sam Snead	Ash Wood, Virginia	05-27-1912
70-3	James Braid	Earlsferry, Fife, Scotland	02-06-1870
70-4	Henry Cotton	Cheshire, England	01-26-1907
70-5	Tony Jacklin	Scunthrope, England	07-07-1944
70-6	John Daly	Carmichael, California	04-28-1966
70-7	Tom Morris, Sr.	St. Andrews, Fife, Scotland	06-16-1821
70-8	Mark O'Meara	Goldsboro, North Carolina	01-13-1957
70-9	Sandy Lyle	Shrewsbury, England	02-09-1958
70-10	Ted Ray	Isle of Jersey	03-28-1877
70-11	Greg Norman	Mount Isa, Queensland, Australia	02-10-1955
70-12	Bobby Locke	Germiston, South Africa	11-20-1917
70-13	Denny Shute	Cleveland, Ohio	10-25-1904
70-14	Seve Ballesteros	Pedrena, Spain	04-09-1957
70-15	Nick Faldo	Welwyn Garden City, England	07-18-1957
70-16	J.H. Taylor	Devon, England	03-19-1871
70-17	Nick Price	Durban, South Africa	01-28-1957
70-18	Peter Thomson	Melbourne, Australia	08-23-1929
70-19	Paul Runyan	Hot Springs, Arkansas	07-12-1908
70-20	Jimmy Demaret	Houston, Texas	05-24-1910

71-1   Between Lee Trevino (1971) and Tiger Woods (1997), name the other PGA player(s) who won the AP Athlete of the Year Award.

71-2   What major championship did Jack Nicklaus win, to win the "Modern Grand Slam" twice?

71-3   What was Jimmy Demaret speaking of when he said, "You could have combed North Africa with it and Rommel wouldn't have gotten past Casablanca."

71-4   **T or F** Five-time winner of the British Open J.H. Taylor was the designer of Royal Birkdale.

71-5   What did Padraig Harrington shoot to win his second consecutive British Open in 2008?

71-6   When and where did Jack Nicklaus break Hogan's 72-hole scoring record in the U.S. Open?

71-7   How many dog-leg holes did Hazeltine National Golf Club have during the 1970 U.S. Open?

71-8   What player missed a three-foot putt on the last hole which would have set up the first sudden-death play-off at the Masters Tournament?

71-9   Which former British Open winner was leading the 2008 PGA Championship after 54 holes?

71-10   How many years did Jack Nicklaus have a double-major championship winning season?

71-11   Sam Snead won seven major championships; how many did he win in a play-off?

71-12   Who was the first U.S. Amateur Public Links Champion to win the Masters Tournament?

71-13   Before Tiger Woods' double win of the U.S. and British Open Championships in the same year (2000), who did it last?

71-14   **T or F** Bobby Jones, Jack Nicklaus, Arnold Palmer and Sam Snead have all been a runner-up four times in the U.S. Open Championship.

71-15   What is the longest course in major championship history at 7,536 yards?

71-16   Seven players have shot a 63 in the British Open Championship. Who is the only one to go on and win through 2008?

71-17   Who beat not only the field, but the whole U.S. Ryder Cup Team, to win the British Open Championship at Carnoustie?

71-18   On which shot would Jack Nicklaus have liked to have a "mulligan," in his major championship play?

71-19   Which major course was a secret training ground for troops by the OSS during World War II?

71-20   Jones, Sarazen, Armour, Farrell and Diegel all played in their first U.S. Open when and where?

ANSWERS

71-1   None! Tiger Woods won in 1997, 1999, 2000 and 2006

71-2   1971 PGA Championship at PGA National Golf Club in Palm Beach Gardens, FL

71-3   The furrowed sand traps at Oakmont Country Club

71-4   True, built in 1922

71-5   69 final round, finishing plus three for the championship

71-6   1967 at Baltusrol Golf Club (Lower), Jack shot 275 vs. Hogan record of 276

71-7   13! Not real popular at the time

71-8   Hubert Green, 1978 losing to Gary Player

71-9   Ben Curtis, two under par, only three players were under par

71-10   Five times: 1963, 1966, 1972, 1975 and 1980

71-11   One, 1954 Masters Tournament beating Ben Hogan 70 to 71

71-12   Trevor Immelman, 2008

71-13   1982, Tom Watson; U.S. Open Championship at Pebble Beach Golf Links, British Open
        Championship at Royal Troon Golf Club

71-14   True

71-15   Whistling Straits, Kohler, WI, PGA Championship 2004

71-16   Greg Norman, 1986 at Turnberry (Ailsa Course), Turnberry, Scotland

71-17   Henry Cotton, 1937

71-18   1980 British Open, #6 at Carnoustie; he hit it Out-of-Bounds, lost by two shots
        to Gary Player

71-19   Congressional Country Club, Bethesda, MD

71-20   1920 at The Inverness Club, Toledo, OH. They won eight U.S. Opens, five British Opens
        and six PGA Championships in the next 13 years.

GROUP

72 QUESTIONS

72-1   Who would have won six U.S. Opens and tied four others if he would have shot a 69 in the fourth and final round?

72-2   If the "Gutty" ball had been restored after 1902, who stated he would never lose another British Open Championship?

72-3   In the PGA Championship, who finished 4th at the age of 60 in 1972, 9th in 1973 and tied for third in 1974 at the age of 62?

72-4   Which major championship player left his player's badge at his hotel during a lunch break and had to pay half-a-crown to regain entrance to complete his round and win the championship?

72-5   **T or F** Jones, Hagen, Sarazen, Snead, Hogan, Palmer and Nicklaus have all lost a play-off in the U.S. Open Championship.

72-6   What does the only commemorative marker at Royal Birkdale recognize?

72-7   What is the "White Fang?"

72-8   What was the winner's purse in each of the 2008 major championships?

72-9   What was the toughest hole at the 2008 PGA Championship at Oakland Hills?

72-10   What did Scotland's Braid and Ireland's Harrington accomplish 102 years apart?

72-11   What major championship golf course is the ultimate test for strategic golf?

72-12   **T or F** Ben Hogan played the same pin placements in the last 36 holes (same day) at Carnoustie in 1953, winning the British Open Championship.

72-13   What major golf course did major winners Jack Burke, Jr. and Jimmy Demaret build in Houston?

72-14   Who was the first European to win the PGA Championship in the stroke-play era?

72-15   Who was the last player through 2008 to win a major after 36 holes being beyond the top five?

72-16   Who is the only player to have had two holes-in-one in the U.S. Open Championship?

72-17   **T or F** The Inverness Club, in hosting four U.S. Opens, has never had par broken by the winner.

72-18   What U.S. Open Championship was the first to have a radio broadcast?

72-19   Which U.S. Open Championship winner carried two putters; a long one for long putts, the other one for holing out short putts?

72-20   What was different about the experimental "Balloon" golf ball?

ANSWERS

72-1   Sam Snead, he never won a U.S. Open Championship

72-2   James Braid: A master with the "Gutty" ball

72-3   Sam Snead

72-4   Bobby Jones, 1926 at Royal Lytham & St. Annes Golf Club, Lancashire, England

72-5   False, all have lost except Walter Hagen

72-6   Arnold Palmer's six-iron out of the rough to secure victory in 1961

72-7   Jack Nicklaus' putter he used to win the 1967 U.S. Open Championship at Baltusrol Lower Course, beating Arnold Palmer 275 to 279

72-8   Masters Tournament $1,360,000.00, U.S. Open Championship $1,350,000.00, British Open Championship $1,498,875.00 and PGA Championship $1,350,000.00

72-9   #18, 498 yards, Par 4

72-10   Both won consecutive British Opens as Europeans. James Braid 1905 and 1906, Padraig Harrington 2007 and 2008

72-11   Augusta National Golf Club...you must get into the correct position to score well.

72-12   True, they did not change the pin placements between rounds three and four

72-13   Champions Golf Club (1957), hosting the 1969 U.S. Open Championship and other tour events

72-14   Padraig Harrington

72-15   Mark O'Meara, 1998, the Masters Tournament

72-16   Tom Weiskopf, 1987 at Cherry Hills Country Club and 1982 at Pebble Beach Golf Links

72-17   True, 1920 (Par 72, 295), 1931 (Par 71, 292), 1957 (Par 70, 282) and 1979 (Par 71, 284)

72-18   1930 at Interlachen Country Club, MN, Bobby Jones' last U.S. Open win

72-19   Sam Parks, Jr. 1935 at Oakmont Country Club, Oakmont, PA

72-20   It weighed only 1.55 ounces; Billy Burke won the 1931 U.S. Open Championship playing one.

73 QUESTIONS

"Who said?"

73-1   "If a lot of people gripped a knife and fork as poorly as they do a golf club, they'd starve to death."

73-2   "Victory is everything. You can spend the money, but you can never spend the memories."

73-3   "What other people may find in poetry or art museums, I find in the flight of a good drive."

73-4   "It's the most fun I've ever had with my clothes on."

73-5   "May thy ball lie in green pastures, and not in still waters."

73-6   "You've just got one problem. You stand too close to the ball after you've hit it."

73-7   "It does not matter if you look like a beast before or after the hit, as long as you look like a beauty at the moment of impact."

73-8   "The only shots you can be dead sure of are those you've had already."

73-9   "I don't say my golf game is bad, but if I grew tomatoes they'd come up sliced."

73-10   "A lot of guys who have never choked, have never been in the position to do so."

73-11   "There are two things you can do with your head down—play golf and pray."

73-12   "If you try to fight the course, it will beat you."

73-13   "Many shots are spoiled at the last instant by efforts to add a few more yards."

73-14   "Golf is a game invented by the same people who think music comes out of bagpipes."

73-15   "Lay off for three weeks, and then quit for good."

73-16   "Golf is an awkward set of bodily contortions designed to produce a graceful result."

73-17   "Golf puts a man's character to the anvil and his richest qualities of patience, poise and restraint, to the flame."

73-18   "If you are going to throw a club, it is important to throw it ahead of you, down the fairway, so you don't have to waste energy going back to pick it up."

73-19   "No one who ever had lessons would have a swing like mine."

73-20   "You can't go into a shop and buy a good game of golf."

ANSWERS

GROUP

73

"Who said?"

73-1   Sam Snead

73-2   Ken Venturi

73-3   Arnold Palmer

73-4   Lee Trevino

73-5   Ben Hogan

73-6   Sam Snead

73-7   Seve Ballesteros

73-8   Byron Nelson

73-9   Arnold Palmer

73-10   Tom Watson

73-11   Lee Trevino

73-12   Lou Graham

73-13   Bobby Jones

73-14   Lee Trevino

73-15   Sam Snead

73-16   Tommy Armour

73-17   Billy Casper

73-18   Tommy Bolt

73-19   Lee Trevino

73-20   Sam Snead

74 QUESTIONS

74-1   Who was the first three-time winner of the Masters Tournament?

74-2   Who scored the greatest come from behind victory in a PGA Championship?

74-3   What golf club did Arnold Palmer tee-off with, then hit again, in all four rounds on the "Railway Hole" #11, Par 5, at Royal Troon to win the British Open in 1961?

74-4   On what British Open Championship venue did Australia's Peter Thomson win his first and fifth British Open Championship?

74-5   **T or F** Ted Ray drove the same hole four times and made three birdies in a U.S. Open.

74-6   After two holes in the 1994 U.S. Open Championship play-off at Oakmont Country Club, how many total strokes over par were the three players?

74-7   How many players broke par on the first day at the 1974 U.S. Open at Winged Foot Golf Club?

74-8   Which five players have led or shared the Masters' lead after the previous years' victory?

74-9   What has been the shortest course in the U.S. Open Championship history?

74-10   What year did Byron Nelson make the cut for the last time in the Masters Tournament?

74-11   What is the lowest adjusted scoring average (60 rounds minimum) for the Vardon Trophy?

74-12   How many total holes were needed to win (the longest on record) the 1931 U.S. Open at the Inverness Club in Toledo, OH?

74-13   **T or F** The United States leads all countries in the total number of victories for all four major championships.

74-14   What is the lowest 72-hole score ever shot in any major championship?

74-15   What year did the Masters start to award crystal for the day's low round, eagles and holes-in-one?

74-16   Who designed the first 18-hole golf course in the United States which hosted the U.S. Open Championships in 1897, 1900 and 1911?

74-17   Who is the oldest Top 10 finisher at the Masters Tournament?

74-18   How many consecutive major championships did Jack Nicklaus compete in when he was eligible?

74-19   Who set a new 72-hole scoring record of 275 (1967) and lowered it to 272 (1980) at Baltusrol during the U.S. Open Championship?

74-20   In which major championship, and on which course was the "coming of age" for Tom Watson?

ANSWERS

GROUP
74

74-1   Jimmy Demaret, 1940, 1947 and 1950

74-2   John Mahaffey, 1978 at Oakmont Country Club, eight shots behind

74-3   One-iron, winning by six shots, made a par, two birdies and an eagle

74-4   Royal Birkdale Golf Club, Southport, England, 1954 and 1965

74-5   True! #7, Par 4, 320 yards at the Inverness Club, Toledo, OH, 1920

74-6   Eight shots over par! Ernie Els, Loren Roberts and Colin Montgomerie. Ernie Els won on the second sudden-death hole with a par.

74-7   None! "The Massacre at Winged Foot" as stated by Dick Schapp

74-8   Jack Burke, Jr. (1957), Arnold Palmer (1961), Gary Player (1962), Jack Nicklaus (1966) and Jose Maria Olazabal (1995)

74-9   Shinnecock Hills Golf Club, 4,423 yards long in 1896

74-10   1965, tied for 15th place

74-11   67.79 strokes; done twice by Tiger Woods in 2000 and 2007

74-12   144 holes; two 36-hole play-offs, Billy Burke beat George Von Elm by one stroke

74-13   False; Masters Tournament, U.S Open and PGA Championships, but not the British Open Championship. U.S. is third place behind the United Kingdom and Scotland

74-14   265 (66-65-65-69) 15 under by David Toms, 2001 PGA Championship at Atlanta Athletic Club, Highlands Course, Duluth, GA

74-15   1954, same year Sam Snead beat Ben Hogan in an 18-hole play-off

74-16   Charles Blair Macdonald, "Father of American Golf Course Architects"

74-17   Jack Nicklaus, age 58, tied for 6th place, 1998

74-18   154, withdrew due to left hip replacement surgery

74-19   Jack Nicklaus

74-20   1975, the British Open at Carnoustie. The first of his eight major championship wins including five British Opens, two Masters, and one U.S. Open Championship.

GROUP 75 QUESTIONS

75-1   Who is the only player to have played on the same course in five U.S. Open Championships?

75-2   Which five players have not defended their U.S. Open Championships?

75-3   **T or F** Bobby Jones, Walter Hagen, Johnny Miller and Arnold Palmer all won a British Open by a six-shot margin.

75-4   What was the first major championship to implement a sudden-death play-off?

75-5   **T or F** Walter Hagen lead after each round of his 1914 U.S. Open Championship win.

75-6   What did Padraig Harrington shoot on #18 at Carnoustie in 2007 and yet still won the British Open Championship in a play-off?

75-7   Golf historians call which PGA Championship in the match-play format, "Golf's Greatest Match?"

75-8   **T or F** Johnny Miller started his record-setting 4th round in the 1973 U.S. Open Championship at Oakmont Country Club with four straight birdies.

75-9   During the 1920s, which three players won all the PGA Championships from 1921 to 1929?

75-10   What does "Tam Arte Quam Marte," the Royal Troon club motto, translate to in English?

75-11   On which U.S. Open course did then amateurs, Bobby Jones and Jack Nicklaus, make their debuts?

75-12   How many Vardon Trophies did Byron Nelson win?

75-13   **T or F** NBC television announced Ben Hogan the winner of his fifth U.S. Open Championship at the Olympic Club in 1955 before it was all over.

75-14   What are the three toughest starting holes, based on the handicap system, on a U.S. Open Championship course?

75-15   In what year and on which course did Sam Snead debut in the U.S. Open Championship?

75-16   Name the three non-winners of the British Open Championship to shoot four rounds under 70.

75-17   Who was the first player to shoot "under par" for 72 holes in the U.S. Open Championship?

75-18   **T or F** Tiger Woods never three-putted in his record-setting victory at the 1997 Masters.

75-19   **T or F** All three of the U.S. Open Championships played at The Country Club (Brookline, MA) have ended with a play-off champion.

75-20   Which three former U.S. Open Championship winners tied for fourth place, three shots back of Johnny Miller's win at Oakmont Country Club in 1973?

ANSWERS

75-1   Arnold Palmer, Oakmont Country Club; 1953 (Amateur), 1962, 1973, 1983 and 1994

75-2   Harry Vardon (1901), Alex Smith (1907), Bobby Jones (1931), Ben Hogan (1949) and Payne Stewart (2000)

75-3   True! Jones (1927), Hagen (1929), Palmer (1962) and Miller (1976)

75-4   The PGA Championship starting in 1977

75-5   True, 68-74(142), 75(217), 73 = 290

75-6   Double-bogey six, two balls in Barry Burn, beat Sergio Garcia plus one in the play-off

75-7   1923, Gene Sarazen vs. Walter Hagen: Sarazen winning on first extra hole finale in PGA Championship history.

75-8   True! He also birdied #11, #12 and #13 in a row on his way to a 63 and victory.

75-9   Walter Hagen (1921, 1924, 1925, 1926 and 1927), Gene Sarazen (1922 and 1923), Leo Diegel (1928 and 1929)

75-10   "As much by skill as by strength"

75-11   The Inverness Club, Toledo, OH; Bobby Jones 1920 and Jack Nicklaus 1957

75-12   Just one in 1939, won 54 PGA events in 13 year career

75-13   True! But Jack Fleck came in later to tie Ben Hogan, and then beat Hogan the next day in an 18-hole play-off, 69 to 72.

75-14   Oakmont Country Club, Handicaps one, five and three

75-15   1937 at Oakland Hills Country Club; first round he shot 69 to tie for the lead

75-16   Ernie Els (1993), Jasper Parnevik (1994) and Ernie Els again (2004)

75-17   John McDermott, 1912 (74-75-74-71 = 294), par was 74 = 296 at the Country Club of Buffalo

75-18   True! A great display of putting on some of the world's greatest and toughest greens

75-19   True: Francis Ouimet (1913), Julius Boros (1988) and Curtis Strange (1988)

75-20   Jack Nicklaus, Arnold Palmer and Lee Trevino (282s), they all tied for fourth place

GROUP
1

The Ryder Cup QUESTIONS

1-1   Through 2008, how many biennial Ryder Cup matches have been played?

1-2   **T or F** Ben Hogan and Sam Snead both Captained the USA Ryder Cup Team on three occasions.

1-3   Which two Ryder Cups have ended in a tie?

1-4   Which USA Ryder Cup Team is considered by many to be the best one ever assembled?

1-5   What is the Ryder Cup Trophy made of?

1-6   In 2004 and 2006, what was the winning score for the European Ryder Cup Team?

1-7   Which European player has won the most matches in Ryder Cup competition?

1-8   Where were the inaugural Ryder Cup matches contested?

1-9   What three formats are used in the Ryder Cup Matches?

1-10   Who is the current Ryder Cup player with the most appearances?

1-11   On average, who is the leading point winner for the European Team?

1-12   Name the five players (three USA; two European) to win the five points in a single Ryder Cup match.

1-13   **T or F** Jack Nicklaus and Tom Watson, as partners, won all of their 1981 matches at Walton Heath Golf Club.

1-14   When was the last time the European team tied to retain the Ryder Cup?

1-15   Which European player has halved the most matches?

1-16   When was the first time the European Ryder Cup Team won on American soil?

1-17   Which Captain stated, "I'm a big believer in fate."?

1-18   **T or F** For the first time the 2008 European Ryder Cup Team had all 12 players in the Top 50 World Golf rankings.

1-19   What two players have played 12 consecutive matches without a loss?

1-20   Who designed Valhalla Golf Club in Louisville, KY, the host club of the 37th version of the Ryder Cup in 2008?

The Ryder Cup ANSWERS

GROUP
1

1-1   2008 was number 37, starting with the first one in 1927

1-2   True; Ben Hogan 1947, 1949 and 1967; Sam Snead 1951, 1959 and 1969

1-3   1969 at Royal Birkdale Golf Club; 1989 at The Belfry; 14 to 14

1-4   1981 victorious USA Team, every member except one was a major championship winner

1-5   Solid Gold! Weighs four pounds, measures 17 inches high and nine inches wide from the handles. Crafted by Mappin & Webb, golfer image on top of Abe Mitchell

1-6   2004 Oakland Hills and 2006 The K Club; same score both times 18-1/2 to 9-1/2

1-7   Nick Faldo with 23 wins

1-8   1927 Worcester Country Club in Massachusetts

1-9   Foursome matches (alternate shot), four-ball matches (best ball by team) and singles matches (standard match-play)

1-10   Phil Mickelson with seven, through 2008, needs one more to tie Billy Casper, Raymond Floyd and Lanny Wadkins with a record of eight

1-11   Sergio Garcia (3.20 points); only player averaging over three points

1-12   USA Team: Larry Nelson 1979, Gardner Dickinson 1967, Arnold Palmer 1967; European Team: Peter Alliss 1965 and Tony Jacklin 1969

1-13   True 4 to 0, played four times, won four, lost none, halved none

1-14   1989, 14 to 14 at The Belfry

1-15   Tony Jacklin, eight halves

1-16   Muirfield Village Golf Club, Dublin, OH, 1987

1-17   Ben Crenshaw 1999, when the USA Team came from behind to win 14-1/2 to 13-1/2 at The Country Club, Brookline, MA

1-18   True!

1-19   Arnold Palmer (USA Team); Lee Westwood (European Team)

1-20   Jack Nicklaus, 1986

The Ryder Cup QUESTIONS

2-1 Which major championship golf course was the first one to host the Ryder Cup in the United States of America?

2-2 Who is the youngest player so far from either side to compete in the Ryder Cup matches?

2-3 Which two USA Team players have won a singles match 8 & 7?

2-4 **T or F** The Ryder Cup was founded on prestige, and not money.

2-5 Who is the leading American point winner through 2008?

2-6 Next to leader England (52); which European country is second in the number of appearances in the Ryder Cup?

2-7 Which non-major championship winner has the best winning percentage in the Ryder Cup?

2-8 Name the best partnership from each team over the history of the Ryder Cup.

2-9 When was the first time the Ryder Cup was held in Scotland?

2-10 When and why did the Ryder Cup move to even-numbered years?

2-11 What years did the USA Team compete against the three different team formats from Europe?

2-12 Who is the only USA Team player to be undefeated 6-0-0 having played in three Ryder Cups?

2-13 Who did Bernhard Langer halve his singles match with at Kiawah Island in 1991?

2-14 Who were the original "Dream Team" (two-man partnership) for the USA Ryder Cup Team?

2-15 Which American player has taken the worst drumming in Ryder Cup Single Matches?

2-16 Which three American players, with only one major win, have played in six or more Ryder Cups?

2-17 In 1947, the USA Team won 11 to 1 at the Portland Golf Club, who lost the one point?

2-18 **T or F** Between 1927 and 1959 all matches were played to a maximum of 36 holes.

2-19 Which American player hit a shot through a refreshment stand to win his singles match 7 & 6?

2-20 Name the Top Five American Ryder Cup players of all time.

The Ryder Cup ANSWERS

2-1   Scioto Country Club, 1931, Upper Arlington, OH

2-2   Sergio Garcia (European Team) 19 years old; Horton Smith (USA Team) 21 years old

2-3   Tom Kite, 1989 vs. Howard Clark; Fred Couples 1997 vs. Ian Woosnam

2-4   True! The Ryder Cup is truly one of the world's greatest sporting events.

2-5   Billy Casper, 23.5 points in eight Ryder Cup matches

2-6   Spain is second with 35 appearances, Scotland is third with 33 appearances

2-7   Colin Montgomerie, .653%, 20-9-7

2-8   USA Team: Arnold Palmer and Gardner Dickinson (5-0-0) 5 points;
      European Team: Seve Ballesteros and Jose Maria Olazabal (11-2-2) 12 points

2-9   1973 at Muirfield

2-10 2001, because of the 9-11 attacks; The Ryder Cup was cancelled and moved to 2002
      and even years.

2-11 Great Britain (1927–1971); Great Britain and Ireland (1973–1977) and Europe
      (1979–2008+)

2-12 Jimmy Demaret

2-13 Hale Irwin

2-14 Walter Hagen and Gene Sarazen

2-15 Walter Hagen losing to George Duncan 10 & 8, 1929 at Moortown Golf Club,
      Leeds, Yorkshire, England

2-16 Davis Love III (6), Tom Kite (7) and Lanny Wadkins (8)

2-17 Herman Keiser losing 4 & 3 to Sam King in a singles match

2-18 True! Four, foursome (alternate Shot) matches; eight single matches for a total of
      twelve points

2-19 Gene Sarazen, 1931, at Scioto Country Club, Upper Arlington, OH, #4, Par 3. Refreshment
      stand is still there and still comes in to play on this hole. *Author knows, as he has lost shots
      here!*

2-20 Billy Casper (8) 62%, Jimmy Demaret (3) 100%, Walter Hagen (5) 83%,
      Arnold Palmer (6) 70% and Lanny Wadkins (8) 63%

GROUP

3 *The Ryder Cup* QUESTIONS

3-1   How many times did Walter Hagen Captain the USA Ryder Cup Team?

3-2   Who was the original founder of the Transatlantic Competition which grew into the Ryder Cup in 1927?

3-3   **T or F** The European Team has never won three Ryder Cup Matches in a row.

3-4   Which two golf organizations administer the Ryder Cup Matches?

3-5   Who is the oldest player to compete in the Ryder Cup?

3-6   Which European has had the most appearances in the Ryder Cup matches?

3-7   Which player from both teams has the best winning percentage with over 15 matches?

3-8   In 1999, what did the USA Team shoot in the final singles matches to win?

3-9   When was the last time the Ryder Cup USA Team tied to retain the Ryder Cup?

3-10   What is the highest number of points won by either team in the singles matches?

3-11   Which American player has won the most matches?

3-12   What is the highest number of points scored by any American in a single Ryder Cup Match?

3-13   Which course has hosted the Ryder Cup the most times?

3-14   What was the USA Team's winning score in 2008 at Valhalla, Captained by Paul Azinger?

3-15   Which Ryder Cup is considered the best-ever, as 18 of the 32 matches was determined on the last hole?

3-16   In 1985 at The Belfry, who birdied the 18th hole to win the first Ryder Cup for Team Europe?

3-17   Which team, USA or Great Britain and Ireland/Europe combined, has scored the most points in 37 Ryder Cup Matches?

3-18   Which two American players have played five matches without losing any of them?

3-19   Who did Walter Hagen and Denny Shute beat 10 & 9 in 1931 at Scioto Country Club in a 36-hole match?

3-20   Through 2008, which European (third place all-time) point winner never won a major championship tournament?

The Ryder Cup ANSWERS

3-1   Six times: the first six Ryder Cups (1927, 1929, 1931, 1933, 1935 and 1937)

3-2   James Hartnett, first held at Gleneagles, Scotland in 1921, won by England 9 to 3

3-3   False; they won 2002, 2004 and 2006, but lost in 2008

3-4   USA: PGA of America; Europe: PGA European Tour

3-5   Raymond Floyd, USA Team, 51 years old

3-6   Nick Faldo, 11 times as a player (most from either team) and 2008 European Captain

3-7   USA: Arnold Palmer (.719) 22-8-2; Europe: Sergio Garcia (.667) 14-6-4

3-8   8-3-1 first victory since 1993, winning 14-1/2 to 13-1/2 after trailing going into the single matches

3-9   1969, 16 to 16 at Royal Birkdale Golf Club

3-10   Seven points; Europe: Neil Coles, Colin Montgomerie; USA: Billy Casper, Arnold Palmer and Lee Trevino

3-11   Arnold Palmer with 22 wins

3-12   Five points: Arnold Palmer, Gardner Dickinson, Larry Nelson, Tony Lema and Jack Nicklaus

3-13   The Belfry: four times (1985, 1989, 1993 and 2002)

3-14   16-1/2 to 11-1/2 points

3-15   1969 Royal Birkdale Golf Club, ending in a tie (16 to 16) with Jack Nicklaus' "Concession"

3-16   Sam Torrance beating Andy North

3-17   USA Team: 476 points; Great Britain and European Teams: 368 points

3-18   Jimmy Demaret 6-0 and Bobby Nichols 4-0-1

3-19   Great Britain's George Duncan and Arthur Havers

3-20   Colin Montgomerie, 23.5 points (3rd), point average 2.94 (2nd)

GROUP

4

The Ryder Cup QUESTIONS

4-1 Between 1937 and 1947, how many Ryder Cup Matches were held during World War II?

4-2 What is Jack Nicklaus' record as USA Team Captain vs. the European Team Captained by Tony Jacklin?

4-3 What business was Samuel Ryder, for whom the Ryder Cup is named, involved in?

4-4 Who sank the winning putt to secure victory for the European Team in 2004 at Oakland Hills?

4-5 **T or F** The winner of each match scores a single point (1) for their team; a half (1/2) point is won by each team for a match tied after 18 holes.

4-6 Which team has had the most "Holes-in-One?"

4-7 Which year(s) did the "Challenge" Matches replace the Ryder Cup Matches?

4-8 Which American has played the most singles matches in Ryder Cup history through 2008?

4-9 How many times was Billy Casper unbeaten in any one single Ryder Cup Match?

4-10 Which four Americans have lost the most single match points in the Ryder Cup?

4-11 Who are the only two cousins to play in the Ryder Cup?

4-12 Which was the first team to win the Ryder Cup on the other team's domain golf course?

4-13 Which Ryder Cup Matches were labeled the "War on the Shore?"

4-14 Who wrote, after the 1977 Ryder Cup Matches at Royal Lytham and St. Annes, "In America, the Ryder Cup win rates somewhere between Tennessee Frog Jumping and the Alabama Melon-pip Spitting Championship."

4-15 Who was the only player to beat Sam Snead in seven single matches?

4-16 Which USA Team captain gave himself four captain's picks instead of the usual two picks?

4-17 Which Ryder Cup was the first one to be contested in Ireland?

4-18 **T or F** Before 2008, the USA Team had lost five of the previous Ryder Cup Matches.

4-19 Which two European players have competed in 10 Ryder Cup Matches?

4-20 Which European player has won the most foursome matches?

The Ryder Cup ANSWERS

GROUP 4

4-1 None, 1937 at Southport and Ainsdale, Lancashire, England and 1947 at Portland Golf Club, Portland, Oregon

4-2 1 to 1; won 1983 14-1/2 to 13-1/2 at PGA National Golf Club. Palm Beach Gardens, FL, lost in 1987 15 to 13 at Muirfield Village, Dublin, OH

4-3 He was an English seed merchant and entrepreneur

4-4 Colin Montgomerie

4-5 True. It takes 14 points to retain the Ryder Cup, 14-1/2 points to win the Ryder Cup outright

4-6 Europe with five, USA with only one

4-7 1940–1943, during World War II, to raise money for the American Red Cross and other service organizations

4-8 Arnold Palmer, 11 matches, winning six times

4-9 Twice, 1963 and 1967, 4-1/2 points out of five points both times, four wins and one halved match

4-10 Four points: Raymond Floyd, Jack Nicklaus, Mark O'Meara and Phil Mickelson (five points)

4-11 Jack Burke and Dave Marr, they are also both major championship winners

4-12 1937 USA Team at Southport and Ainsdale Golf Club, Lancashire, England

4-13 1991, at Kiawah Island, SC, won by the USA Team 14 to 13

4-14 Sportswriter Peter Dobereiner

4-15 Harry Weetman, winning one up, 1953 at the Wentworth Club, Surrey, England

4-16 Paul Azinger, 2008

4-17 2006 at the K Club, in Straffan, County Kildare, Ireland

4-18 True; lost 1995, 1997, 2002, 2004, 2006, only won one time in 1999

4-19 Christy O'Connor, Sr. and Bernhard Langer

4-20 Bernhard Langer, 11 out of 18, winning 11.5 points

GROUP 5

The Ryder Cup QUESTIONS

5-1 What is "The Concession?"

5-2 **T or F** Only American-born players were allowed to play on the first USA Team.

5-3 What was the first year that Continental European players could compete in the Ryder Cup Matches?

5-4 How many Ryder Cups did the Great Britain & Ireland (GB&I) Team win in the years they were together as a team?

5-5 Name the three players who have averaged over three points in the Ryder Cup Matches.

5-6 Which two players have the largest margin of victory in a four-ball match?

5-7 How many times did 2008 Captains Azinger and Faldo play against each other in the Ryder Cup?

5-8 How many times has the Augusta National Golf Club hosted the Ryder Cup Matches?

5-9 Who was the first captain for the English Ryder Cup Team in 1927?

5-10 Which major championship winner pitched the idea to increase the selection procedures in Continental Europe to enhance the past prestige of the Ryder Cup?

5-11 How many times was Gene Sarazen unbeaten in a singles Ryder Cup Match?

5-12 **T or F** Tom Watson was selected for the 1979 USA Team, but did not compete.

5-13 Which year was the largest margin win for the USA Team?

5-14 Through 2008, how many times have European Teams won the Ryder Cup on American soil?

5-15 Who beat Jack Nicklaus twice in the same day in singles matches?

5-16 Who made the putt "Heard Around the World" to win a Ryder Cup?

5-17 Which two players did not score a single point in the 2004 defeat for the USA Team at Oakland Hills Country Club?

5-18 **T or F** The USA Team has twice won seven consecutive Ryder Cups.

5-19 Which partnership was unbeaten against eight different players in four matches at the Country Club, Brookline, MA, 1999?

5-20 When did the Ryder Cup format change to 24 matches of 18 holes maximum, instead of 12 matches of 36 holes?

The Ryder Cup ANSWERS

GROUP
5

5-1   Jack Nicklaus' "Concession" to Tony Jacklin in the 1969 Ryder Cup at Royal Birkdale Golf Club, ending in a tied Ryder Cup (16 to 16). *Considered one of the greatest sportsmanship moments in all of sports.*

5-2   True!

5-3   1979 at the Greenbrier in West Virginia

5-4   None, 0-3-0 in 1973, 1975 and 1977

5-5   Lee Trevino (3.33), Arnold Palmer (3.29) and Jack Nicklaus (3.08)

5-6   USA teammates Lee Trevino & Jerry Pate defeated Nick Faldo & Sam Torrance of Europe 7 & 5, 1981

5-7   Four times: two four-ball matches and one each foursome and singles. Paul Azinger won two and tied two of the matches.

5-8   Never; and has not been scheduled at anytime in the future

5-9   Abe Mitchell, however he had appendicitis and Ted Ray filled in. Abe Mitchell did play in the 1931 and 1933 Ryder Cup

5-10 Jack Nicklaus, 1977 at Royal Lytham & St. Annes

5-11 Three Times: 1927, 1933 and 1937; 1-1/2 points out of two points

5-12 True

5-13 1967 at The Champions Golf Club, Houston, TX, 23-1/2 to 8-1/2

5-14 Three times: 1987 Muirfield Village, 1995 Oak Hill and 2004 Oakland Hills

5-15 Billy Barnes 4 & 2, and 2 & 1, 1975 at Laurel Valley Golf Club in Ligonier, PA

5-16 Justin Leonard, 1999, making a 45-foot long putt at the Country Club, Brookline, MA

5-17 Fred Funk and Kenny Perry

5-18 True! 1935–1955 and 1971–1983

5-19 Known as "The Odd Couple" Sergio Garcia and Jesper Parnevik; won three, lost none and halved one for 3-1/2 points

5-20 1961, 14th Ryder Cup at Royal Lytham & St. Annes, won by the USA Team 14-1/2 to 9-1/2 points

The Presidents Cup QUESTIONS

1-1   When and where was the first Presidents Cup contested?

1-2   Name the U.S. Presidents who have been honorary Chairmen of the Presidents Cup.

1-3   How many times has Jack Nicklaus been the Captain of the United States Team in the Presidents Cup?

1-4   **T or F** The Presidents Cup is the United States vs. an International Team, not including Europe.

1-5   Which two players have appeared in all seven Presidents Cups through 2007?

1-6   What is the United States win/loss record through 2007, in the first seven Presidents Cups?

1-7   Which of the Presidents Cups had the largest winning margin by the United States Team?

1-8   Who are the two overall point winners for the U.S. and International Presidents Cup teams?

1-9   Who were the first Captains of the Presidents Cup in 1994?

1-10   Which two players represented their teams in a sudden-death play-off which was called because of darkness...still ending in a tie for the Presidents Cup?

1-11   **T or F** Both teams use the same qualifying figures for the players to make their respective team.

1-12   What two former major championship winners have been Captains for the International Team three times each?

1-13   The Presidents Cup is a match-play event, differing from the Ryder Cup. How many points are needed to win the Presidents Cup?

1-14   How many matches are played in the Presidents Cup?

1-15   For the 2009 Presidents Cup, what is par and how long is the Harding Park Golf Club in San Francisco, CA?

1-16   **T or F** The Presidents Cup is held biennially on odd-numbered years, and hosted alternately between the United States and elsewhere in the world.

1-17   What is the purse for the Presidents Cup?

1-18   Who started and organized the Presidents Cup?

1-19   Who made a 15-foot birdie putt on the 18th hole in his singles match to clinch a victory for the United States Team in the sixth Presidents Cup?

1-20   Who are the two Captains for the eighth Presidents Cup, Oct 8–11, 2009

The Presidents Cup ANSWERS

GROUP
1

1-1 September 16–18, 1994 at the Robert Trent Jones Golf Club in Gainesville, FL

1-2 1994, Gerald R. Ford, 1996 George H.W. Bush, 2000 Bill Clinton, 2005 George W. Bush

1-3 Four times: 1998, 2003, 2005 and 2007

1-4 True; Europe competes against the U.S. Team in the Ryder Cup.

1-5 Phil Mickelson, U.S. Team; Vijay Singh, International Team

1-6 5 -1-1; lost in 1998, tied in 2003

1-7 Fourth Presidents Cup, 2000 at Robert Trent Jones Golf Club, 11 point victory

1-8 U.S. Team Davis Love III 16-8-4; International Team Vijay Singh 14-15-6;
both with 20 points

1-9 U.S. Team Hale Irwin; International Team David Graham

1-10 2003, Ernie Els International Team; Tiger Woods U.S. Team. Captains Jack Nicklaus and
Gary Player agreed to share the Presidents Cup in the spirit of competition after being tied
17 all.

1-11 False; U.S. Team, official two years of earning through the PGA Championship of the year
the Cup is contested; International Team, official World Golf Rankings through PGA
Championship (No European members). Both teams get two Captains' picks.

1-12 Peter Thomson (1996, 1998 and 2000); Gary Player (2003, 2005 and 2007)

1-13 17.5 points; Sunday single matches are continued if tied after 18 holes until an outright
winner is determined. Presidents Cup is six extra matches over the Ryder Cup format.

1-14 34 matches; 11 foursomes, 11 four-ball and 12 singles all worth 1 point each or
34 total points

1-15 Par 71, 7137 yards; starts and ends with a Par 5

1-16 True, moved to odd-numbered years because of the terrorist attacks on 9-11-2001.
Ryder Cup is biennially on even-numbered years.

1-17 There is no purse (prize money). The net proceeds are distributed to various charities
nominated by the players and Captains.

1-18 The PGA Tour

1-19 Chris DiMarco, one up over Appleby

1-20 U.S. Team, Fred Couples; International Team, Greg Norman. Both are major championship
winners and have been players in the Presidents Cup...a first!

THE MASTERS TOURNAMENT

AUGUSTA NATIONAL GOLF CLUB
AUGUSTA, GEORGIA, USA

YEAR	CHAMPION	COUNTRY	WINNER'S SCORE	WINNERS TO PAR	MARGIN
2015					
2014					
2013					
2012					
2011					
2010					
2009					
2008	TREVOR IMMELMAN	SOUTH AFRICA	280	−8	3
2007	ZACH JOHNSON	USA	289	+1	2
2006	PHIL MICKELSON	USA	281	−7	2
2005	TIGER WOODS	USA	276	−12	PLAY-OFF (2)
2004	PHIL MICKELSON	USA	279	−9	1
2003	MIKE WEIR	CANADA	281	−7	PLAY-OFF (2)
2002	TIGER WOODS	USA	276	−12	3
2001	TIGER WOODS	USA	272	−16	2
2000	VIJAY SINGH	FIJI	278	−10	3
1999	JOSE MARIA OLAZABAL	SPAIN	280	−8	2
1998	MARK O'MEARA	USA	279	−9	1
1997	TIGER WOODS	USA	270	−18	12
1996	NICK FALDO	ENGLAND	276	−12	5
1995	BEN CRENSHAW	USA	274	−14	1
1994	JOSE MARIA OLAZABAL	SPAIN	279	−9	2
1993	BERNHARD LANGER	GERMANY	277	−11	4
1992	FRED COUPLES	USA	275	−13	2
1991	IAN WOOSNAM	WALES	277	−11	1
1990	NICK FALDO	ENGLAND	278	−10	PLAY-OFF (2)
1989	NICK FALDO	ENGLAND	283	−5	PLAY-OFF (2)
1988	SANDY LYLE	SCOTLAND	281	−7	1
1987	LARRY MIZE	USA	285	−3	PLAY-OFF (3)

THE MASTERS TOURNAMENT (CONTINUED)

AUGUSTA NATIONAL GOLF CLUB
AUGUSTA, GEORGIA, USA

YEAR	CHAMPION	COUNTRY	WINNER'S SCORE	WINNERS TO PAR	MARGIN
1986	JACK NICKLAUS	USA	279	−9	1
1985	BERNHARD LANGER	GERMANY	282	−6	2
1984	BEN CRENSHAW	USA	277	−11	2
1983	SEVE BALLESTEROS	SPAIN	280	−8	4
1982	CRAIG STADLER	USA	284	−4	PLAY-OFF (2)
1981	TOM WATSON	USA	280	−8	2
1980	SEVE BALLESTEROS	SPAIN	275	−13	4
1979	FUZZY ZOELLER	USA	280	−8	PLAY-OFF (3)
1978	GARY PLAYER	SOUTH AFRICA	277	−11	1
1977	TOM WATSON	USA	276	−12	2
1976	RAYMOND FLOYD	USA	271	−17	8
1975	JACK NICKLAUS	USA	276	−12	1
1974	GARY PLAYER	SOUTH AFRICA	278	−10	2
1973	TOMMY AARON	USA	283	−5	1
1972	JACK NICKLAUS	USA	286	−2	3
1971	CHARLES COODY	USA	279	−9	2
1970	BILLY CASPER	USA	279	−9	PLAY-OFF (2)
1969	GEORGE ARCHER	USA	281	−7	1
1968	BOB GOALBY	USA	277	−11	1
1967	GAY BREWER	USA	280	−8	1
1966	JACK NICKLAUS	USA	EVEN	0	PLAY-OFF (3)
1965	JACK NICKLAUS	USA	271	−17	9
1964	ARNOLD PALMER	USA	276	−12	6
1963	JACK NICKLAUS	USA	286	−2	1
1962	ARNOLD PALMER	USA	280	−8	PLAY-OFF (3)
1961	GARY PLAYER	SOUTH AFRICA	280	−8	1
1960	ARNOLD PALMER	USA	282	−6	1
1959	ART WALL, JR.	USA	284	−4	1
1958	ARNOLD PALMER	USA	284	−4	1

THE MASTERS TOURNAMENT (CONTINUED)
AUGUSTA NATIONAL GOLF CLUB
AUGUSTA, GEORGIA, USA

YEAR	CHAMPION	COUNTRY	WINNER'S SCORE	WINNERS TO PAR	MARGIN
1957	DOUG FORD	USA	283	−5	3
1956	JACK BURKE, JR.	USA	289	+1	1
1955	CARY MIDDLECOFF	USA	279	−9	7
1954	SAM SNEAD	USA	289	+1	PLAY-OFF (2)
1953	BEN HOGAN	USA	274	−14	5
1952	SAM SNEAD	USA	286	−2	4
1951	BEN HOGAN	USA	280	−8	2
1950	JIMMY DEMARET	USA	283	−5	2
1949	SAM SNEAD	USA	282	−6	3
1948	CLAUDE HARMON	USA	279	−9	5
1947	JIMMY DEMARET	USA	281	−7	2
1946	HERMAN KEISER	USA	282	−6	1
1945	N/A WORLD WAR II				
1944	N/A WORLD WAR II				
1943	N/A WORLD WAR II				
1942	BYRON NELSON	USA	280	−8	PLAY-OFF (2)
1941	CRAIG WOOD	USA	280	−8	3
1940	JIMMY DEMARET	USA	280	−8	4
1939	RALPH GULDAHL	USA	279	−9	1
1938	HENRY PICARD	USA	285	−3	2
1937	BYRON NELSON	USA	283	−5	2
1936	HORTON SMITH	USA	285	−3	1
1935	GENE SARAZEN	USA	282	−6	PLAY-OFF (2)
1934	HORTON SMITH	USA	284	−4	1

U.S. OPEN CHAMPIONSHIP

YEAR	CHAMPION	COUNTRY	VENUE	VENUE LOCATION	WINNER'S SCORE
2015			CHAMBERS BAY	UNIVERSITY PLACE, WA	
2014			PINEHURST RESORT COURSE #2	PINEHURST, NC	
2013			MERION G C EAST	ARDMORE, PA	
2012			OLYMPIC CLUB -LAKE	DALY CITY, CA	
2011			CONGRESSIONAL C C BLUE	BETHESDA, MD	
2010			PEBBLE BEACH G L	PEBBLE BEACH, CA	
2009			BETHPAGE STATE PARK (BLACK)	FARMINGDALE, NY	
2008	TIGER WOODS	USA	TORREY PINES G C SOUTH	SAN DIEGO, CA	283 (−1) PO
2007	ANGEL CABRERA	ARGENTINA	OAKMONT C C	OAKMONT, PA	285 (+5)
2006	GEOFF OGILVY	AUSTRALIA	WINGED FOOT WEST	MAMARONECK, NY	285 (+5)
2005	MICHAEL CAMPBELL	NEW ZEALAND	PINEHURST RESORT COURSE #2	PINEHURST, NC	280 (E)
2004	RETIEF GOOSEN	SOUTH AFRICA	SHINNECOCK HILLS	SHINNECOCK HILLS, NY	276 (−4)
2003	JIM FURYK	USA	OLYMPIA FIELDS, NORTH COURSE	OLYMPIA FIELDS, IL	272 (−8)
2002	TIGER WOODS	USA	BETHPAGE STATE PARK (BLACK)	FARMINGDALE, NY	277 (−3)
2001	RETIEF GOOSEN	SOUTH AFRICA	SOUTHERN HILLS C C	TULSA, OK	276 (−4) PO
2000	TIGER WOODS	USA	PEBBLE BEACH G L	PEBBLE BEACH, CA	272 (−12)
1999	PAYNE STEWART	USA	PINEHURST RESORT COURSE #2	PINEHURST, CA	279 (−1)
1998	LEE JANZEN	USA	OLYMPIC CLUB (LAKE)	DALY CITY, CA	280 (E)
1997	ERNIE ELS	SOUTH AFRICA	CONGRESSIONAL BLUE	BETHESDA, MD	276 (−4)
1996	STEVE JONES	USA	OAKLAND HILLS SOUTH	BLOOMFIELD HILLS, MI	278 (−2)
1995	COREY PAVIN	USA	SHINNECOCK HILLS	SHINNECOCK HILLS, NY	280 (E)
1994	ERNIE ELS	SOUTH AFRICA	OAKMONT C C	OAKMONT, PA	279 (−5) PO
1993	LEE JANZEN	USA	BALTUSROL (LOWER)	SPRINGFIELD, NJ	272 (−8)
1992	TOM KITE	USA	PEBBLE BEACH G L	PEBBLE BEACH, CA	285 (−3)
1991	PAYNE STEWART	USA	HAZELTINE NATIONAL	CHASKA, MN	282 (−6) PO

U.S. OPEN CHAMPIONSHIP (CONTINUED)

YEAR	CHAMPION	COUNTRY	VENUE	VENUE LOCATION	WINNER'S SCORE
1990	HALE IRWIN	USA	MEDINAH C C #3	MEDINAH, IL	280 (−8) PO
1989	CURTIS STRANGE	USA	OAK HILL C C EAST	ROCHESTER, NY	278 (−2)
1988	CURTIS STRANGE	USA	THE COUNTRY CLUB	BROOKLINE, MA	278 (−6) PO
1987	SCOTT SIMPSON	USA	OLYMPIC CLUB- LAKE	DALY CITY, CA	277 (−3)
1986	RAYMOND FLOYD	USA	SHINNECOCK HILLS	SHINNECOCK HILLS, NY	279 (−1)
1985	ANDY NORTH	USA	OAKLAND HILLS SOUTH	BLOOMFIELD HILLS, MI	279 (−1)
1984	FUZZY ZOELLER	USA	WINGED FOOT WEST	MAMARONECK, NY	276 (−4) PO
1983	LARRY NELSON	USA	OAKMONT C C	OAKMONT, PA	280 (−4)
1982	TOM WATSON	USA	PEBBLE BEACH G L	PEBBLE BEACH, CA	282 (−6)
1981	DAVID GRAHAM	AUSTRALIA	MERION G C EAST	ARDMORE, PA	273 (−7)
1980	JACK NICKLAUS	USA	BALTUSROL- LOWER	SPRINGFIELD, NJ	272 (−8)
1979	HALE IRWIN	USA	INVERNESS CLUB	TOLEDO, OH	284 (E)
1978	ANDY NORTH	USA	CHERRY HILLS C C	CHERRY HILLS, CO	285 (+1)
1977	HUBERT GREEN	USA	SOUTHERN HILLS C C	TULSA, OK	278 (−2)
1976	JERRY PATE	USA	ATLANTA ATHLETIC CLUB (HIGHLANDS)	DULUTH, GA	277 (−3)
1975	LOU GRAHAM	USA	MEDINAH C C #3	MEDINAH, IL	287 (+3) PO
1974	HALE IRWIN	USA	WINGED FOOT WEST	MAMARONECK, NY	287 (+7)
1973	JOHNNY MILLER	USA	OAKMONT C C	OAKMONT, PA	279 (−5)
1972	JACK NICKLAUS	USA	PEBBLE BEACH G L	PEBBLE BEACH, CA	290 (+2)
1971	LEE TREVINO	USA	MERION G C EAST	ARDMORE, PA	280 (E) PO
1970	TONY JACKLIN	ENGLAND	HAZELTINE NATIONAL	CHASKA, MN	281 (−7)
1969	ORVILLE MOODY	USA	CHAMPIONS G C CYPRESS CREEK	HOUSTON, TX	281 (+1)
1968	LEE TREVINO	USA	OAK HILL C C EAST	ROCHESTER, NY	275 (−5)
1967	JACK NICKLAUS	USA	BALTUSROL (LOWER)	SPRINGFIELD, NJ	275 (−5)
1966	BILLY CASPER	USA	OLYMPIC CLUB (LAKE)	DALY CITY, CA	278 (−2) PO
1965	GARY PLAYER	SOUTH AFRICA	BELLERIVE C C	ST. LOUIS, MO	282 (+2) PO
1964	KEN VENTURI	USA	CONGRESSIONAL C C BLUE	BETHESDA, MD	278 (−2)
1963	JULIUS BOROS	USA	THE COUNTRY CLUB	BROOKLINE, MA	293 (+9) PO
1962	JACK NICKLAUS	USA	OAKMONT C C	OAKMONT, PA	283 (-1) PO

U.S. OPEN CHAMPIONSHIP (CONTINUED)

YEAR	CHAMPION	COUNTRY	VENUE	VENUE LOCATION	WINNER'S SCORE
1961	GENE LITTLER	USA	OAKLAND HILLS C C SOUTH	BLOOMFIELD HILLS, MI	281 (+1)
1960	ARNOLD PALMER	USA	CHERRY HILLS CC	CHERRY HILLS, CO	280 (−4)
1959	BILLY CASPER	USA	WINGED FOOT WEST	MAMARONECK, NY	282 (+2)
1958	TOMMY BOLT	USA	SOUTHERN HILL C C	TULSA, OK	283 (+3)
1957	DICK MAYER	USA	INVERNESS CLUB	TOLEDO, OH	282 (+2) PO
1956	CARY MIDDLECOFF	USA	OAK HILL C C EAST	ROCHESTER, NY	281 (+1)
1955	JACK FLECK	USA	OLYMPIC CLUB (LAKE)	DALY CITY, CA	287 (+7) PO
1954	ED FURGOL	USA	BALTUSROL (LOWER)	SPRINGFIELD, NJ	284 (+4)
1953	BEN HOGAN	USA	OAKMONT C C	OAKMONT, PA	283 (−5)
1952	JULIUS BOROS	USA	NORTHWOOD CLUB	DALLAS, TX	281 (+1)
1951	BEN HOGAN	USA	OAKLAND HILLS C C SOUTH	BLOOMFIELD HILLS, MI	287 (+7)
1950	BEN HOGAN	USA	MERION G C EAST	ARDMORE, PA	287 (+7) PO
1949	CARY MIDDLECOFF	USA	MEDINAH CC #3	MEDINAH, IL	286 (+2)
1948	BEN HOGAN	USA	RIVIERA C C	PACIFIC PALISADES, CA	276 (−8)
1947	LEW WORSHAM	USA	ST. LOUIS C C	ST. LOUIS, MO	282 (−2) PO
1946	LLOYD MANGRUM	USA	CANTERBURY G C	BEACHWOOD, OH	284 (−4) PO
1945	N/A WORLD WAR II				
1944	N/A WORLD WAR II				
1943	N/A WORLD WAR II				
1942	N/A WORLD WAR II				
1941	CRAIG WOOD	USA	COLONIAL C C	FORT WORTH, TX	284 (+4)
1940	LAWSON LITTLE	USA	CANTERBURY G C	BEACHWOOD, OH	284 (−4)
1939	BYRON NELSON	USA	PHILADELPHIA C C	GLADWYNE, PA	284 (+8)
1938	RALPH GULDAHL	USA	CHERRY HILLS C C	CHERRY HILLS, CO	284 (E)
1937	RALPH GULDAHL	USA	OAKLAND HILLS C C SOUTH	BLOOMFIELD HILLS, MI	281 (−7)
1936	TONY MANERO	USA	BALTUSROL (UPPER)	SPRINGFIELD, NJ	282 (−6)
1935	SAM PARKS, JR.	USA	OAKMONT C C	OAKMONT, PA	299 (+11)
1934	OLIN DUTRA	USA	MERION G C EAST	ARDMORE, PA	293 (+13)
1933	JOHNNY GOODMAN ★	USA	NORTH SHORE C C	GLENVIEW, IL	287 (−1)

U.S. OPEN CHAMPIONSHIP (CONTINUED)

YEAR	CHAMPION	COUNTRY	VENUE	VENUE LOCATION	WINNER'S SCORE
1932	GENE SARAZEN	USA	FRESH MEADOW C C	GREAT NECK, NY	286 (+6)
1931	BILLY BURKE	USA	INVERNESS CLUB	TOLEDO, OH	292 (+8) PO
1930	BOBBY JONES ★	USA	INTERLACHEN C C	EDINA, MN	287 (−1)
1929	BOBBY JONES ★	USA	WINGED FOOT-WEST	MAMARONECK, NY	294 (+6) PO
1928	JOHNNY FARRELL	USA	OLYMPIA FIELDS C C	OLYMPIA FIELDS, IL	294 (+10) PO
1927	TOMMY ARMOUR	USA	OAKMONT C C	OAKMONT, PA	301 (+13) PO
1926	BOBBY JONES ★	USA	SCIOTO C C	COLUMBUS, OH	293 (+5)
1925	WILLIE MacFARLANE	SCOTLAND	WORCESTER C C	WORCESTER, MA	291 (+7) PO
1924	CYRIL WALKER	ENGLAND	OAKLAND HILLS CC SOUTH	BLOOMFIELD HILLS, MI	297 (+9)
1923	BOBBY JONES ★	USA	INWOOD C C	INWOOD, NY	296 (+8) PO
1922	GENE SARAZEN	USA	SKOKIE C C	GLENCOE, IL	288 (+8)
1921	JIM BARNES	USA	COLUMBIA C C	CHEVY CHASE, MD	289 (+9)
1920	TED RAY	ENGLAND	INVERNESS CLUB	TOLEDO, OH	295 (+7)
1919	WALTER HAGEN	USA	BRAE BURN MAIN	WEST NEWTON, MA	301 (+17) PO
1918	N/A WORLD WAR I				
1917	N/A WORLD WAR I				
1916	CHICK EVANS ★	USA	MINIKAHDA CLUB	MINNEAPOLIS, MN	286 (+2)
1915	JEROME TRAVERS ★	USA	BALTUSROL G C REVISED COURSE	SPRINGFIELD, NJ	297 (+1)
1914	WALTER HAGEN	USA	MIDLOTHIAN C C	MIDLOTHIAN, IL	290 (+2)
1913	FRANCIS OUIMET ★	USA	THE COUNTRY CLUB	BROOKLINE, MA	304 (+8) PO
1912	JOHN MCDERMOTT	USA	C C OF BUFFALO	BUFFALO, NY	294 (−2)
1911	JOHN MCDERMOTT	USA	CHICAGO GOLF CLUB	WHEATON, IL	307 (+3) PO
1910	ALEX SMITH	SCOTLAND	PHILADELPHIA CRICKET CLUB	PHILADELPHIA, PA	298 (+6) PO
1909	GEORGE SARGENT	ENGLAND	ENGLEWOOD G C	ENGLEWOOD, NJ	290 (+2)
1908	FRED MCLEOD	SCOTLAND	MYOPIA HUNT CLUB	SOUTH HAMILTON, MA	322 (N/A) PO
1907	ALEC ROSS	SCOTLAND	PHILADELPHIA CRICKET CLUB	PHILADELPHIA, PA	302 (+10)
1906	ALEX SMITH	SCOTLAND	ONWENTSIA CLUB	LAKE FOREST, IL	295 (−33)
1905	WILLIE ANDERSON	SCOTLAND	MYOPIA HUNT CLUB	SOUTH HAMILTON, MA	314 (N/A)
1904	WILLIE ANDERSON	SCOTLAND	GLEN VIEW CLUB	GOLF, IL	303 (N/A)

U.S. OPEN CHAMPIONSHIP (CONTINUED)

YEAR	CHAMPION	COUNTRY	VENUE	VENUE LOCATION	WINNER'S SCORE
1903	WILLIE ANDERSON	SCOTLAND	BALTUSROL G C	SPRINGFIELD, NJ	307 (N/A) PO
1902	LAURIE AUCHTERLONIE	SCOTLAND	GARDEN CITY G C	GARDEN CITY, NY	307 (N/A)
1901	WILLIE ANDERSON	SCOTLAND	MYOPIA HUNT CLUB	SOUTH HAMILTON, MA	331 (N/A) PO
1900	HARRY VARDON	ENGLAND	CHICAGO GOLF CLUB	WHEATON, IL	313 (+9)
1899	WILLIE SMITH	SCOTLAND	BALTIMORE C C EAST	LUTHERVILLE -TIMONIUM, MD	315 (+7)
1898	FRED HERD	SCOTLAND	MYOPIA HUNT CLUB	SOUTH HAMILTON, MA	328 (+24)
1897	JOE LLOYD	ENGLAND	CHICAGO GOLF CLUB	WHEATON, IL	162 (+10)
1896	JAMES FOULIS	SCOTLAND	SHINNECOCK HILLS	SHINNECOCK HILLS, NY	152 (+12)
1895	HORACE RAWLINS	ENGLAND	NEWPORT C C	NEWPORT, RI	173 (N/A)

★ = Amateur
PO = Playoff
N/A = Not Applicable
C C = Country Club
G C = Golf Course
G L = Golf Links

THE BRITISH OPEN CHAMPIONSHIP

YEAR	CHAMPION	COUNTRY	VENUE	VENUE LOCATION	WINNER'S SCORE
2015					
2014					
2013					
2012			ROYAL LYTHAM & ST. ANNES G C	LANCASHIRE, ENGLAND	
2011			ROYAL ST. GEORGE'S	SANDWICH, ENGLAND	
2010			ST. ANDREWS	ST. ANDREWS, SCOTLAND	
2009			WESTIN TURNBERRY	TURNBERRY, SCOTLAND	
2008	PADRAIG HARRINGTON	IRELAND	ROYAL BIRKDALE G C	SOUTHPORT, ENGLAND	283 (+3)
2007	PADRAIG HARRINGTON	IRELAND	CARNOUSTIE G L	CARNOUSTIE, SCOTLAND	277 (−7) PO
2006	TIGER WOODS	USA	ROYAL LIVERPOOL G C	HOYLAKE, ENGLAND	270 (−18)
2005	TIGER WOODS	USA	ST. ANDREWS	ST. ANDREWS, SCOTLAND	274 (−14)
2004	TODD HAMILTON	USA	ROYAL TROON G C	TROON, SCOTLAND	274 (−10) PO
2003	BEN CURTIS	USA	ROYAL ST. GEORGE'S	SANDWICH, ENGLAND	283 (−1)
2002	ERNIE ELS	SOUTH AFRICA	MUIRFIELD	GULLANE, SCOTLAND	278 (−6) PO
2001	DAVID DUVAL	USA	ROYAL LYTHAM & ST. ANNES G C	LANCASHIRE, ENGLAND	274 (−10)
2000	TIGER WOODS	USA	ST. ANDREWS	ST. ANDREWS, SCOTLAND	269 (−19)
1999	PAUL LAWRIE	SCOTLAND	CARNOUSTIE G L	CARNOUSTIE, SCOTLAND	290 (+6) PO
1998	MARK O'MEARA	USA	ROYAL BIRKDALE G C	SOUTHPORT, ENGLAND	280 (E) PO
1997	JUSTIN LEONARD	USA	ROYAL TROON G C	TROON, SCOTLAND	272 (−12)
1996	TOM LEHMAN	USA	ROYAL LYTHAM & ST. ANNES G C	LANCASHIRE, ENGLAND	271 (−13)
1995	JOHN DALY	USA	ST. ANDREWS	ST. ANDREWS, SCOTLAND	282 (−6) PO
1994	NICK PRICE	ZIMBABWE	TURNBERRY	TURNBERRY, SCOTLAND	268 (−12)
1993	GREG NORMAN	AUSTRALIA	ROYAL ST. GEORGE'S	SANDWICH, ENGLAND	267 (−13)
1992	NICK FALDO	ENGLAND	MUIRFIELD	GULLANE, SCOTLAND	272 (−12)
1991	IAN BAKER-FINCH	AUSTRALIA	ROYAL BIRKDALE G C	SOUTHPORT, ENGLAND	272 (−8)

THE BRITISH OPEN CHAMPIONSHIP (CONTINUED)

YEAR	CHAMPION	COUNTRY	VENUE	VENUE LOCATION	WINNER'S SCORE
1990	NICK FALDO	ENGLAND	ST. ANDREWS	ST. ANDREWS, SCOTLAND	270 (−18)
1989	MARK CALCAVECCHIA	USA	ROYAL TROON G C	TROON, SCOTLAND	275 (−13) PO
1988	SEVE BALLESTEROS	SPAIN	ROYAL LYTHAM & ST. ANNES	LANCASHIRE, ENGLAND	273 (−11)
1987	NICK FALDO	ENGLAND	MUIRFIELD	GULLANE, SCOTLAND	295 (−5)
1986	GREG NORMAN	AUSTRALIA	TURNBERRY	TURNBERRY, SCOTLAND	280 (E)
1985	SANDY LYLE	SCOTLAND	ROYAL ST. GEORGE'S	SANDWICH, ENGLAND	282 (+2)
1984	SEVE BALLESTEROS	SPAIN	ST. ANDREWS	ST. ANDREWS, SCOTLAND	276 (−12)
1983	TOM WATSON	USA	ROYAL BIRKDALE G C	SOUTHPORT, ENGLAND	275 (−9)
1982	TOM WATSON	USA	ROYAL TROON G C	TROON, SCOTLAND	284 (−4)
1981	BILL ROGERS	USA	ROYAL ST GEORGE'S	SANDWICH, ENGLAND	276 (−4)
1980	TOM WATSON	USA	MUIRFIELD	GULLANE, SCOTLAND	271 (−13)
1979	SEVE BALLESTEROS	SPAIN	ROYAL LYTHAM & ST. ANNES G C	LANCASHIRE, ENGLAND	283 (−1)
1978	JACK NICKLAUS	USA	ST. ANDREWS	ST. ANDREWS, SCOTLAND	281 (−7)
1977	TOM WATSON	USA	TURNBERRY	TURNBERRY, SCOTLAND	268 (−12)
1976	JOHNNY MILLER	USA	ROYAL BIRKDALE	SOUTHPORT, ENGLAND	279 (−9)
1975	TOM WATSON	USA	CARNOUSTIE G L	CARNOUSTIE, SCOTLAND	279 (−5) PO
1974	GARY PLAYER	SOUTH AFRICA	ROYAL LYTHAM & ST. ANNES G C	LANCASHIRE, ENGLAND	282 (−2)
1973	TOM WEISKOPF	USA	ROYAL TROON	TROON, SCOTLAND	276 (−12)
1972	LEE TREVINO	USA	MUIRFIELD	GULLANE, SCOTLAND	278 (−6)
1971	LEE TREVINO	USA	ROYAL BIRKDALE	SOUTHPORT, ENGLAND	278 (−10)
1970	JACK NICKLAUS	USA	ST. ANDREWS	ST. ANDREWS, SCOTLAND	283 (−5) PO
1969	TONY JACKLIN	ENGLAND	ROYAL LYTHAM & ST. ANNES G C	LANCASHIRE, ENGLAND	280 (−4)
1968	GARY PLAYER	SOUTH AFRICA	CARNOUSTIE	CARNOUSTIE, SCOTLAND	289 (+5)
1967	ROBERTO DE VICENZO	ARGENTINA	ROYAL LIVERPOOL	HOYLAKE, ENGLAND	278 (−10)
1966	JACK NICKLAUS	USA	MUIRFIELD	GULLANE, SCOTLAND	282 (−2)

THE BRITISH OPEN CHAMPIONSHIP (CONTINUED)

YEAR	CHAMPION	COUNTRY	VENUE	VENUE LOCATION	WINNER'S SCORE
1965	PETER THOMSON	AUSTRALIA	ROYAL BIRKDALE	SOUTHPORT, ENGLAND	285 (−3)
1964	TONY LEMA	USA	ST. ANDREWS	ST. ANDREWS, SCOTLAND	279 (−5)
1963	BOB CHARLES	NEW ZEALAND	ROYAL LYTHAM & ST. ANNES G C	LANCASHIRE, ENGLAND	277 (−5) PO
1962	ARNOLD PALMER	USA	ROYAL TROON	TROON, SCOTLAND	276 (−12)
1961	ARNOLD PALMER	USA	ROYAL BIRKDALE	SOUTHPORT, ENGLAND	284 (−4)
1960	KEL NAGLE	AUSTRALIA	ST. ANDREWS	ST. ANDREWS, SCOTLAND	278 (−10)
1959	GARY PLAYER	SOUTH AFRICA	MUIRFIELD	GULLANE, SCOTLAND	284 (E)
1958	PETER THOMSON	AUSTRALIA	ROYAL LYTHAM & ST. ANNES G C	LANCASHIRE, ENGLAND	274 (−8) PO
1957	BOBBY LOCKE	SOUTH AFRICA	ST. ANDREWS	ST. ANDREWS, SCOTLAND	279 (−5)
1956	PETER THOMSON	AUSTRALIA	ROYAL LIVERPOOL	HOYLAKE, ENGLAND	286 (−2)
1955	PETER THOMSON	AUSTRALIA	ST. ANDREWS	ST. ANDREWS, SCOTLAND	281 (−3)
1954	PETER THOMSON	AUSTRALIA	ROYAL BIRKDALE	SOUTHPORT, ENGLAND	283 (−5)
1953	BEN HOGAN	USA	CARNOUSTIE	CARNOUSTIE, SCOTLAND	282 (−2)
1952	BOBBY LOCKE	SOUTH AFRICA	ROYAL LYTHAM & ST. ANNES G C	LANCASHIRE, ENGLAND	287 (+5)
1951	MAX FAULKNER	ENGLAND	ROYAL PORTRUSH	NORTHERN IRELAND	285 (−3)
1950	BOBBY LOCKE	SOUTH AFRICA	ROYAL TROON	TROON, SCOTLAND	279 (−9)
1949	BOBBY LOCKE	SOUTH AFRICA	ROYAL ST GEORGE'S	SANDWICH, ENGLAND	283 (+3)
1948	HENRY COTTON	ENGLAND	MUIRFIELD	GULLANE, SCOTLAND	284 (E)
1947	FRED DALY	NO. IRELAND	ROYAL LIVERPOOL	HOYLAKE, ENGLAND	293 (+5)
1946	SAM SNEAD	USA	ST. ANDREWS	ST. ANDREWS, SCOTLAND	290 (+2)
1945	N/A WORLD WAR II				
1944	N/A WORLD WAR II				
1943	N/A WORLD WAR II				
1942	N/A WORLD WAR II				
1941	N/A WORLD WAR II				
1940	N/A WORLD WAR II				

THE BRITISH OPEN CHAMPIONSHIP (CONTINUED)

YEAR	CHAMPION	COUNTRY	VENUE	VENUE LOCATION	WINNER'S SCORE
1939	RICHARD BURTON	ENGLAND	ST. ANDREWS	ST. ANDREWS, SCOTLAND	290 (+2)
1938	REG WHITCOMBE	ENGLAND	ROYAL ST. GEORGE'S	SANDWICH, ENGLAND	295 (+15)
1937	HENRY COTTON	ENGLAND	CARNOUSTIE	CARNOUSTIE, SCOTLAND	290 (+6)
1936	ALF PADGHAM	ENGLAND	ROYAL LIVERPOOL	HOYLAKE, ENGLAND	297 (−1)
1935	ALF PERRY	ENGLAND	MUIRFIELD	GULLANE, SCOTLAND	283 (−1)
1934	HENRY COTTON	ENGLAND	ROYAL ST. GEORGE'S	SANDWICH, ENGLAND	283 (+3)
1933	DENNY SHUTE	USA	ST. ANDREWS	ST. ANDREWS, SCOTLAND	292 (+4) PO
1932	GENE SARAZEN	USA	PRINCE'S GOLF CLUB	SANDWICH, ENGLAND	283 (−1)
1931	TOMMY ARMOUR	USA	CARNOUSTIE	CARNOUSTIE, SCOTLAND	296 (+12)
1930	BOBBY JONES ★	USA	ROYAL LIVERPOOL	HOYLAKE, ENGLAND	291 (+3)
1929	WALTER HAGEN	USA	MUIRFIELD	GULLANE, SCOTLAND	292 (+8)
1928	WALTER HAGEN	USA	ROYAL ST. GEORGE'S	SANDWICH, ENGLAND	292 (+12)
1927	BOBBY JONES ★	USA	ST. ANDREWS	ST. ANDREWS, SCOTLAND	285 (−3)
1926	BOBBY JONES ★	USA	ROYAL LYTHAM & ST. ANNES G C	LANCASHIRE, ENGLAND	291 (+9)
1925	JIM BARNES	USA	PRESTWICK G C	PRESTWICK, SCOTLAND	300 (+16)
1924	WALTER HAGEN	USA	ROYAL LIVERPOOL	HOYLAKE, ENGLAND	301 (+13)
1923	ARTHUR HAVERS	ENGLAND	ROYAL TROON	TROON, SCOTLAND	295 (+7)
1922	WALTER HAGEN	USA	ROYAL ST. GEORGE'S	SANDWICH, ENGLAND	300 (+20)
1921	JOCK HUTCHISON	USA	ST. ANDREWS	ST. ANDREWS, SCOTLAND	296 (+8) PO
1920	GEORGE DUNCAN	SCOTLAND	ROYAL CINQUE PORTS	DEAL, ENGLAND	303 (+15)
1919	N/A WORLD WAR I				
1918	N/A WORLD WAR I				
1917	N/A WORLD WAR I				
1916	N/A WORLD WAR I				
1915	N/A WORLD WAR I				
1914	HARRY VARDON	ENGLAND	PRESTWICK G C	PRESTWICK, SCOTLAND	306 (+22)

THE BRITISH OPEN CHAMPIONSHIP (CONTINUED)

YEAR	CHAMPION	COUNTRY	VENUE	VENUE LOCATION	WINNER'S SCORE
1913	JOHN HENRY TAYLOR	ENGLAND	ROYAL LIVERPOOL	HOYLAKE, ENGLAND	304 (+16)
1912	EDWARD RAY	ENGLAND	MUIRFIELD	GULLANE, SCOTLAND	295 (+15)
1911	HARRY VARDON	ENGLAND	ROYAL ST. GEORGE'S	SANDWICH, ENGLAND	303 (+23) PO
1910	JAMES BRAID	SCOTLAND	ST. ANDREWS	ST. ANDREWS, SCOTLAND	299 (+11)
1909	JOHN HENRY TAYLOR	ENGLAND	ROYAL CINQUE PORTS	DEAL, ENGLAND	291 (+3)
1908	JAMES BRAID	SCOTLAND	PRESTWICK G C	PRESTWICK, SCOTLAND	291 (+3)
1907	ARNAUD MASSY	FRANCE	ROYAL LIVERPOOL	HOYLAKE, ENGLAND	312 (+24)
1906	JAMES BRAID	SCOTLAND	MUIRFIELD	GULLANE, SCOTLAND	300 (+20)
1905	JAMES BRAID	SCOTLAND	ST. ANDREWS	ST. ANDREWS, SCOTLAND	318 (+30)
1904	JACK WHITE	SCOTLAND	ROYAL ST. GEORGE'S	SANDWICH, ENGLAND	296 (+8)
1903	HARRY VARDON	ENGLAND	PRESTWICK G C	PRESTWICK, SCOTLAND	300 (+12)
1902	SANDY HERD	SCOTLAND	ROYAL LIVERPOOL	HOYLAKE, ENGLAND	307 (+19)
1901	JAMES BRAID	SCOTLAND	MUIRFIELD	GULLANE, SCOTLAND	309 (+29)
1900	JOHN HENRY TAYLOR	ENGLAND	ST. ANDREWS	ST. ANDREWS, SCOTLAND	309 (+21)
1899	HARRY VARDON	ENGLAND	ROYAL ST. GEORGE'S	SANDWICH, ENGLAND	310 (+22)
1898	HARRY VARDON	ENGLAND	PRESTWICK G C	PRESTWICK, SCOTLAND	307 (+19)
1897	HAROLD HILTON ★	ENGLAND	ROYAL LIVERPOOL	HOYLAKE, ENGLAND	314 (+26)
1896	HARRY VARDON	ENGLAND	MUIRFIELD	GULLANE, SCOTLAND	316 (+36)
1895	JOHN HENRY TAYLOR	ENGLAND	ST. ANDREWS	ST. ANDREWS, SCOTLAND	332 (+44)
1894	JOHN HENRY TAYLOR	ENGLAND	ROYAL ST. GEORGE'S	SANDWICH, ENGLAND	326 (+38)
1893	WM. AUCHTERLONIE	SCOTLAND	PRESTWICK G C	PRESTWICK, SCOTLAND	322 (+34)
1892	HAROLD HILTON ★	ENGLAND	MUIRFIELD	GULLANE, SCOTLAND	305 (+27)
1891	HUGH KIRKALDY	SCOTLAND	ST. ANDREWS	ST. ANDREWS, SCOTLAND	166
1890	JOHN BALL (AM)	ENGLAND	PRESTWICK G C	PRESTWICK, SCOTLAND	164
1889	WILLIE PARK, JR.	SCOTLAND	MUSSELBURGH LINKS	E. LOTHIAN, SCOTLAND	155 PO

THE BRITISH OPEN CHAMPIONSHIP (CONTINUED)

YEAR	CHAMPION	COUNTRY	VENUE	VENUE LOCATION	WINNER'S SCORE
1888	JACK BURNS	SCOTLAND	ST. ANDREWS	ST. ANDREWS, SCOTLAND	171
1887	WILLIE PARK, JR.	SCOTLAND	PRESTWICK G C	PRESTWICK, SCOTLAND	161
1886	DAVID BROWN	SCOTLAND	MUSSELBURGH LINKS	E. LOTHIAN, SCOTLAND	157
1885	BOB MARTIN	SCOTLAND	ST. ANDREWS	ST. ANDREWS, SCOTLAND	171
1884	JACK SIMPSON	SCOTLAND	PRESTWICK G C	PRESTWICK, SCOTLAND	160
1883	WILLIE FERNIE	SCOTLAND	MUSSELBURGH LINKS	E. LOTHIAN, SCOTLAND	159 PO
1882	BOB FERGUSON	SCOTLAND	ST. ANDREWS	ST. ANDREWS, SCOTLAND	171
1881	BOB FERGUSON	SCOTLAND	PRESTWICK G C	PRESTWICK, SCOTLAND	170
1880	BOB FERGUSON	SCOTLAND	MUSSELBURGH LINKS	E. LOTHIAN, SCOTLAND	162
1879	JAMIE ANDERSON	SCOTLAND	ST. ANDREWS	ST. ANDREWS, SCOTLAND	169
1878	JAMIE ANDERSON	SCOTLAND	PRESTWICK G C	PRESTWICK, SCOTLAND	157
1877	JAMIE ANDERSON	SCOTLAND	MUSSELBURGH LINKS	E. LOTHIAN, SCOTLAND	160
1876	BOB MARTIN	SCOTLAND	ST. ANDREWS	ST. ANDREWS, SCOTLAND	176
1875	WILLIE PARK, SR.	SCOTLAND	PRESTWICK G C	PRESTWICK, SCOTLAND	166
1874	MUNGO PARK	SCOTLAND	MUSSELBURGH LINKS	E.LOTHIAN, SCOTLAND	159
1873	TOM KIDD	SCOTLAND	ST. ANDREWS	ST. ANDREWS, SCOTLAND	179
1872	TOM MORRIS, JR.	SCOTLAND	PRESTWICK G C	PRESTWICK, SCOTLAND	166
1871	NO CHAMPIONSHIP				
1870	TOM MORRIS, JR.	SCOTLAND	PRESTWICK G C	PRESTWICK, SCOTLAND	149
1869	TOM MORRIS, JR.	SCOTLAND	PRESTWICK G C	PRESTWICK, SCOTLAND	154
1868	TOM MORRIS, JR.	SCOTLAND	PRESTWICK G C	PRESTWICK, SCOTLAND	157

THE BRITISH OPEN CHAMPIONSHIP (CONTINUED)

YEAR	CHAMPION	COUNTRY	VENUE	VENUE LOCATION	WINNER'S SCORE
1867	TOM MORRIS, SR.	SCOTLAND	PRESTWICK G C	PRESTWICK, SCOTLAND	170
1866	WILLIE PARK, SR.	SCOTLAND	PRESTWICK G C	PRESTWICK, SCOTLAND	169
1865	ANDREW STRATH	SCOTLAND	PRESTWICK G C	PRESTWICK, SCOTLAND	162
1864	TOM MORRIS, SR.	SCOTLAND	PRESTWICK G C	PRESTWICK, SCOTLAND	167
1863	WILLIE PARK, SR.	SCOTLAND	PRESTWICK G C	PRESTWICK, SCOTLAND	168
1862	TOM MORRIS, SR.	SCOTLAND	PRESTWICK G C	PRESTWICK, SCOTLAND	163
1861	TOM MORRIS, SR.	SCOTLAND	PRESTWICK G C	PRESTWICK, SCOTLAND	163
1860	WILLIE PARK, SR.	SCOTLAND	PRESTWICK G C	PRESTWICK, SCOTLAND	174

★   = Amateur
PO = Playoff
N/A = Not Applicable
G C = Golf Course
G L = Golf Links

PGA CHAMPIONSHIP
STROKE-PLAY ERA

YEAR	CHAMPION	COUNTRY	VENUE	VENUE LOCATION	WINNER'S SCORE
2016			BALTUSROL (LOWER)	SPRINGFIELD, NJ	
2015			WHISTLING STRAITS	SHEBOYGAN, WI	
2014			TBA		
2013			OAK HILL CC EAST	PITTSFORD, NY	
2012			KIAWAH ISLAND OCEAN COURSE	KIAWAH ISLAND, SC	
2011			ATLANTA ATHLETIC CLUB – HIGHLANDS	DULUTH, GA	
2010			WHISTLING STRAITS	SHEBOYGAN, WI	
2009			HAZELTINE NATIONAL	CHASKA, MN	
2008	PADRAIG HARRINGTON	IRELAND	OAKLAND HILLS C C	BLOOMFIELD HILLS, MI	277 (−3)
2007	TIGER WOODS	USA	SOUTHERN HILLS C C	TULSA, OK	27 (−8)
2006	TIGER WOODS	USA	MEDINAH #3	MEDINAH, IL	270 (−18)
2005	PHIL MICHELSON	USA	BALTUSROL (LOWER)	SPRINGFIELD, NJ	276 (−4)
2004	VIJAY SINGH	FIJI	WHISTLING STRAITS	SHEBOYGAN, WI	280 (−8) PO
2003	SHAUN MICHEEL	USA	OAK HILL C C EAST	ROCHESTER, NY	276 (−4)
2002	RICH BEEN	USA	HAZELTINE NATIONAL	CHASKA, MN	278 (−10)
2001	DAVID TOMS	USA	ATLANTA ATHLETIC CLUB – HIGHLANDS	DULUTH, GA	265 (−15)
2000	TIGER WOODS	USA	VALHALLA G C	LOUISVILLE, KY	270 (−18) PO
1999	TIGER WOODS	USA	MEDINAH #3	MEDINAH,IL	277 (−11)
1998	VIJAY SINGH	FIJI	SAHALEE C C	SAMMAMISH, WA	271 (−9)
1997	DAVIS LOVE III	USA	WINGED FOOT WEST	MAMARONECK, NY	269 (−11)
1996	MARK BROOKS	USA	VALHALLA G C	LOUISVILLE, KY	277 (−11) PO
1995	STEVE ELKINGTON	USA	RIVIERA C C	PACIFIC PALISADES, CA	267 (−17) PO
1994	NICK PRICE	ZIMBABWE	SOUTHERN HILLS C C	TULSA, OK	269 (−11)
1993	PAUL AZINGER	USA	INVERNESS CLUB	TOLEDO, OH	272 (−12) PO
1992	NICK PRICE	ZIMBABWE	BELLERIVE C C	ST. LOUIS, MO	278 (−6)
1991	JOHN DALY	USA	CROOKED STICK G C	CARMEL, IN	276 (−12)
1990	WAYNE GRADY	AUSTRALIA	SHOAL CREEK G C C	BIRMINGHAM, AL	282 (−6)
1989	PAYNE STEWART	USA	KEMPER LAKES G C	LONG GROVE, IL	276 (−12)

PGA CHAMPIONSHIP (CONTINUED)
STROKE-PLAY ERA

YEAR	CHAMPION	COUNTRY	VENUE	VENUE LOCATION	WINNER'S SCORE
1988	JEFF SLUMAN	USA	OAK TREE G C	EDMOND, OK	272 (−12)
1987	LARRY NELSON	USA	PGA NATIONAL RESORT & SPA	PALM BEACH GARDENS, FL	287 (−1) PO
1986	BOB TWAY	USA	INVERNESS CLUB	TOLEDO, OH	276 (−8)
1985	HUBERT GREEN	USA	CHERRY HILLS C C	CHERRY HILLS, CO	278 (−10)
1984	LEE TREVINO	USA	SHOAL CREEK G C C	BIRMINGHAM, AL	273 (−15)
1983	HAL SUTTON	USA	RIVIERA C C	PACIFIC PALISADES, CA	274 (−10)
1982	RAYMOND FLOYD	USA	SOUTHERN HILLS C C	TULSA, OK	272 (−8)
1981	LARRY NELSON	USA	ATLANTA ATHLETIC CLUB – HIGHLANDS	DULUTH, GA	273 (−7)
1980	JACK NICKLAUS	USA	OAK HILL C C EAST	ROCHESTER, NY	274 (−6)
1979	DAVID GRAHAM	AUSTRALIA	OAKLAND HILLS C C	BLOOMFIELD HILLS, MI	272 (−8) PO
1978	JOHN MAHAFFEY	USA	OAKMONT C C	OAKMONT, PA	276 (−8) PO
1976	DAVE STOCKTON	USA	CONGRESSIONAL C C	BETHESDA, MD	281 (+1)
1975	JACK NICKLAUS	USA	FIRESTONE C C SOUTH	AKRON, OH	276 (−4)
1974	LEE TREVINO	USA	TANGLEWOOD PARK	CLEMMONS, NC	276 (−4)
1973	JACK NICKLAUS	USA	CANTERBURY G C	BEACHWOOD, OH	277 (−7)
1972	GARY PLAYER	SOUTH AFRICA	OAKLAND HILLS C C SOUTH	BLOOMFIELD HILLS, MI	281 (+1)
1971	JACK NICKLAUS	USA	PGA NATIONAL G C	PALM BEACH GARDENS,FL	281 (−7)
1970	DAVE STOCKTON	USA	SOUTHERN HILLS C C	TULSA, OK	279 (−1)
1969	RAYMOND FLOYD	USA	NCR C C SOUTH	DAYTON, OH	276 (−8)
1968	JULIUS BOROS	USA	PECAN VALLEY G C	SAN ANTONIO, TX	281 (+1)
1967	DON JANUARY	USA	COLUMBINE C C	COLUMBINE VALLEY, CO	281 (−7) PO
1966	AL GEIBERGER	USA	FIRESTONE C C SOUTH	AKRON, OH	280 (E)
1965	DAVE MARR	USA	LAUREL VALLEY G C	LIGONIER, PA	280 (−4)
1964	BOBBY NICHOLS	USA	COLUMBUS C C	COLUMBUS, OH	271 (−9)
1963	JACK NICKLAUS	USA	DALLAS A C BLUE	DALLAS, TX	279 (−5)

PGA CHAMPIONSHIP (CONTINUED)
STROKE-PLAY ERA

YEAR	CHAMPION	COUNTRY	VENUE	VENUE LOCATION	WINNER'S SCORE
1962	GARY PLAYER	SOUTH AFRICA	ARONIMINK G C	NEWTOWN SQUARE, PA	278 (−2)
1961	JERRY BARBER	USA	OLYMPIA FIELDS C C	OLYMPIA FIELDS, IL	277 (−3) PO
1960	JAY HEBERT	USA	FIRESTONE C C	AKRON, OH	281 (+1)
1959	BOB ROSBURG	USA	MINNEAPOLIS G C	MINNEAPOLIS, MN	277 (-3)
1958	DOW FINSTERWALD	USA	LLANERCH C C	HAVERTOWN, PA	276 (-14)

PGA CHAMPIONSHIP
MATCH-PLAY ERA

YEAR	CHAMPION	RUNNER-UP	SCORE	VENUE	VENUE LOCATION
1957	LIONEL HEBERT	DOW FINSTERWALD	2 & 1	MIAMI VALLEY C C	DAYTON, OH
1956	JACK BURKE, JR.	TED KROLL	3 & 2	BLUE HILL C C	CANTON, MA
1955	DOUG FORD	CARY MIDDLECOFF	4 & 3	MEADOWBROOK	DETROIT, MI
1954	CHICK HARBERT	WALTER BURKEMO	4 & 3	KELLER G C	ST. PAUL, MN
1953	WALTER BURKEMO	FELICE TORZA	2 & 1	BIRMINGHAM C C	BIRMINGHAM, MI
1952	JIM TURNESA	CHICK HARBERT	1 UP	BIG SPRING C C	LOUISVILLE, KY
1951	SAM SNEAD	WALTER BURKEMO	7 & 6	OAKMONT C C	OAKMONT, PA
1950	CHANDLER HARPER	HENRY WILLIAMS	4 & 3	SCIOTO C C	COLUMBUS, OH
1949	SAM SNEAD	JOHNNY PALMER	3 & 2	HERMITAGE C C	RICHMOND, VA
1948	BEN HOGAN	MIKE TURNESA	7 & 6	NORWOOD HILLS	ST. LOUIS, MO
1947	JIM FERRIER	CHICK HARBERT	2 & 1	PLUM HOLLOW C C	DETROIT, MI
1946	BEN HOGAN	ED OLIVER	6 & 4	PORTLAND C C	PORTLAND, OR
1945	BYRON NELSON	SAM BYRD	4 & 3	MORAINE C C	DAYTON, OH
1944	BOB HAMILTON	BYRON NELSON	1 UP	MANITO G & C C	SPOKANE, WA
1943	N/A WORLD WAR II				
1942	SAM SNEAD	JIM TURNESA	2 & 1	SEAVIEW C C	ATLANTIC CITY, NJ
1941	VIC GHEZZI	BYRON NELSON	38*	CHERRY HILLS C C	CHERRY HILLS, CO
1940	BYRON NELSON	SAM SNEAD	1 UP	HERSHEY CC WEST	HERSHEY, PA
YEAR	CHAMPION	RUNNER-UP	SCORE	VENUE	VENUE LOCATION
1939	HENRY PICARD	BYRON NELSON	37*	POMONOK C C	FLUSHING, NY
1938	PAUL RUNYAN	SAM SNEAD	8 & 7	SHAWNEE INN RESORT	SMITHFIELD TWP., PA
1937	DENNY SHUTE	HAROLD McSPADEN	37*	PITTSBURGH FIELD	O'HARA TWP., PA
1936	DENNY SHUTE	JIMMY THOMSON	3 & 2	PINEHURST # 2	PINEHURST, NC
1935	JOHNNY REVOLTA	TOMMY ARMOUR	5 & 4	TWIN HILLS G & CC	OKLAHOMA CITY, OK
1934	PAUL RUNYAN	CRAIG WOOD	38*	THE PARK C C	WILLIAMSVILLE, NY
1933	GENE SARAZEN	WILLIE GOGGIN	5 & 4	BLUE MOUND G & C	WAUWATOSA, WI
1932	OLIN DUTRA	FRANK WALSH	4 & 3	KELLER GOLF CLUB	ST. PAUL, MN
1931	TOM CREAVY	DENNY SHUTE	2 & 1	WANNAMOISETT	RUMFORD, RI
1930	TOMMY ARMOUR	GENE SARAZEN	1 UP	FRESH MEADOW C C	GREAT NECK, NY
1929	LEO DIEGEL	JOHNNY FARRELL	6 & 4	HILLCREST C C	LOS ANGELES, CA

PGA CHAMPIONSHIP (CONTINUED)

MATCH-PLAY ERA

1928	LEO DIEGEL	AL ESPINOSA	6 & 5	BALTIMORE CC EAST	TIMONIUM, MD
1927	WALTER HAGEN	JOE TURNESA	1 UP	CEDAR CREST C C	DALLAS, TX
1926	WALTER HAGEN	LEO DIEGEL	5 & 3	SALISBURY, RED	EAST MEADOW NY
1925	WALTER HAGEN	BILL MEHLHORN	6 & 5	OLYMPIA FIELDS C C	OLYMPIA FIELDS, IL
1924	WALTER HAGEN	JIM BARNES	2 UP	FRENCH LINK, HILL	FRENCH LINK, IN
1923	GENE SARAZEN	WALTER HAGEN	38*	PELHAM C C	PELHAM MANOR, NY
1922	GENE SARAZEN	EMMET FRENCH	4 & 3	OAKMONT C C	OAKMONT, PA
1921	WALTER HAGEN	JIM BARNES	3 & 2	INWOOD C C	INWOOD, NY
1920	JOCK HUTCHISON	J. DOUGLAS EDGAR	1 UP	FLOSSMOOR C C	FLOSSMOOR, IL
1919	JIM BARNES	FRED MCLEOD	6 & 5	ENGINEERS C C	ROSLYN HARBOR, NY
1918	N/A WORLD WAR I				
1917	N/A WORLD WAR I				
1916	JIM BARNES	JOCK HUTCHISON	1 UP	SIWANOY C C	EASTCHESTER, NY

THE RYDER CUP

YEAR	VENUE	WINNING TEAM	USA SCORE	EUROPE SCORE	LOSING TEAM	CAPTAINS USA – EUROPE
2016	HAZELTINE NATIONAL G C					
2014	GLENEAGLES HOTEL					
2012	MEDINAH COUNTRY CLUB					
2010	CELTIC MANOR RESORT					
2008	VALHALLA GOLF CLUB	USA	16.5	11.5	EUROPE	AZINGER – FALDO
2006	THE K CLUB – PALMER COURSE	EUROPE	9.5	18.5	USA	LEHMAN – WOOSNAM
2004	OAKLAND HILLS C C	EUROPE	9.5	18.5	USA	SUTTON – LANGER
2002*	THE BELFRY	EUROPE	12.5	15.5	USA	STRANGE – TORRANCE
1999	THE COUNTRY CLUB	USA	14.5	13.5	EUROPE	CRENSHAW – JAMES
1997	VALDERRAMA G C	EUROPE	13.5	14.5	USA	KITE – BALLESTEROS
1995	OAK HILL COUNTRY CLUB	EUROPE	13.5	14.5	USA	WADKINS – GALLACHER
1993	THE BELFRY	USA	15	13	EUROPE	WATSON – GALLACHER
1991	KIAWAH ISLAND G R	USA	14.5	13.5	EUROPE	STOCKTON – GALLACHER
1989	THE BELFRY	TIED	14	14	TIED	FLOYD – JACKLIN
1987	MUIRFIELD VILLAGE	EUROPE	13	15	USA	NICKLAUS – JACKLIN
1985	THE BELFRY	EUROPE	11.5	16.5	USA	TREVINO – JACKLIN
1983	PGA NATIONAL G C	USA	14.5	13.5	EUROPE	NICKLAUS – JACKLIN
1981	WALTON HEATH G C	USA	18.5	9.5	EUROPE	MARR – JACOBS
1979	THE GREENBRIER	USA	17	11	EUROPE	CASPER – JACOBS
1977	ROYAL LYTHAM & ST. ANNES	USA	12.5	7.5	GB & I	FINSTERWALD – HUGGETT
1975	LAUREL VALLEY GOLF CLUB	USA	21	11	GB & I	PALMER – HUNT
1973	MUIRFIELD LINKS	USA	19	13	GB & I	BURKE, JR. – HUNT
1971	OLD WARSON C C	USA	18.5	13.5	BRITAIN	HEBERT – BROWN
1969	ROYAL BIRKDALE GOLF CLUB	TIED	16	16	TIED	SNEAD – BROWN
1967	CHAMPIONS GOLF CLUB	USA	23.5	8.5	BRITAIN	HOGAN – REES
1965	ROYAL BIRKDALE GOLF CLUB	USA	19.5	12.5	BRITAIN	NELSON – WEETMAN
1963	ATLANTA ATHLETIC CLUB	USA	23	9	BRITAIN	PALMER – FALLON
1961	ROYAL BIRKDALE GOLF CLUB	USA	14.5	9.5	BRITAIN	BARBER – REES
1959	ELDORADO GOLF CLUB	USA	8.5	3.5	BRITAIN	SNEAD – REES
1957	LINDRICK GOLF CLUB	BRITAIN	4.5	7.5	USA	BURKE, JR. – REES
1955	THUNDERBIRD C C	USA	8	4	BRITAIN	HARBERT – REES

THE RYDER CUP (CONTINUED)

YEAR	VENUE	WINNING TEAM	USA SCORE	EUROPE SCORE	LOSING TEAM	CAPTAINS USA – EUROPE
1953	WENTWORTH CLUB	USA	6.5	5.5	BRITAIN	MANGRUM – COTTON
1951	PINEHURST RESORT	USA	9.5	2.5	BRITAIN	SNEAD – LACEY
1949	GANTON GOLF CLUB	USA	7	5	BRITAIN	HOGAN – WHITCOMBE
1947	PORTLAND GOLF CLUB	USA	11	1	BRITAIN	HOGAN – COTTON
1937	SOUTHPORT & AINSDALE G C	USA	8	4	BRITAIN	HAGEN – WHITCOMBE
1935	RIDGEWOOD C C	USA	9	3	BRITAIN	HAGEN – WHITCOMBE
1933	SOUTHPORT & AINSDALE GC	BRITAIN	5.5	6.5	USA	HAGEN – J.H. TAYLOR
1931	SCIOTO COUNTRY CLUB	USA	9	3	BRITAIN	HAGEN – WHITCOMBE
1929	MOORTOWN GOLF CLUB	BRITAIN	5	7	USA	HAGEN – DUNCAN
1927	WORCESTER COUNTRY CLUB	USA	9.5	2.5	BRITAIN	HAGEN – RAY

*Delayed for one year because of 9-11-2001 attacks. 1929–1969 Team Great Britain, 1973–1977 Team Great Britain & Ireland, 1979-plus Team Europe. WWII canceled 1939, 1941, 1943 & 1945 Ryder Cup matches.

THE PRESIDENTS CUP

YEAR	VENUE	WINNING TEAM	USA SCORE	INT'L SCORE	LOSING TEAM	CAPTAINS USA – INTERNATIONAL
2015						
2013						
2011	ROYAL MELBOURNE GC					
2009	HARDING PARK GC					
2007	ROYAL MONTREAL GC	USA	19.5	14.5	INT'L	NICKLAUS – PLAYER
2005	ROBERT TRENT JONES GC	USA	18.5	15.5	INT'L	NICKLAUS – PLAYER
2003	FANCOURT HOTEL & CCE	TIED	17	17	TIED	NICKLAUS – PLAYER
2000	ROBERT TRENT JONES GC	USA	21.5	10.5	INT'L	VENTURI – THOMSON
1998	ROYAL MELBOURNE GC	INT'L	20.5	11.5	USA	NICKLAUS – THOMSON
1996	ROBERT TRENT JONES GC	USA	16.5	15.5	INT'L	PALMER – THOMSON
1994	ROBERT TRENT JONES GC	USA	20	12	INT'L	IRWIN – GRAHAM

MAJOR CHAMPIONSHIP WINNERS

YEAR	THE MASTERS TOURNAMENT	U.S. OPEN CHAMPIONSHIP	BRITISH OPEN CHAMPIONSHIP	PGA CHAMPIONSHIP
2015				
2014				
2013				
2012				
2011				
2010				
2009				
2008	Trevor Immelman	Tiger Woods	Padraig Harrington	Padraig Harrington
2007	Zach Johnson	Angel Cabrera	Padraig Harrington	Tiger Woods
2006	Phil Mickelson	Geoff Ogilvy	Tiger Woods	Tiger Woods
2005	Tiger Woods	Michael Campbell	Tiger Woods	Phil Mickelson
2004	Phil Mickelson	Retief Goosen	Todd Hamilton	Vijay Singh
2003	Mike Weir	Jim Furyk	Ben Curtis	Shaun Micheel
2002	Tiger Woods	Tiger Woods	Ernie Els	Rick Beem
2001	Tiger Woods	Retief Goosen	David Duval	David Toms
2000	Vijay Singh	Tiger Woods	Tiger Woods	Tiger Woods
1999	Jose Maria Olazabal	Payne Stewart	Paul Lawrie	Tiger Woods
1998	Mark O'Meara	Lee Janzen	Mark O'Meara	Vijay Singh
1997	Tiger Woods	Ernie Els	Justin Leonard	Davis Love II
1996	Nick Faldo	Steve Jones	Tom Lehman	Mark Brooks
1995	Ben Crenshaw	Corey Pavin	John Daly	Steve Elkington
1994	Jose Maria Olazabal	Ernie Els	Nick Price	Nick Price
1993	Bernhard Langer	Lee Janzen	Greg Norman	Paul Azinger
1992	Fred Couples	Tom Kite	Nick Faldo	Nick Price
1991	Ian Woosnam	Payne Stewart	Ian Baker-Finch	John Daly
1990	Nick Faldo	Hale Irwin	Nick Faldo	Wayne Grady
1989	Nick Faldo	Curtis Strange	Mark Calcavecchia	Payne Stewart
1988	Sandy Lyle	Curtis Strange	Seve Ballesteros	Jeff Sluman
1987	Larry Mize	Scott Simpson	Nick Faldo	Larry Nelson
1986	Jack Nicklaus	Raymond Floyd	Greg Norman	Bob Tway
1985	Bernhard Langer	Andy North	Sandy Lyle	Hubert Green

MAJOR CHAMPIONSHIP WINNERS (CONTINUED)

YEAR	THE MASTERS TOURNAMENT	U.S. OPEN CHAMPIONSHIP	BRITISH OPEN CHAMPIONSHIP	PGA CHAMPIONSHIP
1984	Ben Crenshaw	Fuzzy Zoeller	Seve Ballesteros	Lee Trevino
1983	Seve Ballesteros	Larry Nelson	Tom Watson	Hal Sutton
1982	Craig Stadler	Tom Watson	Tom Watson	Raymond Floyd
1981	Tom Watson	David Graham	Bill Rogers	Larry Nelson
1980	Seve Ballesteros	Jack Nicklaus	Tom Watson	Jack Nicklaus
1979	Fuzzy Zoeller	Hale Irwin	Seve Ballesteros	David Graham
1978	Gary Player	Andy North	Jack Nicklaus	John Mahaffey
1977	Tom Watson	Hubert Green	Tom Watson	Lanny Wadkins
1976	Raymond Floyd	Jerry Pate	Johnny Miller	Dave Stockton
1975	Jack Nicklaus	Lou Graham	Tom Watson	Jack Nicklaus
1974	Gary Player	Hale Irwin	Gary Player	Lee Trevino
1973	Tommy Aaron	Johnny Miller	Tom Weiskopf	Jack Nicklaus
1972	Jack Nicklaus	Jack Nicklaus	Lee Trevino	Gary Player
1971	Charles Coody	Lee Trevino	Lee Trevino	Jack Nicklaus
1970	Billy Casper	Tony Jacklin	Jack Nicklaus	Dave Stockton
1969	George Archer	Orville Moody	Tony Jacklin	Raymond Floyd
1968	Bob Goalby	Lee Trevino	Gary Player	Julius Boros
1967	Gay Brewer	Jack Nicklaus	Roberto DeVicenzo	Don January
1966	Jack Nicklaus	Billy Casper	Jack Nicklaus	Al Geiberger
1965	Jack Nicklaus	Gary Player	Peter Thomson	Dave Marr
1964	Arnold Palmer	Ken Venturi	Tony Lema	Bobby Nichols
1963	Jack Nicklaus	Julius Boros	Bob Charles	Jack Nicklaus
1962	Arnold Palmer	Jack Nicklaus	Arnold Palmer	Gary Player
1961	Gary Player	Gene Littler	Arnold Palmer	Jerry Barber
1960	Arnold Palmer	Arnold Palmer	Kel Nagle	Jay Hebert
1959	Art Wall, Jr.	Billy Casper	Gary Player	Bob Rosburg
1958	Arnold Palmer	Tommy Bolt	Peter Thomson	Dow Finsterwald
1957	Doug Ford	Dick Mayer	Bobby Locke	Lionel Hebert
1956	Jack Burke, Jr.	Cary Middlecoff	Peter Thomson	Jack Burke, Jr.
1955	Cary Middlecoff	Jack Fleck	Peter Thomson	Doug Ford
1954	Sam Snead	Ed Furgol	Peter Thomson	Chick Harbert

MAJOR CHAMPIONSHIP WINNERS (CONTINUED)

YEAR	THE MASTERS TOURNAMENT	U.S. OPEN CHAMPIONSHIP	BRITISH OPEN CHAMPIONSHIP	PGA CHAMPIONSHIP
1953	Ben Hogan	Ben Hogan	Ben Hogan	Walter Burkemo
1952	Sam Snead	Julius Boros	Bobby Locke	Jim Turnesa
1951	Ben Hogan	Ben Hogan	Max Faulkner	Sam Snead
1950	Jimmy Demaret	Ben Hogan	Bobby Locke	Chandler Harper
1949	Sam Snead	Cary Middlecoff	Bobby Locke	Sam Snead
1948	Claude Harmon	Ben Hogan	Henry Cotton	Ben Hogan
1947	Jimmy Demaret	Lew Worsham	Fred Daly	Jim Ferrier
1946	Herman Keiser	Lloyd Mangrum	Sam Snead	Ben Hogan
1945	N/A World War II	N/A World War II	N/A World War II	Byron Nelson
1944	N/A World War II	N/A World War II	N/A World War II	Bob Hamilton
1943	N/A World War II	N/A World War II	N/A World War II	N/A World War II
1942	Bryon Nelson	N/A World War II	N/A World War II	Sam Snead
1941	Craig Wood	Craig Wood	N/A World War II	Vic Ghezzi
1940	Jimmy Demaret	Lawson Little	N/A World War II	Byron Nelson
1939	Ralph Guldahl	Byron Nelson	Richard Burton	Henry Picard
1938	Henry Picard	Ralph Guldahl	Reg Whitcombe	Paul Runyan
1937	Byron Nelson	Ralph Guldahl	Henry Cotton	Denny Shute
1936	Horton Smith	Tony Manero	Alf Padgham	Denny Shute
1935	Gene Sarazen	Sam Parks, Jr.	Alf Perry	Johnny Revolta
1934	Horton Smith	Olin Dutra	Henry Cotton	Paul Runyan
1933	Not Yet Founded (NYF)	Johnny Goodman	Denny Shute	Gene Sarazen
1932	NYF	Gene Sarazen	Gene Sarazen	Olin Dutra
1931	NYF	Billy Burke	Tommy Armour	Tom Creavy
1930	NYF	Bobby Jones	Bobby Jones	Tommy Armour
1929	NYF	Bobby Jones	Walter Hagen	Leo Diegel
1928	NYF	Johnny Farrell	Walter Hagen	Leo Diegel
1927	NYF	Tommy Armour	Bobby Jones	Walter Hagen
1926	NYF	Bobby Jones	Bobby Jones	Walter Hagen
1925	NYF	Willie MacFarlane	Jim Barnes	Walter Hagen
1924	NYF	Cyril Walker	Walter Hagen	Walter Hagen
1923	NYF	Bobby Jones	Arthur Havers	Gene Sarazen

MAJOR CHAMPIONSHIP WINNERS (CONTINUED)

YEAR	THE MASTERS TOURNAMENT	U.S. OPEN CHAMPIONSHIP	BRITISH OPEN CHAMPIONSHIP	PGA CHAMPIONSHIP
1922	NYF	Gene Sarazen	Walter Hagen	Gene Sarazen
1921	NYF	Jim Barnes	Jock Hutchison	Walter Hagen
1920	NYF	Ted Ray	George Duncan	Jock Hutchison
1919	NYF	Walter Hagen	N/A World War I	Jim Barnes
1918	NYF	N/A World War I	N/A World War I	N/A World War I
1917	NYF	N/A World War I	N/A World War I	N/A World War I
1916	NYF	Chick Evans	N/A World War I	Jim Barnes
1915	NYF	Jerome Travers	N/A World War I	Not Yet Founded
1914	NYF	Walter Hagen	Harry Vardon	NYF
1913	NYF	Francis Ouimet	John Henry Taylor	NYF
1912	NYF	John McDermott	Ted Ray	NYF
1911	NYF	John McDermott	Harry Vardon	NYF
1910	NYF	Alex Smith	James Braid	NYF
1909	NYF	George Sargent	John Henry Taylor	NYF
1908	NYF	Fred McLeod	James Braid	NYF
1907	NYF	Alec Ross	Arnaud Massy	NYF
1906	NYF	Alex Smith	James Braid	NYF
1905	NYF	Willie Anderson	James Braid	NYF
1904	NYF	Willie Anderson	Jack White	NYF
1903	NYF	Willie Anderson	Harry Vardon	NYF
1902	NYF	Laurie Auchterlonie	Sandy Herd	NYF
1901	NYF	Willie Anderson	James Braid	NYF
1900	NYF	Harry Vardon	John Henry Taylor	NYF
1899	NYF	Willie Smith	Harry Vardon	NYF
1898	NYF	Fred Herd	Harry Vardon	NYF
1897	NYF	Joe Lloyd	Harold Hilton	NYF
1896	NYF	James Foulis	Harry Vardon	NYF
1895	NYF	Horace Rawlins	John Henry Taylor	NYF
1894	NYF	Not Yet Founded	John Henry Taylor	NYF
1893	NYF	NYF	Willie Auchterlonie	NYF
1892	NYF	NYF	Harold Hilton	NYF

MAJOR CHAMPIONSHIP WINNERS (CONTINUED)

YEAR	THE MASTERS TOURNAMENT	U.S. OPEN CHAMPIONSHIP	BRITISH OPEN CHAMPIONSHIP	PGA CHAMPIONSHIP
1891	NYF	NYF	Hugh Kirkaldy	NYF
1890	NYF	NYF	John Ball, Jr.	NYF
1889	NYF	NYF	Willie Park, Jr.	NYF
1888	NYF	NYF	Jack Burns	NYF
1887	NYF	NYF	Willie Park, Jr.	NYF
1886	NYF	NYF	David Brown	NYF
1885	NYF	NYF	Bob Martin	NYF
1884	NYF	NYF	Jack Simpson	NYF
1883	NYF	NYF	Willie Fernie	NYF
1882	NYF	NYF	Bob Ferguson	NYF
1881	NYF	NYF	Bob Ferguson	NYF
1880	NYF	NYF	Bob Ferguson	NYF
1879	NYF	NYF	Jamie Anderson	NYF
1878	NYF	NYF	Jamie Anderson	NYF
1877	NYF	NYF	Jamie Anderson	NYF
1876	NYF	NYF	Bob Martin	NYF
1875	NYF	NYF	Willie Park, Sr.	NYF
1874	NYF	NYF	Mungo Park	NYF
1873	NYF	NYF	Tom Kidd	NYF
1872	NYF	NYF	Tom Morris, Jr.	NYF
1871	NYF	NYF	N/A Not Played	NYF
1870	NYF	NYF	Tom Morris, Jr.	NYF
1869	NYF	NYF	Tom Morris, Jr.	NYF
1868	NYF	NYF	Tom Morris, Jr.	NYF
1867	NYF	NYF	Tom Morris, Sr.	NYF
1866	NYF	NYF	Willie Park, Sr.	NYF
1865	NYF	NYF	Andrew Strath	NYF
1864	NYF	NYF	Tom Morris, Sr.	NYF
1863	NYF	NYF	Willie Park, Sr.	NYF
1862	NYF	NYF	Tom Morris, Sr.	NYF
1861	NYF	NYF	Tom Morris, Sr.	NYF
1860	NYF	NYF	Willie Park, Sr.	NYF

TOP MAJOR CHAMPIONSHIP WINNERS
5 WINS OR MORE

PLAYER	THE MASTERS TOURNAMENT	U.S. OPEN CHAMPIONSHIP	BRITISH OPEN CHAMPIONSHIP	PGA CHAMPIONSHIP	TOTAL
Jack Nicklaus	6	4	3	5	18
Tiger Woods	4	3	3	4	14
Walter Hagen	0	2	4	5	11
Ben Hogan	2	4	1	2	9
Gary Player	3	1	3	2	9
Tom Watson	2	1	5	0	8
Harry Vardon	N/A	1	6	0	7
Gene Sarazen	1	2	1	3	7
Bobby Jones	0	4	3	0	7
Sam Snead	3	0	1	3	7
Arnold Palmer	4	1	2	0	7
Nick Faldo	3	0	3	0	6
Lee Trevino	0	2	2	2	6
Seve Ballesteros	2	0	3	0	5
James Braid	N/A	0	5	N/A	5
Byron Nelson	2	1	0	2	5
J.H. Taylor	N/A	0	5	0	5
Peter Thomson	0	0	5	0	5

THE 13 ORIGINAL RULES OF GOLF

Written by
The Gentlemen Golfers of Leith,
now the Honourable Company of Edinburgh Golfers based at Muirfield

1744

1. "You must tee your ball within a club's length of the hole."

2. "Your tee must be on the ground."

3. "You are not to change the ball which you strike off the tee."

4. "You are not to remove stones, bones or any break club for the sake of playing your ball, except upon the fair green, and that only within a club's length of the ball."

5. "If your ball comes among watter, or any wattery filth, you are at liberty to take out your ball and bringing it behind the hazard and teeing it, you may play it with any club and allow your adversary a stroke for so getting out your ball."

6. "If your balls be found anywhere touching one another you are to lift the first ball till you play the last."

7. "At holling you are to play your ball honestly at the hole, and not to play upon your adversary's ball, not lying in your way to the hole."

8. "If you should lose your ball, by its being taken up, or any other way, you are to go back to the spot where you struck last and drop another ball and allow your adversary a stroke for the misfortune."

9. "No man holling his ball is to be allowed to mark his way to the hole with his club or anything else.

10. "If a ball be stopp'd by any person, horse, dog, or any thing else, the ball so stopp'd must be played where it lyes."

11. "If you draw your club in order to strike and proceed so far in the stroke as to be bring down your club, if then your club should break in any way, it is to be accounted a stroke."

12. "He whose ball lyes farthest from the hole is obliged to play first."

13. "Neither trench, ditch, or dyke made for the preservation of the links, nor the Scholars' Holes or the soldiers' lines shall be accounted a harzard but the ball is to be taken out, teed and play'd with any iron club."

In 1897, The Royal & Ancient Golf Club of St. Andrews formed a Rules Committee.